In memory of Alex Coutselos

Contents

TURKEY

Al Malikiyah ★

Erbil △
Mosul △
Tikrit △
Tigris
Baghdad ✦
Karbala △
Iraqi Marshes
Basra △
KUWAIT ✦
Kuwait

Euphrates

SYRIA

IRAQ

Palmyra ★
Homs ★
Bekaa Valley
Damascus ✦
Sea of Galilee
Byblos
LEBANON

ISRAEL
Tel Aviv
Jerusalem ✦
Bethlehem

JORDAN

Amman △

Petra ★

Dead
Sea
Wadi Rum ★
Aqaba ★

Al Ula △

SAUDI

Medina ★

Mecca ★
Jeddah ★

HEJAZ

EGYPT

Red

0   miles   400

ARABIA

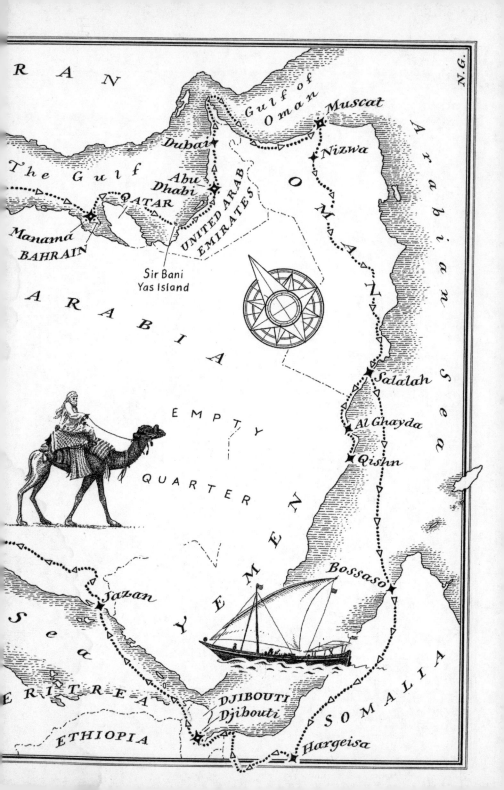

I R A N

Gulf of Oman

Muscat

The Gulf

Dubai

Nizwa

Abu
Dhabi

QATAR

UNITED ARAB
EMIRATES

Manama
BAHRAIN

O
M
A
N

A
r
a
b
i
a
n

S
e
a

Sir Bani
Yas Island

A R A B I A

E M P T Y

Salalah

Al Ghayda

QUARTER

Qishn

Y
E
M
E
N

Bossaso

Jazan

S
e
a

E R I T R E A

DJIBOUTI
Djibouti

S O M A L I A

ETHIOPIA

Hargeisa

For me, exploration was a personal venture. I did not go to the Arabian desert to collect plants nor to make a map; such things were incidental . . . I went there to find peace in the hardship of desert travel and the company of desert peoples . . . To others my journey would have little importance. It would produce nothing except a rather inaccurate map which no one was ever likely to use. It was a personal experience, and the reward had been a drink of clean, nearly tasteless water. I was content with that.

Wilfred Thesiger, *Arabian Sands*

Introduction

The so-called Arab Spring of 2011 had brought about a hope of change in a troubled region. Dictatorships had been toppled and, in some places, democracy flourished. Social media had evoked a new-found love of freedom of expression and for the first time in decades, there appeared to be a shift in the collective consciousness of what it meant to be an Arab. The stereotypes no longer applied, and the young rose up to show the bearded and gold-clad autocrats who really mattered.

But, just a few years later, the dream lay in tatters. Where there had been dictators, there were now terrorists or foreign armies. Wars were still raging at either end of the peninsula in Syria, Yemen and Iraq, raising an infinite number of questions.

Had the initial optimism from the revolutions brought about any change at all? What did the conflict between Sunni and Shi'a Islam mean for the prospects of peace in the region. Did Saudi Arabia, backed by the West, hold the key to stability in this notorious land, and was Iran really to blame for the volatility in places like Lebanon and Yemen? How is it that seventy years after the creation of a Jewish state in Israel, there is still daily conflict?

More broadly, in times of technological advancement, how has development and rapid change arrived in a place with so much history and tradition. Many people suspect that it was oil that caused the American invasion of Iraq, but with fluctuating economies and a new desire to move away from fossil fuels – what does this mean for the future of the Gulf? And indeed, what on earth does being a Bedouin nomad mean in the modern era?

I was interested in discovering more about these and many other topics, and I hope my travels might offer at least some insight to those curious about Arabia and the Arabs, even if they can't provide any definitive answers.

This is a journey through a land steeped in history. It is also mired in controversy, jealousy and tarnished by seemingly endless war. This book, however, doesn't intend to present a comprehensive geo-political narrative, nor does it pretend to cover the vast legacy of this complex and often misunderstood area. Instead, it attempts to showcase a region usually misrepresented.

This account is aimed at those who want to learn a little about Arabian culture in the modern day, and to read my musings on these questions by hearing from the people themselves. I travelled through thirteen countries over the autumn and winter of 2017– 18, meeting men and women (although sadly far fewer of the latter than I would have liked), who told me their stories. I have, of course, tried to be objective when it comes to political allegiances, and yet it is impossible to cover every viewpoint, and every group and organisations' agenda.

There are plenty of volumes that will go into great detail about the history of Islam, or the Middle East's current affairs, and there are yet more tales of voyages and adventures that will describe the Arabia of yesteryear. But only so much can fit within the pages of this book and anyway, travel is a very personal matter, and what follows is simply my snapshot of one moment in time.

I'd hope that people reading this will take the title of this book with a pinch of salt. Don't get hung up by the appropriation of the name Arabia. I have no doubt that there may be some who point an accusatory finger at the apparent peddling of outdated orientalist notions. What right has a white man – a non-Muslim, and more meddlesome still, an Englishman – to prance across the desert in an age of such sensitivity, amid conflicts and strife; let alone to have the nerve to call this land by its ancient name?

I knew from the outset that any journey in the Middle East would be contentious, and simply by undertaking to cross such a loaded region, it would garner criticism. It is exactly for that reason that I thought I *should* travel across these borders, because despite its controversy, there is nowhere else quite like it.

The truth is – there is no Arabia.

Arabia is an imagined construct and always has been: any attempt to define this land will always be met with censure. The Arabs themselves could never agree on what constituted Arabia, so what chance does anyone else have?

These days, when referring to the Arabian Peninsula, geographers include the Gulf States of Kuwait, Bahrain, Qatar, the United Arab Emirates and Oman, as well as Yemen and, of course, the largest country – Saudi Arabia. Some would say that Jordan is within the peninsula, others would not. But what about Iraq, Syria and the Holy Lands? Jerusalem, Damascus, Jericho and Baghdad all sit at the heart of the Arabian legacy, so it seems impossible to ignore them in a journey around the most enigmatic place on earth. In the spirit of the Bedouin of old, I have defied these borders and gone on to cross them in spite of their existence.

Until recently, the entire Arabian Peninsula was very much at the mercy of nature, and by that, I mean the desert – a landscape so hostile to man that only the hardiest nomads could survive in it. Since history began, Arabia has offered no comfortable welcome to the stranger, or much beyond austerity to its own people, and yet, from this barren land has emerged the root of all civilisation and the commandments of God Himself, giving rise to three great religions and a culture that has spread across the continents.

The legacy of those original desert dwellers must never be underestimated. Once upon a time, on the south-western coast, in what is now Yemen, there ruled a king named Yarab, descendant of Noah, whose name will forever be remembered for saving all humanity (and the animals, too), when the great flood came to punish man for his sins. Yarab's offspring, mythology aside, were the original Semites, and his seed soon spread far and wide – over the Red Sea to Africa, and north to mingle with the Sumerians of the Iraqi Marshes.

They left us with an alphabet and the written word, and yet as a people, they vanished into multiplicity. Mobile, elusive and disparate, these nomads became the Babylonians, the Assyrians and the Chaldeans; they were the mercantile Phoenicians, the monotheistic Hebrews, the beautiful Ethiopians and the industrious Arameans; then and now, they were the Bedu, the Arabs – the survivors.

Before Islam and the advent of nations, the old Arab tribes simply broke the region down into north and south – Al Sham (Syria) and Al Yaman (Yemen) – which was all well and good in the days before borders got in the way. The fact is that Arabia did not exist, because the Arabs did not exist. In those earlier times, the Arabs were simply a loose collection of disparate tribes that were always on the move and cared little for such definitions. Frontiers and identity existed only in the imagination of the beholder.

Forced by the environment to form family clans based around this wadi or that oasis, a sort of micro-nationalism emerged along the invisible ridges of the sands. There were the Hashemites and the Qurashi; the Abd Shams and the Nadir; the Hilal, Talil, Khalid and the Hajjar. This loose affiliation of blood gangs once roamed the valleys in search of plunder and pasture. Some were Jews, some were Christian and many more were animists, at once at ease and in constant battle with the forces of nature. And then in AD 571, something happened that changed the face of Arabia forever – the Prophet Muhammad was born, and with him a new religion emerged.

The old tribes had fought one another for women, frankincense and camels for generations, but now they had another reason to fight – Islam and identity – and it's a fight that continues to this day. And yet, in spite of so much bloodshed, these desert dwellers could also live in peace as a result of an unwritten code of hospitality that emerged, perhaps because of this collective geographical struggle. Even mortal enemies were welcomed as guests as soon as they had crossed the threshold of the tent, and generosity became synonymous with the new religion. In the context of the desert, it was the only way to ensure survival. Hospitality and war went hand in hand.

For me, this was a journey of discovery through a forbidden, mysterious land. I travelled at the mercy of Arabian hospitality – sometimes on foot, at other times by camel, mule, donkey and battle tank. It was the culmination of fifteen years' work and a lifelong fascination with the history of the Middle East. I have followed in the footsteps of some of the great explorers such as T.E. Lawrence, Richard Burton, Ibn Battutah, Wilfred Thesiger and a whole host of other giants that shaped the course of history in the region, but I have necessarily tried to keep my historical meanderings on a tight leash.

This book is a story of my own wanderings set against a backdrop of interesting times. I have tried to challenge the prevailing winds where possible and contest stereotypes, hopefully smashing a few myths along the way.

I

The Edge of Arabia

*Of the gladdest moments in human life, methinks, is the departure upon
a distant journey into unknown lands. Shaking off with one mighty
effort the fetters of Habit, the leaden weight of Routine, the cloak of
many Cares and the slavery of Civilisation, man feels once more happy.*

Richard Francis Burton

Rojava, Syria:
September 2017

In the distance was the border, a little over two miles away. The
hills were brown, sunburnt after a long summer, and the grass
was withered and dry. A solitary shepherd braved the midday
glare, slowly shuffling behind his flock across the dusty plain.
No-man's-land lay to the north across the fields, which were
pockmarked by abandoned and half-built concrete houses. On
the far side were the mountains of Turkey, and the Turks lined
the northern edge of Arabia.

Al-Malikiyah sprawled across the plain. It was like many
provincial towns in the Middle East: charmless and dusty. It
resembled a building site, and the greys of the breeze-block
mansions blended seamlessly with the piles of rubble, left over
from forgotten projects. Minarets vied for the skyline with the
spires of churches, seemingly compatible, and high walls with

6

creaky gates hid families from their neighbours. It was a Sunday and the streets were quiet, but as I walked through the suburban maze, the sounds of an alien world grew closer.

The call to prayer echoed across the main street, as some children scuttled from an alleyway to kick a football into the waste ground. Women carrying heavy bags of shopping waddled across the road. Most were unveiled, revealing jet-black or peroxide-blonde hair; many had bright red lipstick and piercing eyes.

Al-Malikiyah seemed to be very sleepy and life appeared to be going on as normal. But it didn't calm my nerves. This was Syria, in the middle of the deadliest war of the twenty-first century. Al-Malikiyah was a stone's throw away from Turkey, and for the local Kurds, these were the enemy – known for shelling the border villages frequently with impunity.

Just a few months before, the outskirts of the town had been bombarded with artillery shells from the Turkish army's mountain bases. Al-Malikiyah hadn't seen any close-quarter fighting on its streets yet, but it was full of families fleeing from the conflict only a few miles away.

Raqqa, at this time still occupied by ISIS, was a mere hundred and sixty miles to the south-west, and the front line was only fifty miles down the road. Equally bad as ISIS was the Nusra Front, an Islamist terror group that was busy roaming the countryside plundering the towns and murdering anyone who got in their way. A cluster of other rebel groups held positions all over central and eastern Syria, fighting both President Bashar al-Assad and each other, and even here in Rojava, the Kurds themselves were struggling to fight a battle on both fronts with almost no international support.

This was where my journey began. I'd convinced a Syrian

Kurdish official to let me in across the border without a visa, on the promise that I'd head straight for Iraq and not hang around. Quite why he'd agreed to let me go wandering about is anyone's guess, but I supposed that they thought a foreign writer might shine the spotlight on their cause. Either way, I had to be out within thirty-six hours or face arrest. It was already afternoon and the Iraqi border lay some twenty-odd miles to the east across an open plain, all in sight of the Turkish bomber jets and watchtowers, and so I thought it best to find somewhere to spend the night.

So far, I'd had no problems, though. I could blend in pretty well most places in the Middle East. I'd opted to wear a pair of old jeans, a dusty Belstaff jacket and some plain old desert boots, so I felt as though I could pass for a Kurd or an Arab.

'*Salam*,' a voice said from across the road. I looked up and saw a police checkpoint with two men in uniform, stood leaning against a compound wall covered with murals drawn by school children.

'Salam,' I replied. I noticed the flags hoisted above the wall. They weren't Syrian national flags. A combination of red, yellow and green signified the lands of Rojava; another was in yellow with a red star in the centre, surrounded by the letters YPG. These were the flags of the Kurdish militia, responsible for protecting the interests of the Kurds in Syria. Above them both was another one, this time green, with the socialist star surrounded by a yellow sun. This was the insignia of the Kurdistan Workers' Party – the PKK – a designated terrorist organisation to some, but for the Kurds, these were the saviours and freedom fighters of a lost nation.

'Who are you?' said one of the men, stubbing out a cigarette against the wall. He ambled over, casually swinging his AK-47 rifle by its wooden handle.

So much for blending in, I thought.

'I'm looking for a hotel,' I told him, as if it was the most normal thing in the world, while handing him my passport and an official-looking media pass I'd had printed off the internet.

He shrugged lazily, assuming I had permission to be here, and pointed down the street. 'Ask for Yasim. He usually has rooms.'

I walked down the main road of the town, relieved, passing bakeries and butchers' shops. The bells of the church tolled and I walked by a couple of girls with long flowing hair. They were Assyrian Christians and they giggled at me. I realised that my backpack gave me away as an outsider. Nobody carried backpacks here. I passed a little kiosk selling second-hand mobile phones and sim cards and it reminded me that I should probably buy one, in case I got into trouble and needed to make a call. A young man barely out of his teens was loitering around outside, inspecting the colourful phone cases.

'Is that an iPhone 7 Plus?' he said in passable English.

'It is,' I replied, somewhat surprised.

'What do you need? A Samsung?'

'No, thanks, I just need a Syrian sim card and some credit.'

The boy said something in Arabic to the man behind the kiosk, acting as my translator. The man shuffled under the counter for a plastic card with the sim, which he broke loose and handed to me in exchange for some Syrian pounds with President Assad's head on them. I took out my UK sim card and replaced it with the Syrian one. After a few seconds, I received a message from the provider: *Ministry of Tourism welcomes you in Syria, please call 137 for information and complaints.*

I'm not sure how many tourists Syria had received in the last seven years since the conflict began, but at least the people were optimistic.

'What's your name?' I asked the lad.

'Bassam,' he replied. 'I'm from Raqqa. But even though I'm an Arab, I knew I had to escape when Daesh came. I was studying computer science at the university, but they destroyed it. So I came here and now I'm looking for work.'

'Why Al-Malikiyah?' I asked, surprised that he'd chosen to come to a predominantly Kurdish and Christian town.

'It's tolerant here,' he said with a smile. 'Everyone is welcome. There's Kurds, Assyrian Christians, Armenians and Arabs, all living together in peace. Look at the churches and mosques side by side. We're all friends here and it's peaceful for now. Daesh are far away and I don't think they'll win now the government is taking back control. The only people we have to worry about are the Turks over there.'

He motioned to the north, flicking his head in the direction of the mountains. 'They bombed this town in April. But it's still better than Raqqa. My house has been destroyed there and most of my family are gone.'

He led me down the street, past some children wearing white robes. Not Arabic ones, though – these were karate uniforms.

'They love karate here,' Bassam said, imitating a martial-arts stance and chopping through the air with a vocal swoosh.

'Like I say, the Kurds are very nice. They're stuck in this little corner of Syria and they're really the only ones fighting Daesh properly. Nobody gives them any help and even the Americans who promise them the world have deserted them now. You're not American, are you?' Bassam looked at me apologetically.

'No,' I replied.

'Good,' he said, shaking his head. 'The whole place is a mess. And everybody knows that it's the Americans who started it.'

'Do people really think that? What about the revolution, about the Arab Spring and the uprising against Assad?' I asked, wanting to try to understand something of the background to this infernal civil war from those who had witnessed it first-hand.

'Pfft,' he snorted. 'Think it? They know it. The revolution was a joke. This whole war is just a game between the big countries. Iran, Israel, America, Russia and Saudi Arabia. They just come and screw around with things until they get what they want.'

'And what do they want?' I asked.

Bassam laughed. 'How long have you been on this journey for?'

'This is my first day,' I told him.

'Then I suppose you'll find out,' he said.

With that he walked off and disappeared down an alleyway in the market. The sun was setting and I figured that I'd better find a place to stay before it got dark. Even though normality seemed to prevail in this little oasis of calm, I kept reminding myself that this was a country at war, and nothing should be taken for granted.

I found the hotel a few blocks away. As the policeman had directed, it was on a side street near to a church. I knocked on the iron gates of the three-storey building and sent a cat bounding down the road. A young man in a tight red T-shirt opened the door to the gate and welcomed me inside the courtyard. He looked like a body-builder. I noticed a tattoo on his rippling biceps only half covered by a sleeve. It was the face of Jesus and some hands praying, surrounded by a rosary.

'I'm Yasim.' He smiled, flashing some gold teeth. His grip was iron-like.

'Where are you from?' he asked.

'England,' I told him.

'I love London. I'm Swedish,' he said, giving me a thumbs-up.

'Swedish?'

'Yes, well I have a Swedish passport now at least. I'm a refugee.'

'Oh,' I said, somewhat taken aback. With his enormous barrel chest and the glint in his eye, he didn't really fit my stereotype of a refugee.

'What are you doing back here?' I asked.

'Here, in Malikiyah?' he said. 'I'm working, of course. This hotel is the family business. I come here every summer and work, so my dad can go on holiday. Then I go to Sweden for a few months and work there. Maybe I'll move to London soon. Who knows.'

I guess that even refugees need to have summer jobs and holidays.

Yasim showed me through the reception into the garden, where a huge swimming pool dominated the neat manicured lawns. It was empty of water.

'No tourists anymore.' Yasim shrugged. 'Only wedding parties.' He pointed to the far side of the lawn, where some seats had been arranged and bouquets of flowers decorated the veranda. Big speakers and a DJ booth had been set up.

'Sorry about the noise later, it'll probably get quite loud. The wedding starts at seven.'

He walked me up to the room, which was basic but clean, and had a view out across the street towards the church. The sun was almost touching the mountains now and the sky was a fiery red. A chorus of prayer erupted across the skyline as the muezzin sang on prerecorded tapes from the city's minarets.

'Kebab for dinner, okay,' said Yasim. 'Do you want beer or whisky with that?' As he spoke, the first wedding guests began to arrive. Men in flared trousers and shiny suits, with slicked black hair and pointy shoes, sauntered through the garden with women in high heels wearing miniskirts and leopard-print jackets. The music kicked in, blaring Arabic pop songs and pumping techno music.

It looked like my first night in Syria was going to set the bar high.

I slept fitfully that night. The racket from the wedding party went on until the early hours, supplemented by sporadic bursts of gunfire that were indistinguishable from the fireworks. At one a.m., there was a bang on the door. It was a Kurdish soldier asking to see my passport. Word had spread there was a foreigner in town and the militia were concerned. He made sure to remind me that tomorrow I should make an early start to leave Syria and get on my way to Iraq.

I left early, after a breakfast of bread and cheese, waved off by Yasim, who was sporting red eyes that gave him away as a wedding crasher. I walked through the deserted streets at seven a.m. and the company was a few feral dogs and a couple of old men sitting at some tables of a chai shop, smoking and drinking tea and reading the morning news.

'Salam.' They waved.

'Salam.' I waved back, and walked east, out of town.

As the buildings grew smaller and the plain opened up in front of me, I took one last glance to my left towards the Turkish border. Large boulders dotted the seemingly endless ploughed fields that were dusty and brown from a long summer, remnants of a volcanic past.

This was the very edge of Arabia, the start of a five-thousand-mile journey, and I was jumping out of the frying pan and into the fire. Ahead, twenty miles away, was the flowing waters of the Tigris River, and on its far bank was Iraq.

2

The Call to Prayer

When you sleep in a house your thoughts are as high as the ceiling,
when you sleep outside they are as high as the stars.

Bedouin proverb

Most people old enough can remember where they were on that tragic day in September 2001. Personally, I was on a long-distance coach taking the cheapest road home from Poland, unable to afford a flight after several months travelling on my very first solo journey at the age of nineteen. I was heading back to England, eager to begin reading history at the university of Nottingham the following week, and I finally felt ready, having travelled all over Africa, Asia and Europe as a backpacker.

I was young, enthusiastic and had a great deal of faith in the kindness of strangers. After five months vagabonding, I had it all worked out; I was on the verge of becoming a hippy, with long hair and fisherman's pants that made me look like a poster boy for a cliché gap-year holiday. I was full of joy and couldn't wait to spend the next three years making new friends, drinking and maybe even learning something new.

The news came over the bus speakers as we drove along the autobahn somewhere near the Dutch border. It was a bulletin that interrupted the German radio station's incessant blaring of 1990s techno music. My school days' German language came in handy as I could just about translate the mumbled reports from New York. The news echoed through the coach and the other passengers began shaking their heads in unison. As the bus transited through the Netherlands and into Belgium the true horrors of the day began to unfold.

I'll never forget the silence on the ferry across the English Channel as returning tourists stared in shock at the television screens, watching on loop as the twin towers came crashing down. Every newspaper shared the same image. Everyone knew that things would never be the same again. A new inter-civilisational war was about to commence and its initiators were lined up on our screens for all to see: dark-eyed, sinister-looking Arabs, intent on the destruction of Western civilisation. They were the perfect enemy.

Of course, there had already been the Gulf War in 1990–1, the Iran–Iraq war before that, and both Afghanistan and Iran were ruled by psychotic religious zealots. In Saudi Arabia they enjoyed chopping hands and heads off, and Beirut was a byword for bombs. But terrorists aside, the stereotype of an Arab was either a shepherd riding a camel across a desert, or a wealthy sheikh dripping in gold, hiding his hawkish face behind a pair of oversized designer sunglasses.

Whatever we thought of Arabs in their own lands, in general it didn't affect our perception of the dishdashi-wearing shopkeepers we would occasionally say hello to on the Edgware Road or Atlantic Avenue. Before 9/11, Muslims had existed in relatively peaceful anonymity in the United States and Europe, but as soon as George W. Bush announced the West's 'War on Terror', a long shadow was cast across the entire region and all of its expatriates.

Much has been said about the rights and wrongs of the Second Iraq War and many people blame it for the ills of the early twenty-first century. It seems to have defined a generation – my generation – in a way that is usually the case for much larger conflicts. By military standards, the Iraq war was a minor skirmish. Lasting only a month, it was really an artillery bombardment followed by a swift *coup d'état*. The war, at least from the American and British perspective, was effective, rapid and, at that time, apparently justified. Casualties were limited to only those military targets that resisted, and the city of Baghdad was left largely undestroyed. Civilian casualties numbered into their hundreds, rather than thousands. It was a job well done.

In May 2003, shortly after the statue of Saddam Hussein had been pulled down by American troops, and the war officially declared won, I had just finished my second year of studies. I remember watching as the American flag was hoisted over Baghdad and thinking to myself what interesting times we lived in, however ominous. Through a combination of chance and curiosity, I'd ended up completing a number of modules of my degree course in Middle Eastern history. I'd studied the early Crusades and examined their impact on medieval Islamic culture in the Levant, and I'd reviewed the consequences of Pan-Arabism in the mid-twentieth century.

I had studied travel literature of the Silk Road and read the journals of eighteenth-century pilgrims who undertook the overland route to Jerusalem. I'd read about the conquests of Alexander the Great and Genghis Khan; the history of Persia; the travels of Ibn Battutah and even dipped into the Qu'ran. But it niggled me that I hadn't seen the places other than in my imagination. I wanted more than anything to see the Dome of the Rock; the Church of the Holy Sepulchre; Petra; Wadi Rum; the gates of Damascus and the souks of Sana'a.

I was having a beer with my housemate Alex in Nottingham to celebrate the end of exams, which is how most interesting journeys begin. Alex was a medical student and young eccentric – highly intelligent, brave, fun to be with and well read – and he had the added charm of never saying no to an adventure.

'Why don't we go to Egypt this summer?' I said. 'We can go and see what Cairo is like. I really want to see the Pyramids.'

A wide grin spread across his face.

'Excellent. I'd been thinking something similar myself,' he said. 'Let's go to Israel as well, and then we could take the boat to Greece and backpack through Europe.'

Alex's father was Greek and lived in Athens, and his mother was Jewish, so it made perfect sense. I knew he'd be game for it.

So, a couple of months later, at the end of July, we boarded a plane to Egypt with a very loose plan and whatever spare change we had left from the term, which wasn't very much.

It was a summer to be reckoned with. We spent a few days exploring the souks of Cairo and the banks of the Nile; then we headed east over the Suez Canal and trekked across the Sinai Desert. We scaled the mountain where Moses received the commandments and saw the remaining twigs of the burning bush. After that, a fortnight was spent admiring the domes of Jerusalem and the churches of Bethlehem. I'd fulfilled a childhood dream of seeing the Levant with my own eyes, and it did not disappoint.

I smelt frankincense in the church of the Holy Sepulchre and looked out across the glinting stillness of the Dead Sea. I walked in the footsteps of Jesus, Moses and Abraham. Memories of Sunday school were still fresh in my mind and I felt a deep joy and sense of satisfaction that I'd seen places none of my peers had at that age, and been to places most of my family could only dream of. I tasted falafel and hummus, and ate fresh fish from the Sea of Galilee. I saw camels in the dunes and even rode a donkey through the gates of Petra.

We stayed as guests of Alex's Israeli relatives in Tel Aviv and watched as the sun set over a golden Mediterranean. The turmoil in Iraq, which had unfolded earlier that year, seemed distant and remote as we swilled beers on the beach and partied with hippies in Eilat.

It was good to be young and carefree. We'd planned to take a boat from Haifa across the Mediterranean to Cyprus and Greece, and from there to hitchhike home through Eastern Europe. But there was no rush; we had a whole six weeks to play with, and as long as we were back in time for the new term in September we could go wherever we wanted.

In spite of our relaxed itinerary, it goes without saying that we weren't prepared for the suddenness with which our plans were dashed when, on 19 August, a Palestinian suicide bomber exploded himself in the city centre of Jerusalem, killing twenty-five civilians and injuring a hundred more. As Alex and I sat on the beach enjoying our holiday, the news spread through Israel like wildfire, and the country went into lockdown.

It was the start of a new wave of violence across the region. Security was beefed up everywhere. As Israeli Special Forces scoured the country searching for terrorists, the boats out of Haifa were cancelled, the border back to Egypt was closed and it appeared that we may well be stuck.

'Leave while you still can,' said Ronnie, Alex's uncle. 'This place is about to explode.'

'But we can't go back to Egypt, and we can't afford to fly home,' said Alex.

Ronnie shrugged and said he wasn't able to give us any money. 'If you go to Jordan today, you'll be able to go north from there into Syria and get to Europe through Turkey that way. Good luck to you, though, even if I was allowed to go myself, I wouldn't go anywhere near those hell holes.'

It seemed we didn't have a choice. We packed our bags and made for the eastern border. The Israelis had halted all incoming traffic over the Allenby Bridge, but they let us leave when Alex told them he was Jewish. We took a bus to Amman and a few hours later we found ourselves in the capital of Jordan.

But just as we celebrated our successful escape out of Israel, it appeared we had jumped out of the frying pan and into the fire. That afternoon, at four-thirty, as we were checking into a cheap hostel, a massive bomb exploded at the UN headquarters in Baghdad, killing the United Nations special representative and dozens of others. This time it was al-Qaeda. Jordan, fragile in its location sandwiched between Israel and Iraq, decided to close its borders too. Now Alex and I really were in a pickle. There was no going back to Israel and Syria was closed off as well.

'There's only one thing for it,' I said to Alex, as we sat on the roof of our grotty little hostel, smoking a shisha.

'What's that? We can't ask for any money; both our parents think we're safe and sound on a beach holiday in Greece. They'd go nuts,' he said.

'We can't let a bomb or two stop us,' I urged. 'There's only one border left open. Let's head east.'

Alex looked at me blankly.

'Are you actually suggesting we cross into Iraq?'

'Yes, if it's our only option. There are Americans on the border, they'll surely let us in. We can say we're journalists or something. Then we can find a way north up to Turkey.'

'Are you mad?'

'Well can you think of a better idea?' I asked him.

In all honesty I couldn't quite believe I was suggesting that we hitchhike to Baghdad, but it seemed a preferable option to asking my parents for money to fly home and admitting defeat.

Alex shrugged. 'No, not really. I suppose it'll make a good story one day. If we survive.'

And so that's what we did.

There were no buses going into Iraq, so we went to a taxi stand by the old Roman theatre and asked how much it would cost to go to the Iraqi border, which we'd been told was five or six hours' drive.

The taxi driver grinned. 'I'll take you all the way to Baghdad if you like?' he said. 'I'm Iraqi anyway and it would be a good excuse to see my mum.'

'How much would that cost?' I asked. It was over nine hundred kilometres and I was expecting the worst.

The man looked us up and down. 'You look poor. I'll do it for twenty dollars each.'

Alex looked as stunned as I did. 'Twenty dollars, is that it?'

'Fuel is cheap,' the taxi man said, with a shrug. 'Are you coming or what? It's a long drive.'

So that's how we ended up taking a taxi for ten hours across the Syrian desert into Iraq, only recently conquered by the Americans. A National Guardsman from Alabama stood sentry on the quiet border post. He looked at our passports, welcomed us to the newly liberated country and suggested we buy some guns when we get to the nearest town.

'There's still a lot of bad guys out there,' was his sage advice.

The journey was fairly uneventful, apart from a slightly unnerving hour when our driver cut off the main highway to drive across the desert in a bid to circumvent the town of Fallujah, which was apparently infested with al-Qaeda.

That night we found ourselves arriving in the darkness on the edge of the green zone at the Palestine Hotel, overlooking the notorious roundabout where Saddam's statue had been ripped down a few months before, although the man himself was nowhere to be found. Our taxi driver was convinced the Americans had spirited him away and the whole thing was a conspiracy. Either way, we were at least fairly safe behind the concrete chicanes and razor wire of the compound.

When we discovered that the price of a room was a princely one hundred dollars, Alex suggested we sleep on the roof among the rubble for free instead. A few weeks before, an American tank commander had blown the top off the hotel when he mistook an Iraqi cameraman for an insurgent, killing the innocent journalist and demolishing the rooftop terrace simultaneously.

As I was about to suggest a compromise by camping in the gardens instead, we were approached by a Scottish journalist who was there covering the war. Martin Geissler was the ITV news correspondent, and he seemed rather surprised to see us.

'You pair of idiots. Who let you in?' he said.

We explained the rationale for our unexpected journey.

'Well, we can't have you sleeping on the roof, can we?' He tutted and shook his head. 'You know you are probably the first tourists in Iraq since the war? We have a spare room for the cameras and equipment, so you can stay there.'

And so Alex and I found ourselves with a decent suite on the tenth floor, with great views of the Tigris River. By day we drank cocktails by the pool, listening to stories of the mercenaries who went out hunting for terrorists in disguise, and by night we watched as Black Hawk helicopters flew over the city, patrolling the skies. Often we'd hear the crack of gunfire in the distance, or the rumble of a faraway explosion. It was all very surreal at the age of twenty-one, but an experience we'd never forget.

We ended up staying for a week and eventually managed to blag a free ride all the way to Turkey with some ex-SAS soldiers, who were now security guards responsible for looking after journalists. We travelled through Mosul and Tikrit, where, unbeknown to us at the time, Saddam Hussein was hiding in a hole while US Special Forces searched high and low for him.

Alex and I did make it to Greece in the end, and from there we hitchhiked home through Europe, back to England in time for the next semester, with more than a few tales to tell.

I'd held a fascination for the deserts of Arabia since my childhood. I think deep down there had been a psychological draw to a place of such controversial allure ever since I'd been read stories from the Bible and *One Thousand and One Arabian Nights* as a child. Like many, I'd been captivated by the Middle East, where blurred lines of myth and legend have torn at the souls of travellers for eons. One of my earliest memories perhaps goes some way to explaining why I undertook this journey.

The snow had been falling heavily outside. The fields were glistening white and the little red-breasted robins danced in the holly bushes of my garden. It was 1987 and magical. I'd spent the weekend before we broke up for the Christmas holidays sledging with my father down the slopes of Park Hall Hills. I was only six years old and nothing could beat the thrill of being hurled down what seemed like a mountain. I made my first snowman and threw snowballs at my baby brother.

But despite the exhilaration, something had been bothering me. All week the talk at the school had been about the impending nativity play. I was scared stiff and the pressure was mounting, because I had been given a starring role – I was to be a king. All week we'd been learning about the birth of Jesus. I enjoyed the story of how his family had walked all the way from Nazareth to Bethlehem. Having myself had to walk to school twice that week, because of the snow, it was something I could sympathise with.

I also liked how the Holy Family had been turned away from the inn. I remembered the time last week when we'd gone to the shop to buy oatcakes, and they'd all sold out and my mum came out fraught, and we'd had beans on toast instead. It was basically the same thing, I thought.

I didn't really understand the bit about virgin births and angels, but that didn't matter, because the important bit was the fact that baby Jesus was born in a stable next to some donkeys in something called a manger. And even if Mary and Joseph had it tough, they must surely have been cheered up by all the shepherds who came to say hello. Then there were the kings, whose eminent ranks I was to join on Friday in the play. We'd been read stories by our teacher about the Magi, these wise men from the East, who came bearing gifts of gold, frankincense and myrrh.

As a child I knew nothing about the East, other than what I'd learned at Sunday school. I knew there were sand dunes and palm trees. That was certain, because I'd seen pictures of them. I even knew the different types of camel, and the fact that some had two humps and others just one. I was safe in the knowledge that the Holy Land was special somehow, but I wasn't sure exactly why, other than lots of important things had happened there.

For me, Jerusalem was a faraway mythical city where Jesus had been killed by a man called Pontius Pilate for no other reason than claiming to be the son of God. It all sounded a bit far-fetched and I couldn't distinguish between what was real and what was legend.

Now I had to become one of the kings. It seemed that my coronation was the highest priority for Mrs Watts, who was determined that one of her class would have the honoured role of bringing the baby Jesus a present. I was the one to bring frankincense, which I was assured was a very valuable smelly thing.

Even at the age of six, I was fairly certain that in the olden days, they didn't have Santa Claus wrapping paper around their frankincense packages. My mum had made a crown of golden cardboard for me, encrusted with plastic rubies, and Mrs Watts gave me a long red cloak, edged with fur, which I was sure had been recycled from last year's Santa Claus costume, but again, I kept my mouth shut. Even kings should recycle, I supposed.

The role seemed so complex, so intimidating. I had to lead the other two kings; even Jonathan Barclay, who was the king with the gold. Why did I have to go first? Why couldn't Ben Bowler go first with his myrrh? I was even more scared, because I had to give my fake box of frankincense to Mary, who was actually Stacey Hubbard, who I really fancied. It was all going to be a disaster.

On the big day itself, my nerves were at an all-time high. The crowds were gathered, the stage was set. Baby Jesus was already waiting in the crib and Stacey Hubbard was looking magnificent in her blue robes. Ben Bowler was being naughty and spraying his myrrh perfume all over Dominic Cooper, who was doing a sterling effort of being Joseph, even if his beard was on upside down. I was carefully donning my crown in anticipation of a regal entrance. I was terrified it might fall off.

But then Mrs Watts came storming into the classroom, where we were all getting changed into our costumes.

'We have an emergency,' she said with real alarm. 'There's a change of plan. Poor Andrew Mitchell isn't feeling well and has to drop out. Levison, you'll have to stand in.'

I froze, not sure whether to laugh or cry. Andrew Mitchell, the sneaky little bastard. I knew for a fact he wasn't poorly, he just didn't want to be in the play.

'But, but, but . . .,' I stammered.

'Hush,' said Mrs Watts. 'We need someone who is co-ordinated and can manage the very important job of walking without looking. We can't have a holy animal with no back legs.'

And with that, my crown and robe were confiscated and handed over to Mark Knapper, who grinned with delight. He'd been promoted from being a palm tree, and I'd been relegated to being the back end of the donkey.

3

Yalla

All men dream: but not equally. Those who dream by night in the dusty recesses of their minds wake in the day to find that it was vanity: but the dreamers of the day are dangerous men, for they may act their dreams with open eyes, to make it possible.

T.E. Lawrence

My subsequent encounters with the Middle East were a little more productive. After my exploits with Alex in 2003, I had cause to return to the region a few times over the next fifteen years. In 2010, I drove across Turkey, Syria and Jordan into Africa delivering ambulances. I'd hitchhiked along the Silk Road studying Islamic culture and spent more time than I could remember in Afghanistan, both as a civilian and as an officer in the Parachute Regiment. I'd been to Egypt in the wake of the Arab Spring and in 2012 I returned to Iraq to trek among the Zagros Mountains on the Iranian border.

After I'd left the army, I'd dedicated my life to travel, and as an occasional photojournalist I'd spent as much time on the road as possible undertaking several expeditions to some of the most remote and far-flung reaches of the earth, and yet still I was pulled back to the place that for me held the most fascination. Often, I wonder why it was that I couldn't help being drawn to a place so full of hardship and danger.

Possibly I missed the excitement I'd felt in war zones in the army? Perhaps I felt an affinity to people who seemed to relish a simple life, or maybe it was because I wanted to see those deserts that were ingrained in my soul after a Church of England upbringing – a sense of purity and authenticity maybe, to counterbalance the reality of a privileged life in rural England? Who knows. Whatever it was, I found myself time and again back in the mountains and deserts of Arabia, always looking for something new, something real.

In 2016, I saw something new alright, and it was very real. I was sent by the *Daily Telegraph* to report on the rise of ISIS and the massacre of Yazidis in the Sinjar Mountains in northern Iraq. It was an assignment that opened my eyes forever to the brutality of this new and evil empire that was growing in strength and numbers across Iraq and Syria.

Even though I'd served in Afghanistan as a soldier, this was something else. In 2014, Abu Bakr al-Baghdadi had announced the formation of the new Caliphate of the Islamic State of Iraq and the Levant from the minaret of the al-Nuri mosque in Mosul. It was a town I'd passed through with Alex years before, and there I was again, standing on its northern fringes, embedded with the Kurdish Peshmerga, looking on as ISIS caused havoc and destruction across the country.

I'd gone to see for myself the devastation they had wrought, and the scenes were beyond anything I could have ever imagined. The stories of mass executions, rape and torture were heartbreaking and incomprehensible. I couldn't believe what I was seeing and hearing: entire towns destroyed, bombs everywhere, relics smashed and museums looted; women and children sold into slavery; an entire civilisation imploding.

Between 2013 until the end of 2017, ISIS – or *Daesh*, as locals prefer to call it – took over great swathes of Iraq and Syria, with branches forming inYemen, Somalia,Afghanistan, Iran and even further afield. The conflict, which began when al-Qaeda split into factions amid the chaos that followed the Iraq war, now seemed to be spilling onto the streets of our own cities.

It was as if Saddam's ghost had finally come back to haunt us all. ISIS, the reincarnation of al-Qaeda, had gone fully global. Suicide bombers had attacked everywhere from Paris to Boston, Jakarta to Mogadishu.There was a surge in shootings, stabbings and a new horrific trend in terror attacks involving cars and lorries running people over.

In the UK, 2017 was named as the year of terror. ISIS-inspired Islamic terrorists had gone on a murderous spree with attacks in Manchester and London; the city I'd chosen as my home in between expeditions.The capital had suffered greatly as a result of this jihadist determination to kill Westerners. I'd seen the carnage of both theWestminster and London Bridge attacks and how fear was being sown in my own country.

That's the point of terrorism; it's not only the tragedy of those killed and injured, it's the deep-rooted anxiety that is born of fear, and how it causes fractures in society. It reinforces divisions and creates an atmosphere of distrust.That was the intention of ISIS all along: to generate isolationism among the Muslim communities of the West.To stop them being accepted by the rest of society and to create a sense of us and them.

In doing so, Muslims everywhere would be forced to choose between integration into their host communities, or going over to the side of extremism. ISIS's real strategy was to win the civil war within Islam; to defeat the Shi'a and to establish a single Caliphate that would become a centre for 'true believers'.

It was a scary prospect indeed, not least for the many millions of Muslims around the world who had no desire whatsoever to be ruled by a mad mullah in Syria. Rarely a day went by without the news of the civil war in that country, the daily murders and executions, or of atrocities committed by these Wahhabi psychopaths. Having already travelled widely in the Islamic world, I was more intrigued than ever to find out more about what made presumably normal young men and women leave their homes to go and fight for a barbaric organisation, hell bent on the destruction of the Western world.

The idea of a journey around Arabia came not as one epiphany, as so many of my others had, but more as a growing concern. I'd walked the Nile, the Himalayas and travelled across the fringes of Europe from Russia to Iran in a bid to try to understand what made people tick, on the fault-lines of the geopolitical arena.

I was determined to learn more about the Middle East, and why it has the reputation as the most contested and dangerous region on earth.

I figured it was time to strike into the very heart of the culture that had drawn me time and again back to its roots. I knew I had to go back, on the eve of the defeat of ISIS, and see for myself what the future might hold.

'Are you serious?' said Dave, sipping on his Guinness. It was number five or six by the time I'd built up the courage to mention my idea to my friends.

'Deadly,' I said.

'A trip round the Middle East . . .' He stroked his beard. 'When are you thinking?'

'Well, this time there's no sponsors. No one will pay for it, they all think it's too risky. So I guess there's no point in hanging around, I'd like to go this autumn.'

For a moment there was silence.

'You're mad,' he said. 'We don't get back from the Caucasus till July. It'll take months to get this off the ground. And how do you propose to pay for it all without any sponsorship?'

'I haven't figured that one out yet. I'll pay for it myself if I have to.'

Dave looked quizzically at me. 'Let me get this right. You want to circumnavigate the entire Arabian Peninsula? It'll take months.'

'Yes. Five, I think. Give or take.'

'And how many countries do you propose to go through?'

'Well, it depends which ones are out of bounds, but at this rate not fewer than eleven. There's a few tricky spots.'

'Tricky spots? That's an understatement. And where do you plan to start this grand adventure?'

'Syria,' I said

'Are you fucking kidding me? You'll get your head cut off. The place is a war zone swarming with ISIS.'

'I know. But we can't go around the Middle East and not go into Syria, can we?'

'We?' He pushed his seat back. 'You're assuming I even want to be involved.'

'Well, do you?' I said.

He stared at me intently for a good thirty seconds before taking the last swig of his pint.

'Well, I can't very well let you go on your own, can I?'

'I can't pay you,' I said.

'For fuck's sake,' he said and strode off to the bar.

I watched him trying to order more Guinness in his thick Belfast drawl. I could barely understand him myself half the time and the Russian barman was giving him a bemused shrug. He wore a check shirt and skinny black jeans and his mousy ginger hair shone under the strip lights of the hotel bar.

Dave couldn't usually blend in outside his native Ireland. That wasn't ideal for a man whose job it was to sneak around unnoticed. But somehow, we'd found ourselves in an Irish bar in the Caucasus Mountains, where his massive red beard had allowed him to pass seamlessly for a Chechen fighter. He'd earned himself the nickname 'The White Mullah' from the locals.

Dave was a man of many talents. We'd met as officer cadets at Sandhurst Military Academy a decade before and served in Afghanistan together. Since then he'd acted as a security consultant on several of my projects and been with me in the ganglands of Central America. He was an academic, an engineer, a bomb disposal expert, an accomplished climber and mountaineer, a yoga instructor and all-round travelling guru. On top of that he was a heroic boozer.

I'd also asked Simon to join the party. Simon was tall, impossibly handsome and muscular. He was a photographer and business consultant, who'd travelled to some of the most remote parts of the world advising companies on how to establish themselves in dodgy places. He was a Cambridge graduate who spoke six languages fluently and a reservist in the Armed Forces.

I knew that if I wanted to do this expedition I'd need them both on board in some capacity, even if it were only to get them to help me with the planning and preparation. Ideally, they would come and help with some of the ground logistics and maybe even join for parts of the expedition itself. It was a tall order.

Simon pushed Dave to one side and ordered the round of drinks in Russian, which he'd picked up in no time. The pair returned with the pints of beer and plonked them on the table.

'Are you going to tell him, or am I?' said Dave.

'What are you boys plotting?' Simon asked.

Dave and I looked at each other. I'd not known Simon as long as I had Dave, but I knew he'd make an invaluable contribution. Even though he didn't speak Arabic, I was sure he'd be able to learn it in a few weeks.

'We're going to circumnavigate the Arabian Peninsula. Are you keen?'

'Are you mad?'

'That's what he said. It'll be a real quest. We'll cross the Empty Quarter and see Dhofar. We'll meet the Marsh Arabs and the Druze and the Yazidis. We'll get camels and horses and trek the Hejaz. It'll be the biggest adventure we've ever done. We'll start in Syria and work our way clockwise around Arabia, all the way to the Mediterranean.'

Simon shook his head and smiled. 'I think we're going to need a few more drinks.'

The following morning, I woke up with a raging hangover and looked at my phone. In our excitement, we'd drawn out a route on Google Maps and scrolling along it now made me feel even more sick than the imported Guinness from the bar. Syria, Iraq, Yemen. Countries that people actively avoided, and for good reason. I went down for breakfast with my tail between my legs. I regretted suggesting that I would pay for it, too. I couldn't afford to take on that kind of financial risk, not to mention the very real danger to our lives.

It suddenly occurred to me that perhaps the whole idea was plain daft. As I sat down to breakfast, I was filled with doubt and embarrassment. How on earth could I expect to ask my mates to be involved in such a hare-brained scheme. Maybe what I really wanted was to just go home and read about the Middle East, rather than actually go and spend five months there.

Dave came over with a plate full of cabbage. 'Well, at least the food might be an improvement there.'

'Dave, listen—,' I said, ready to give him an opt-out clause.

But before I could finish, he interrupted.

'So, I've done a feasibility study,' he said, in his best professional tone. 'I've looked at the route and done a risk assessment.'

Simon came over and sat down as well. 'It's bad. Very bad,' he said.

Dave nodded. 'Syria is fucked. We all know that, but in the north-east the Turks are planning an invasion of Rojava to destroy the Kurds. On top of that, ISIS are still holding Raqqa and most of Mosul in Iraq. The Kurds are planning a referendum for independence, which will probably mean they end up scrapping with Baghdad. All of central Iraq is swarming with Shi'a militia, and trust me, you don't want to get on the wrong side of them. I've been there and fought the bastards myself.'

He looked serious. 'Yemen is getting worse by the day. The Houthi rebels are in control of Sana'a and the civil war has already killed five thousand people and a cholera epidemic has just broken out. There's outright famine in parts, and in any case there's no way of getting in. All foreigner visas have been suspended and even the aid workers are getting chucked out. The coast is a no-go, too. The Gulf of Aden is as full of pirates as it's ever been, and Saudi Arabia is off-limits. There's been some new developments in the royal family. They're saying one of the princes has been selected to take over as king, so no doubt that'll upset the rest of them. They don't give out tourist visas in any case and I haven't heard of anyone being allowed to travel there as a journalist unmolested.'

Dave sighed. 'Israel is getting jip about Gaza and Hamas is still kicking off. God knows what Trump will get up to with his policies there. Then, of course, the situation in western Syria is even worse. Assad doesn't look like he's going anywhere soon and nobody in their right mind would go into the rebel areas. There's gas attacks and Russians bombing, and American drone strikes all over the place, not to mention ISIS, al-Qaeda and the two thousand or so other armed groups. Oh, and don't forget Hezbollah in Lebanon. If they find out you've been to Israel, they'll string you up by the balls. I don't want to put a dampener on things, but it's seriously shit out there right now.'

When is it not, I thought to myself.

'Don't forget the weather,' he carried on. 'Even if you set off in September, it'll be forty-plus degrees in the Gulf. There's a hell of a lot of nasties out there, too. Snakes, scorpions and camel spiders. The desert is full of them. Oh, and don't forget the wolves, hyenas and rabid dogs.'

Simon sat there in silence, listening to Dave's analysis.

I'd thought of all those things, and they all worried me, but none of his points were even valid if I couldn't afford to set off in the first place.

'Look,' I said. 'This is all very well, but at the moment, it's all academic. We won't even have the chance to get chased by pirates or shot at by ISIS if there's no money in the pot, so I won't blame you if you're not interested.' It was my last chance to back out, and one that nobody could really argue with.

'We can do it if we all invest,' said Si. 'We'll all chip in.'

Damn it. Now I had no excuses left.

It was time to start doing my homework. I'd asked Dave and Simon to start looking into the more practical logistics like visas and permits, while I concentrated on figuring out how the hell I'd navigate the complexities of a culture so different to my own. Like my previous journey, I thought that the best place to start was with those who had gone before. I was cheered by the fact that plenty of explorers had been to the region and left a great raft of literature on the subject. I re-read Richard Burton's stories of reckless heroism and Freya Stark's incredible tales of a brave woman in a man's world. Isabella Bird and Gertrude Bell would make most modern men wither in their boots with their exploits in the sand. I trawled through Herodotus and Ibn Battutah and took inspiration from the tales of *Arabian Nights*.

There were the great but obscure journals of Doughty and Philby, which gave me food for thought on the practicalities of crossing deserts and dealing with hostile sheikhs. There was Captain Shakespeare, who'd been the first to cross Arabia in a car, only to get his head cut off meddling in tribal politics, and who could forget that hawk-nosed throwback to the Victorian era, Wilfred Thesiger, whose classics *Arabian Sands* and *The Marsh Arabs* will forever take the reader back to an age before oil changed everything.

But above them all loomed the greatest of all the old Arabists, and one of the most controversial and mysterious British explorers of all time. T.E. Lawrence, known to posterity as

'Lawrence of Arabia', was my childhood hero. For as long as I could remember, I'd dreamt of visiting the Hejaz railway, where he spent two years fighting a guerrilla campaign against the Ottoman Empire during the First World War. As far as dead mentors go, he was as alluring as he was dangerous.

I'd read *Seven Pillars of Wisdom* after watching the film *Lawrence of Arabia* as a child. It's a doorstep of a book and despite it being on numerous academic reading lists, I suspect few people can claim to have ever finished it. It's a cautionary tale that must be taken with a pinch of salt. Lawrence was an undoubtedly great man, whose love for the Arabs was unconditional and real, but rarely reciprocated. He was a visionary and yet he was very much a man of his time. He was a player and a pawn, innocent and guilty, a walking contradiction, much like the people he loved to study. He was the embodiment of Arabia itself. Simple yet complex, pure and deadly, holy and yet immovably material. He, like the place, was an enigma.

Spurred on by tales of derring-do and comforted somewhat by having the backing of good friends, I was ready to embark on the biggest adventure of my life. And so on 14 September 2017, sixteen years and three days after the Twin Towers came down, I got on a plane and flew to Kurdistan on the edge of Arabia.

4

Kurdistan

The Kurds have no friends but the mountains.
Kurdish proverb

Rojava, Syria:
September 2017

I arrived at the banks of the Tigris a few hours later, warmed by
the morning sun, and glad to be on the road again. I'd been
looking forward to this journey for so long, that in spite of its
inherent dangers, I was happy and excited for the road ahead. For
the next five months or so, I would be travelling entirely at the
mercy and kindness of strangers, trying to learn more about the
heart of Arabia by following those ancient routes that once made
this the centre of the world; trying to understand why it was now
the root of so much trouble and bloodshed. I'd been warned against
visiting Syria, but I knew that this was where I'd have to begin.

From now on in, I'd be following the course of the great
Tigris River to the point at which it meets the mighty Euphrates,
and there heading south through Baghdad, I would travel the
length of Iraq past the vast marshes onto Kuwait and the Gulf,
where I knew I'd find a very different Arabia.

Beyond that, I hoped to skirt the jagged coastlines of the Emirates
and Oman, crossing some of the sprawling *Rub' al-Khali* – the

Empty Quarter Desert – before reaching the mysterious mountains of Dhofar. Until now, I'd had no idea how I intended on transiting Yemen, still in the throes of a deadly civil war, and after that, Saudi Arabia, who simply didn't issue visas to independent travellers. Then I was vaguely hopeful to reach Jordan and the Holy Land. But I knew that in order to get there, this would not be my only encounter with Syria and its conflict, whose echoes seemed to reverberate around every corner of this stricken peninsula.

First of all, I had to get through Iraq. It was noon by the time I arrived at the Faysh Khabur crossing point. Two Kurdish soldiers, a man and a woman, both armed to the teeth, stood guard over the boat that would take us to the relative safety of Iraqi Kurdistan. There was a queue of several other people waiting for the boat: Syrian refugees, a couple of aid workers and families wanting to be reunited with their loved ones on the far side of the river. I asked a woman where she was going.

'Erbil,' she said. 'I'm going for the vote.'

'The vote?' I asked. In all of the build-up to the expedition and setting off, I'd lost track of time and the news. I'd forgotten that in just over a week, there was to be the first Kurdish independence referendum.

We shuffled down some steps and clambered onto the little motor boat.

'We're all excited by it,' she said. 'We have been trying to gain our independence from the Iraqis for centuries. They take our oil, they make us fight in their wars and they even forbid us from speaking our own language. And now we've had enough, we will have our own free country of Kurdistan.'

The boat man pulled the engine cord, firing the machine into life with a splutter, and the vessel jolted forward into the swirling eddies of the Tigris.

Despite the fact I'd been in Syria a little over twenty-four hours, I was relieved to be leaving and getting back to Iraq.

I thought back to my previous forays into Iraq. Back in 2003, during the tail-end of the coalition war, I'd travelled overland from Amman to Baghdad with Alex, and then again more recently, I'd been to Erbil a couple of times as a photojournalist to report on the ISIS genocide, but this time was different. I was arriving in the Kurdish autonomous region on the eve of a referendum that might change the course of Middle Eastern history forever. More than that, the Iraqi government had finally retaken Mosul only weeks earlier and had gained the upper hand against ISIS, who were now in retreat. I was planning on travelling the length of Iraq and hoped to see first-hand whether the future was hopeful in light of the recent developments.

To help me, I'd contacted an old friend, Omer 'Chomani' Hussain, a Kurd from the eastern town of Choman in the Zagros Mountains. He was discerning, ambitious and well-connected. I'd met him some years before, when I led a climbing expedition there, and we'd ended up thrown into jail together, but that's another story. Omer was waiting on the far bank of the river standing by a 4x4 Toyota Land Cruiser. It was good to see a friendly face on the threshold of my adventure.

I hauled my rucksack off the boat and walked up the concrete ramp past a security barrier to where Omer was standing. With a thick, manicured bouffant and large Ray Ban sunglasses, he reminded me of a young George Michael.

'Mister Lev!' he shouted, as we embraced. 'Welcome back to Kurdistan. It's so good to see you, I've been waiting for your return. You need to see the mess we're in here.'

I smiled back and thanked him for coming to meet me. 'Meet Firman, too,' he added, introducing me to the driver, a rough-looking man with a pistol in his jeans. I went to shake his hand and was greeted with a mangled stump sprouting a thumb and two half-fingers. I ignored his disfigurement and gripped it as best I could. Omer chuckled out loud.

'He's Peshmerga. He lost his hand in a grenade explosion fighting ISIS a couple of years ago.'

I looked at Firman and gave him a soldierly nod. The Peshmerga are the Kurdish army in Iraq and had fought alone on the front line against Islamic State since 2014 with virtually no help from the Iraqi army.

'Let's go,' said Firman. 'It's a long drive to Erbil.'

He didn't look like a man to argue with, so I got into the car and we set off away from the little border post. We drove east parallel to the Turkish border, past Zakho, where I'd escaped Iraq in 2003, and then south, through Duhok and down into the plains of Nineveh, passing by ancient Assyrian villages made of stone and mud. Shepherds and small flocks of goats blended seamlessly into a flat, beige landscape.

As we sped on into the afternoon, our only companions on the road were occasional lorries bringing supplies to the front line, and sporadic military vehicles patrolling the open countryside. Most of the villages seemed either empty or abandoned and many of the farms had been left to crumble. Firman drove in silence, as Omer filled me in on the goings on in Iraq.

'The situation isn't good. The economy is terrible, all the building has stopped since ISIS took Kirkuk and the Turks are still bombing the northern border. We've had no help from the government and the Peshmerga haven't been paid in months.'

It was a familiar story. Omer had been complaining about the same things a year before, when I was last here.

'But Mosul has been retaken, though, that's a good start, right?' I said, offering a glimmer of hope.

'Yes, and thankfully the Iraqi army didn't run away this time, but it was only down to us Kurds, who've been blockading the east for all these years.'

'What about the Shi'a militias?' I asked, wanting to know more about how the Iranian-backed brigades had been involved. I'd heard all sorts of worrying reports that these powerful armed groups were the biggest threat to Iraq's security. Even though they technically worked for the government, I'd read that they were a law unto themselves.

'They're there alright. Killing everyone that moves, ISIS or not. We fear them as much as we do ISIS, they're just as bad, and mark my words, when ISIS is defeated, they'll be on our doorstep and we'll end up fighting them.'

'You'll fight the Iraqis?'

'You know the old saying, Lev. The Kurds have no friends but the mountains.'

'But what about this referendum in a few days? Surely that will change everything. They won't have a choice but to respect it.'

Omer shook his head.

'It's a joke. It's just a way for the president to show some power, nothing will happen.'

'So you'll vote against it?' I said, rather shocked.

'No, of course not. I'll vote for it. All the Kurds will vote for it, a hundred per cent. But it means nothing, it'll just piss off Baghdad and Istanbul, and nobody will support an actual independent Kurdish state.'

'Why not? You have oil.'

'The oil is on the fringes and most of it is outside our lands.

The Iraqis will lay claim to those oilfields in Kirkuk and we'll be left with nothing. It's all a big game for the Iranians, who are taking over in the south.'

As the sun set behind us, we drove on into the evening. It was still warm, but I was glad that the baking sun wasn't beating down on us anymore. The road continued over the Great Zab River and into Kurdistan proper. The night sky was ablaze with a billion stars and the Zagros Mountains were merely black silhouettes in the far distance marking the boundary of Persia, the ancient enemy of the Arabs. But for the Kurds, this wild frontier was their home, and for centuries they had been persecuted and forced to join nations to which they didn't belong.

We arrived late at night and tired in Erbil, the capital of the Kurdish Regional Government, and Omer took me straight to the Rotana Hotel to get a good night's rest.

'I'll see you in the morning, bright and early. There's much to do.'

I'd originally planned on spending a few days in Erbil, acclimatising to the brutal heat and planning my onward journey. There were permits to arrange, visas to extend and introductions to make, but the bad news came over breakfast when Omer arrived.

'You need to get out of Kurdistan tomorrow.'

'Tomorrow? I've only just arrived. What happened?' I said.

'There's talk of a new civil war,' he said glumly. 'The referendum is in six days and they will close all the borders after tomorrow for a week, maybe two. Even the airport has been shut. So unless you get out now, you'll be stuck here and nobody knows what the situation will be like. All the aid workers and UN staff have been ordered out. All the foreigners should go, and that means you.'

'Do you really think it'll be that dangerous?'

'I don't know, but it's not worth the risk. None of our so-called allies in the West are supporting the referendum. Your Mr Michael Fallon MP is in Erbil right now, telling us not to proceed with the vote and to get back into bed with Baghdad. I'd recommend you go south and get to Baghdad as soon as you can. There you'll be safe. Whatever happens, don't go to Kirkuk or go anywhere near Hawija, that's where the fighting is. I reckon us Kurds have less than a week till the Iraqi army attacks us.'

He was right, of course, but I wasn't really prepared to be moving on so quickly. I knew that to get south to Baghdad, I'd have to travel by way of Mosul and get on the main highway via Tikrit and Samarra, but everything to the east of that road was the front line, and still in ISIS hands. I'd been put in touch with an Iraqi fixer who said he'd help – for a price. He was meant to be an undercover operative for the Hashd, also known as the Popular Mobilisation Forces (PMF), a government-sanctioned paramilitary force set up to defeat ISIS, after the call to jihad by the Shi'a spiritual leader, Ayatollah Ali al-Sistani.

I'd agreed to meet this man, Amar, down near the al-Qayyarah Bridge over the Tigris, fifty miles south-west of Erbil. In our last email exchange, he'd signed off with an ominous piece of advice. 'Bring your body armour.'

Since I didn't have any body armour to hand, I thought I better get hold of some. Omer agreed to drive me through the city to a place that sold military equipment.

Erbil city centre is a microcosm of the region, with its stark contrast of the very old and the very new. Shopping malls, high-rise apartments and landscaped water gardens stand in juxtaposition with ancient walls and medieval fortresses. The citadel is perched on top of a huge hill with its adobe ramparts dominating the town. It's a strong contender for the oldest citadel in the world, with evidence dating back to the fifth millennium BC.

The bazaar descends from the fort and was packed with all sorts of stalls selling everything from sweets and spices to second-hand clothes, children's toys and turbans. There were kebab shops aplenty and tea houses filled with men in brown baggy trousers and traditional cummerbunds. Almost all of them were sporting enormous moustaches and glistening daggers; and the women wore colourful dresses with floral headscarves, gold necklaces and imitation Gucci handbags.

The mood in the air was electric; one of excitement and trepidation. Every shop had its bunting dangling from the window panes, and massive flags filled the archways. Cars honked their horns in unison to celebrate the forthcoming prospect of freedom, and as we dodged the traffic, a small aeroplane flew overhead dragging behind it a banner of the Kurdish colours. Peshmerga soldiers waved their rocket launchers in celebration and posters were stuck on every wall proclaiming a unanimous vote in support of independence, each of them displaying a victorious president of Kurdistan, Masoud Barzani.

We made our way through the crowds to the place where we'd come to go shopping. A row of stores displayed an array of military hardware.

'Welcome, sir,' said the shopkeeper, beaming, a shifty man in a fake leather jacket.

'What do you want? Night vision goggles? A bayonet? Pistol holder? Ammunition belt?'

I felt as if I'd suddenly walked into the Wild West.

'Just some body armour, please. Do you sell flak jackets?' I asked.

'Of course we do. You want ballistic protection or just for show?'

'Erm. The real thing, please, I suppose.'

He shrugged and pulled a heavy black Kevlar-plated chest rig from a coat hanger and lumped it on the counter.

He leant close to me and whispered. 'You need a weapon, too?'

'No thanks,' I said.

Omer had been flicking through the collection of camouflage jackets and US marine pattern trousers, most of it pilfered from American contractors, or the surplus of the previous fifteen years of war.

'You better take one of these, too.' He tossed me a bulletproof helmet, also black.

'It matches the vest.' He smiled.

With that we drove south out of Erbil, leaving the party behind before it even got started. Ahead, to the south, lay the frontier with federal Iraq, which I knew would be a new world entirely. We passed a number of Peshmerga checkpoints, but Firman simply flashed his stumpy hand and they waved us through, until we finally reached Makhmour on the front line of Kurdish control just as the sun was setting.

'This is the last checkpoint,' said Omer nervously. 'Beyond that, it's all Arabs. Us Kurds don't go any further south than this.'

An American Special Forces captain stood next to the Kurdish guard at the makeshift barrier and walked up to the car.

'There's no movement south of here,' he barked in English at Firman. Firman just sniffed.

The American poked his head inside and saw me.

'Who are you and where are you going?'

'I'm British, I'm going to Baghdad,' I told him, holding up my press pass.

'Are you fucking crazy?' He took a step back. 'Who are you with? These Kurds can't go any further than the river.' He pointed towards Al-Qayyarah and the bridge over the Tigris.

I explained to him that I was meeting a man at the bridge called Amar, who was supposedly part of the Hashd PMF and from then on in I'd be under his protection.

The captain shook his head. 'You know from midnight tonight this whole route is closed off. The final offensive begins tomorrow against ISIS in Hawija, and KRG is getting shut down for the referendum.'

I nodded and told him that I knew.

'Well, it's your head,' he said with a shrug. 'You're lucky to get out, but I don't envy you where you're heading, it's a war zone down there. Be careful.'

He signalled for the barrier to be lifted and Omer drove us to the bridge. It was pitch black by the time we got there and all I could see was the cluster of hundreds of vehicles queueing to cross the river. As we entered the fray, I saw that these weren't any old cars, they were what seemed to be an entire Iraqi army brigade. There were artillery pieces, tanks, armoured troop carriers, tractors, Humvees and hundreds of pick-up trucks with massive machine-guns mounted on the back.

A stream of refugees was pouring in from the other side – hundreds of bedraggled families carrying their possessions in wheelbarrows and strapped to the roofs of their cars. Headlights blazed out of the darkness and soldiers rushed around barking orders and frantically waving the vehicles in different directions.

It was utter pandemonium on the bridge itself, as the troops massed, ready for war.

Firman saluted with his mangled hand and said goodbye. Omer looked at me. 'This is the end of the road for us, my friend, I must go back to Erbil. I mustn't miss the vote.' I thanked him for his help so far. As I went to shake his hand, he gave me something in the darkness. I squinted and felt the object that he placed in my palm. It was a commando dagger in a sheath. I looked up at him.

'Keep it with you.' He stared at me in earnest. 'You can't trust the Arabs.'

5

Jihad: This Is War

When the shooting starts, climb on your camel and head for the mountaintops.

Bedouin proverb

Amar was waiting at the side of the road. He was big and burly with a jet-black beard, yet at the same time he looked slightly pear-shaped and wore thick-rimmed glasses and a leather handbag.

'What the fuck took you so long?' he bawled, as I got into his jeep.

'Lots of checkpoints,' I said, perturbed by his immediate rudeness.

'Fucking Kurds,' he muttered to himself, in an American accent. 'It's late. We need to get a move on and get to the safe house.' He hadn't even said hello.

We drove twenty kilometres through the night, following the flow of the military convoy, weaving our way between the tanks and the tractors. As the flash of headlights illuminated the roadside, I could just make out the shadows of the bombed-out buildings and bunkers and barbed-wire entanglements. I could tell we were close to the front line. For the last three years, the western banks of the Tigris had seen some of the heaviest fighting and most devastating destruction in Iraq, as

48

fighting and most devastating destruction in Iraq, as ISIS, the Iraqis and the Kurds had fought for control over Mosul.

Amar drove us to a villa, where he pulled up behind a fortified wall. We were in the outskirts of a town or a village, but the darkness was overwhelming. There were no street lamps at all and the only light was from the glow of cigarettes being inhaled by weary troops sat huddled around in the garden. There were shadowy figures lurking everywhere and the bodies of sleeping soldiers littered the path that led to the main house.

'This way,' said Amar, stepping over the snoring men, whose only pillows were assault rifles and ammunition boxes.

I followed my burly guide up the steps to the veranda and into the house, which was lit by a flickering lightbulb powered by a noisy generator. We walked down the hallway and into a room. It had been someone's living-room once, and was filled with colourful furniture and rugs. There were vases of plastic flowers on the coffee table and chintzy throws on the back of the sofa, and yet the walls were covered in military maps and there were guns stacked up against the wallpaper. In the corner was a group of men drinking tea.

'*T'Fadl*,' said one, 'come and sit down', waving for us to join them. '*Marhaba.*' Welcome.

Amar motioned for me to sit down cross-legged, while a sheikh wearing a white turban and an old American camouflage jacket poured me sweet chai. He had an AK-47 resting between his legs and a radio laid on the floor in front of him, which occasionally squelched. With his dark beard and intense eyes, he looked a bit like Osama bin Laden.

The other three men all sat staring at me, until Amar spoke and introduced me.

'This is an English journalist. He has come to tell the story of our victory over Daesh and show how great the Hashd are. With the grace of Allah and the blessing of our glorious Ayatollah Ali al-Sistani, may he live to go and show the world the greatness of the loyal Shi'a in their fatwa.'

The men mumbled in assent and poured more tea, seemingly satisfied that I wasn't their enemy. Amar had done a good job so far, despite his abrasive demeanour. He wasn't interested in small talk, at least not with me. And he kept the plans to himself; unless I specifically asked what was going on, no translation was forthcoming. Still, it was easy enough to deduce what was happening from the maps and the chatter of the commanders on their radios.

This was the headquarters of the 11th Brigade. Kareem, the sheikh, was the brigade commander and a seasoned soldier.

The next morning, we set off towards Mosul. It was a short drive across the plain and not long until the ruins of the once great city were laid out before us. Thousands of trashed cars littered the roadside on our approach, some of them completely flattened. Craters dented the surrounding fields and gardens, and as we entered the city itself, barely a building was left untouched. The Iraqi army had retaken Mosul by the end of July, only seven weeks ago.

Some people were starting to return to their decimated homes in an attempt to rebuild their lives, but as we grew nearer to the old town, on the west bank of the Tigris, it became clear that no attempt to rebuild this place would be successful. Only by bulldozing the entire city centre and starting again would people be able to come back. The scene of carnage was one unlike any I had seen before.

'Let's walk,' said Amar, bringing the jeep to a halt by an army checkpoint. 'That way you'll really see just how fucked this place is.'

I got out of the car and followed Amar as he spoke to the soldiers.

'We'll need an escort,' he said. 'It's still not clear of booby traps and bombs, so don't go fiddling around in the rubble.'

I certainly didn't have any intention of fiddling around in the rubble. A young Iraqi soldier led the way down what was once the main road to the Great Mosque of al-Nuri. Now it was deserted. The soldier carried a long-barrelled machine-gun and wore a mask over his face decorated with a skull. He looked like the grim reaper incarnate.

On each side of the road were the remains of the old city, once one of the greatest in the world. Buildings lay in utter desolation, some having fallen in completely, others strafed by heavy-calibre bullets. Circular explosion marks could be seen everywhere that rockets had detonated against the concrete. We walked for five hundred metres to the main roundabout. Piles of masonry and bricks and burnt-out twisted cars filled the otherwise vacant streets. Even the feral dogs and cats had fled this haunted place. Only flies and the stench of death remained.

'The bodies are still in there,' said Amar with a grimace, flicking a hand towards the shells of apartment blocks. 'Thousands of them.'

I looked around. There were barrels stacked up against walls with wires sticking out from them: bombs, waiting to be defused. Shredded clothes were strewn about the place and as I looked down, I saw some khaki trousers poking out from under the debris nearby. They were the remains of an ISIS fighter.

'Follow me,' said Amar. 'I want to show you something.'

Amar and the soldier began climbing over the bricks. So much for not fiddling around in the rubble.

He picked a trail, clambering over the charred remains of a taxi, down into a side street. Fridges, microwaves and sofas were strewn across the pavement. The ISIS logo was spray-painted on the walls and the terror group's graffiti decorated the insides of the shops. I wondered what life must have been like for the people living under the brutality of this regime.

'These poor bastards lived under the savages for three whole years. Entire families murdered in cold blood. They blew up the museum and burned down the library.'

Two hundred metres down the street, I saw what remained of perhaps Mosul's most famous building.

'That's all that's left of the al-Nuri Mosque,' said Amar. 'That's where al-Baghdadi gave his speech to proclaim the Caliphate.' He pointed at a huge pile of stones.

I remembered watching it on the news in 2014 with dread and then seeing how ISIS had gone on to overrun most of Iraq and Syria in a matter of months. Now they were all but destroyed, but at what cost? Looking around at the wreckage of the twelfth-century mosque, of which there was nothing left but smashed stones, I wasn't certain.

'And here, in this courtyard, is where Daesh used to decapitate people.' He finished drinking a can of soda and threw it dismissively onto the ground.

'If anyone disagreed with them, or if they just took a disliking to you, they'd bring you out here and chop your head off. The foreigners were the worst. Those motherfuckers from your country led the charge. Jihadi John and all his mates, not to mention the Chechens and the Turks. Plenty of French and Swedish, too. I don't know what bullshit you're letting them get away with over there, but if you'd mind not sending them this way anymore, we'd be very grateful.'

Suddenly there was a loud bang that echoed across the street. I jumped instinctively. Amar laughed. It was clearly a gunshot. Bang. There was another. And another. Bang. They weren't random. They sounded like deliberate shots.

'What's that?' I asked.

'The army is just finishing the job,' he said, with a flash of yellow teeth.

'I thought the city had been cleared weeks ago?'

'That's what the news tells you,' he said, rolling his eyes. 'No, this place is filled with tunnels and bunkers. There's still a few dozen terrorists hiding out. The army is just going around to kill them now.'

'But it's been seven weeks since the city was declared taken.'

'Trust me,' said Amar. 'I don't know what those fuckers are eating, probably rats and their own shit, but some of them are still alive. And they'd rather blow themselves up than surrender, so our boys are out hunting.'

I looked up. An Iraqi army helicopter buzzed overhead.

'Come on, we should leave,' said Amar. 'You don't want to miss the offensive, do you?'

'Which offensive? Hawija?' I remembered what Omer had said about making sure to avoid Hawija at all costs.

'Exactly. It starts in the morning. All those troops down at the bridge will be crossing the front line in the morning, and if you want to get to Baghdad, we'd better go join them.'

Amar smiled now. He was clearly in his element. 'We're all crazy in this country. Fifteen years of war does that. There's not a single bastard in this shithole that doesn't have PTSD. So we just roll with it. Let's go find some action.'

Given that he was my only hope of getting to Baghdad, it seemed I had little choice but to just 'roll with it'.

That afternoon we drove south, following the Tigris River, past the bridge at Qayyarah and on to a new village, where we found Sheikh Kareem, the brigade commander, in a different compound only a mile away from the front line. He was sat in another living-room with his commanders, yet again drinking tea and occasionally whispering orders into his radio. He stood up and shook my hand when Amar and I walked into the room.

'Welcome,' he said with a smile. 'Get some rest, it'll be an early start tomorrow.'

There was no sleeping quarters, so I unfurled my cotton sleeping-bag liner and laid it out on the floor of the living-room. The light stayed on all night as soldiers came and went, stepping over us. There was whispering and heated debate while the plans for the battle tomorrow were deliberated, but eventually I dozed off and dreamt of war.

There were bangs and thuds and the screams of rockets and I felt as though the room rumbled in the wake of mortars. The dream, it seemed, was more of a nightmare. I woke with a start and squinted through sleepy eyes. Amar was snoring loudly next to me, but then there was another thud. I sat up with a start. Perhaps I hadn't been dreaming after all. Boom, boom, boom. No, it was all real. I shuffled up and looked out of the window into the blackness. The dark horizon flashed with not so distant explosions. It must be the Iraqi artillery barrage starting in preparation for the assault. I looked at my watch. It was four a.m. The sun would be up in a couple of hours, and then we'd join the war.

Amar grunted and lit a cigarette. 'I know you think I'm only doing this for the money.' He sneered at me.

I looked at him, surprised by the unsolicited comment.

'But I'm not. I am here showing you this war because the Hashd has a bad reputation. Everyone calls us the Shi'a militia. We're not. We're the fucking saviours of this goddamn country. I lived in America for seven years and came back to do my bit. I've seen more action than you can ever imagine. I've killed more people than you've shaken hands with. I'm a fucking hero.'

I listened to him go on, worried that he might be completely mad.

'I have been on every operation against these savages. Look at you with your body armour. I don't need body armour. I'm invincible. You'll see.'

I kept my mouth shut, thinking it best to let him get whatever it was off his chest. I could tell he held me in contempt and saw me as a rotten journalist, even though he was one himself. I'd done my research on him and his file stated that he was a media spokesman for the PMF and before that, he'd been a translator for the US military. I guess that's how he'd come to live in the States and get himself an American accent.

Half of me wanted to tell him that I'd seen a bit of action myself and had been in the army, but I thought perhaps I'd better not, at least for now.

As the soldiers mustered, we drove on ahead. These were the rear echelon troops and Amar wanted to show me the actual fighting, so he drove us past the logistics convoy to the front line. It wasn't hard to find. We simply followed the sound of the shelling away from the village and into the desert. A mile down the road, we came to a line of trucks and military vehicles lined up next to each other behind a simple dirt embankment.

Hundreds of soldiers were milling about, smoking, chatting and loading their weapons with ammunition.

The men were dressed in all sorts of uniforms. Some looked well-trained and highly professional, with Special Forces outfits and top-of-the-range American assault rifles, whereas others wore robes and flip flops, and torn bandanas around their foreheads. It resembled a ragtag terror organisation more than a professional army unit. I guess to the Kurds, and what was left of the Sunni population, that's exactly what they were.

These were the Hashd, Iraq's feared religious paramilitary. Sworn to protect the Shi'a population of Iraq and heavily sponsored by Iran. Call them what you will, but they were the most effective fighting force in Iraq and the reason that ISIS had been defeated. Each and every one of them was a volunteer, accepting low pay and three years of solid fighting, because the Grand Ayatollah Ali al-Sistani had called a fatwa on ISIS, saying that they were un-Islamic and proclaiming a jihad against them.

We didn't need to wait long before the battle commenced. It happened almost unannounced. The first vehicle spluttered into life – a digger with a big bucket on the front, being driven by a fighter in a cowboy hat – and led the charge across the desert.

The first ISIS village was around two miles away. We could see the low-lying roofs of the adobe houses as speckles in the heat haze. Smoke was already billowing from it, presumably after being bombarded through the night. We parked up the car at the start point, put on our body armour and began walking behind a tank. It was the most surreal experience of my entire life. There seemed to be no strategy, no direction and no tactics, other than a long convoy of vehicles driving in single file straight towards the enemy positions.

The soldiers who strolled among the tanks carried flags and

rocket launchers and were whooping and cheering; some had enormous daggers on their belts and others were dripping in grenades. One fighter, who looked like he'd torn men apart with his bare hands, seemed to be wearing his child's rucksack. In stark contrast to his green fatigues was a pink plastic backpack covered in cartoons. It was as if the cast of *Mad Max* had met Lawrence of Arabia and were off to party.

It was disconcerting to be entering a battle armed with nothing more than a camera and the knife that Omar had given me in Kurdistan. I darted between the cars and the men photographing them. None of them looked in any way fearful. If anything, the gang of baseball-cap-wearing gunmen were joyous, and there was something festive in the atmosphere. They knew they would win; there was no doubt in anyone's mind at all who would come out victorious.

Hawija was the goal, thirty kilometres to the south, not far from Kirkuk. It was one of the last bastions of the Islamic State, and they planned to take it by the end of the week in three days' time. But that meant clearing dozens of villages on the way. Today we would have to cover ten kilometres.

When the digger got to within five hundred metres of the first village, it stopped and rammed its bucket into the earth, creating a bank of dirt that snipers could hide inside. Three tanks lined up and began firing at the houses. The noise was phenomenal as the missiles pummelled the adobe walls and vast columns of dust were kicked up from the impacts. But there seemed to be no resistance. Most of the buildings had already been smashed by the artillery and it wasn't long until the troops ran forward and inspected the damage. There was nobody there. Twenty minutes later, we were off again, covering another four or five kilometres in under an hour. The plains rolled out ahead of us, some of it sandy desert, other parts sparse grassland that a straight dirt road dissected neatly.

'Let's hitch a ride,' shouted Amar, above the din of the crowd and rolling engines. I could tell he wasn't used to walking very far and was already out of breath. A pick-up truck was edging forward and Amar jumped in the back. I tried to follow suit, but the truck didn't stop and suddenly sped off towards the front of the column.

I looked around, and the nearest vehicle was a massive battle tank. The driver, wearing a tight T-shirt, a padded helmet and earphones, gave me a thumbs-up and motioned for me to jump on, so I did. I clambered up onto the metal hulk as the tracks continued to move, and lurched onto the turret next to the barrel. The navigator pulled out his phone and asked if we could take a selfie.

We sped off with a jolt, the tank in hot pursuit of Amar in the pick-up. The navigator was grinning wildly, clearly enjoying the chase. Soldiers waved and cheered as we overtook them. When I was planning this journey, I never once thought I'd be riding a tank into battle against ISIS, on the Ninevah plains, but there I was.

We levelled with the pick-up and found ourselves the second vehicle in the convoy, only behind the digger now. I jumped off and managed to get in the back of the truck with Amar when it slowed down.

He was sneering. 'You fucker. Who told you to get on the tank?'

'You sped off,' I said.

'Well, keep up.'

Before I could tell him to fuck off, I suddenly heard a sharp, cracking sound whip through the air, as if someone had split the atmosphere. Then there was a whoosh and a bang. It happened again and the pick-up lurched to a halt, throwing us forward against the frame of the cabin. Then there was the unmistakable rattle of machine-gun fire from the left-hand side.

'Sheikh Ahmad!' shouted Amar to the driver. 'Contact.'

We'd come under fire from the village a few hundred metres away. The entire convoy stopped, and we all jumped out of the back of the truck and took cover behind it. Bullets began ricocheting off the side of the digger, and I hurried to put my helmet on. The digger immediately sprang into action, digging shell scrapes for the men to jump into and take cover. The cowboy-hat man seemed to enjoy his job, waving and smiling while smoking a cigarette, seemingly unbothered by the amount of lead flying around.

The Hashd began to return fire, spurred on by a mad-looking mullah wearing a pristine white turban and an ammunition belt, who was a spitting image of the Ayatollah himself. It looked like he had fancied a day out on the shooting range. The soldiers lined up behind the tanks and started shooting in the direction of the houses. Then the machine-gunners rattled away and it wasn't long before the tanks all began firing, too. It was an orchestra of violence and I didn't imagine that whoever was shooting at us could survive the barrage. The column began to edge forward.

'Stay with me!' shouted Amar, who waddled forward in the shadow of a tank.

Within minutes, we'd closed in towards a bank of earth that marked the edge of the village. We must have been no further than two hundred metres away from the outlying compounds, as hundreds of the soldiers all massed on the safe side of the bank. While the tanks pounded away, a truck sped towards us and in another bizarre moment, its driver began handing out lunch boxes to the soldiers. I couldn't quite believe what I was seeing. Right in the middle of a battle, only metres away from the enemy, a chap was distributing cheese sandwiches and chicken drumsticks.

'Eat up,' said Amar. 'It's brunch time.'

So I helped myself to a Tupperware box filled with biryani and sat down next to a sniper, who was busy popping off insurgents.

'This is where the real fun begins,' said Amar, pointing at the sky.

I heard them before I could see them. The whirring of rotors filled the air and then, first as little dots that grew bigger and bigger, two American Cobra helicopter gunships appeared overhead. As they zipped past, they let loose a volley of missiles, which whacked straight into the houses, crumpling the earth and shaking the dust for miles around. It caused one soldier to drop his sandwich, earning him a clip around the ear by the mullah.

After the helicopters had done three more salvos and pulverised some of the ISIS trenches, the commander pointed towards the village and signalled for the men to move in. The vehicles once again roared into action and drove around the edge of the compounds to surround the farms and cut off any runaways, while the men climbed over the bank and began strolling leisurely towards the houses.

'Watch out for suicide bombers,' said Amar. 'They're usually waiting, if they're not dead already.'

I got up and followed Amar as we went over the top and walked into the village. I was surprised to find that in spite of the heavy bombardment, many of the buildings were left standing.

The soldiers went around kicking in doors and clearing the buildings, but it wasn't long before we found them.

At first, one old shepherd walked over with his hands raised. He must have been eighty years old, wearing a dirty robe and a Bedouin-style *keffiyeh*, or headscarf, around his head. He lifted his skirts as he approached, showing his bare stomach to indicate to the soldiers that he was not a suicide bomber. Amar shouted to him that we were friendly and to bring out anyone else. The man turned and waved and a little girl ran over, wiping away her tears as she climbed into one of the soldiers' arms. The soldier gave her some water, which she gulped down with joy.

Soon after, more women and children came flooding out from one of the buildings. How they'd survived the onslaught, I have no idea.

'They must have been in a bunker,' said Amar, and he directed them all to line up against a wall. I helped to carry some water and hand it out to the families. The women were crying and many of them were happily tearing off their black burkhas and thanking the soldiers for coming to their rescue.

'We've been stuck here for three years!' one screamed. 'No cold water or good food for three years.' She hugged the commander and kissed his feet.

The woman pointed to a shed. 'In there, they're in there.'

'Who is?' asked Amar.

'Daesh.'

The commander nodded to his men, who ran over and burst open the door, dragging out two men in their thirties. The soldiers ripped off their headscarves and hoisted up their skirts to check their bodies.

'They're looking at the waists and shoulders for rubbing

marks from webbing and rucksacks. Anyone with scars or rubbing is ISIS.'

The women whooped as the two men were dragged out and handcuffed. The soldiers gathered round and began spitting and kicking at the men. One of them slapped the insurgent across the face and another took off his sandal and beat it over one of their heads, until the sheikh came over and ordered the men to calm down. The ISIS men were bundled into the back of the pick-up. They held their heads low in acquiescence, but the fear in their eyes was palpable. They both looked guilty, for what it's worth. Neither of them resisted in the slightest, and both seemed resigned to their fate.

'What will happen to them?' I asked Amar.

He looked me in the eye. 'They'll be dealt with.'

At that moment, a rattle of gunfire erupted on the far side of the buildings.

'Probably one trying to escape,' he said and shrugged, before pointing at a car parked fifty metres away under a lean-to shelter.

'See that? I bet it's a suicide bomber in there.'

I looked across at the rusty Toyota half-hidden by a pile of rubble. As I peered to see if anyone was inside, there was suddenly an ear-cracking explosion. The car blew up, sending smoke and debris flying in all directions. Bits of wood and brick landed nearby and a grey haze obscured what was once the garage.

'One less to worry about,' said Amar, cracking open a can of Coke and taking a long swig. He wiped the sweat from his brow.

'Enough fun for today, let's go get some rest. Tomorrow we'll take Sharqat.'

We drove back to a village where the Hashd's rolling headquarters was currently based. They had taken over a compound and filled it with soldiers and it was now acting as a resupply point. It was dark by the time we arrived, but I could just make out the familiar shape of mine-resistant armoured vehicles, meaning that the American Special Forces were in town. Not wanting to arouse any unwanted questions, Amar suggested we avoid them and bunk up with the Hashd fighters outside in the garden. Everyone was covered in dirt and sweat, but nobody was complaining. It was a hot sticky night and my veins were still pumping with adrenaline as I sat down exhausted by a campfire.

I noticed one of the fighters staring at me. He was a man in his sixties, with a long grey beard. He wore khaki overalls and had big leathery hands. Laid across his lap was the biggest sniper rifle I'd ever seen.

'Where are you from?' he asked.

I told him.

He grunted in acknowledgement. Amar came over and shook the man's massive hand.

'This is Abu Tahsin,' he said, 'the most feared warrior in Iraq. They call him the Hawk Eye. Abu Tahsin, tell this Englishman a bit about your life.'

Abu Tahsin sat and stared at me without a flicker of emotion. I looked him in the eyes. They were cold and grey. I knew that if I wanted to know more about him, I had to hold his stare. He was searching my soul in silence, wanting to know if I was a warrior too, and whether I could be trusted. After a minute, which felt eternal, I felt something akin to acceptance.

'My name is Abu Tahsin al-Salhi,' he said, never taking his eyes away from mine. This was a man who simply didn't blink.

'I am sixty-three years old and I have fought as a Special

Forces sniper in every conflict since 1973. I fought the Israelis, I fought in the Iran–Iraq war, I fought in 1991 against the Americans, I fought in Afghanistan and in Chechnya with the Russians, and in the Balkans, too. I fought in 2003 against your countrymen and during the liberation war for the following ten years. Now I fight Daesh. It's what I do.'

'Ask him how many people he's killed,' whispered Amar in English.

I knew it's a question one should never ask a soldier, especially as a soldier myself. But Abu Tahsin understood.

'Three hundred and forty-three,' he said automatically. 'Confirmed.'

I didn't really know what to say to that.

'I know what you want to ask me,' he said. 'You're a writer. You want to know what I feel, don't you?'

I nodded with a grimace. I didn't feel comfortable asking a man who used to kill British soldiers what he felt about it, but I knew that it was my job.

'I don't feel a thing,' he said. 'It is my job. Allah has granted me these big hands with which to defend my people. Allah has granted me these good eyes with which to shoot straight. I only kill those who mean me harm and only Allah can judge.'

'And what does your wife think about it?' I said, wanting to bring the conversation to a close.

He shrugged and for the first time raised a smile. He slapped me on the back. 'She's pretty understanding.'

We shook hands and exchanged phone numbers. He said that we were friends, regardless of our past, and I promised to send him some photographs and a copy of my book once it was written. With that he got up and slung the six-foot rifle over his shoulder. He looked like an invincible Titan in his shawl and godly beard. He nodded once more and walked away into the shadows. I curled up by the heat of the fire and slept soundly in the knowledge that for now at least, Abu Tahsin – the Hawk Eye – was on my side.

Seven days later, I read in the Iraqi newspaper that Abu Tahsin had been killed on the last day of the fight against ISIS.

6

Holy Destruction

Never trust a fool with a sword.
Arab proverb

The following day we went in search of the 2nd Brigade, a unit that Amar had worked with before and whose commander he knew personally.

'They're good guys,' he said.

We set off out of the village, following a little track into the brown wheat fields. Someone had kindly put out signposts directing troops to the front line. It felt more like an exercise than a real war. Green flags and red ribbons and little arrows pointed latecomers in the right direction, as if it were some sort of Easter egg hunt. We followed the signs out through the fields and beyond to the rocky plain where the tracks petered out.

Somehow in the dust and bright light of the morning sun, we managed to veer off the track and lost sight of the ribbons and flags. In our quest to find Sharqat, we ended up driving around the desert in circles for two hours before we got back on track. At one point, our car broke down and when I looked at the map I realised we were only two kilometres from the nearest ISIS village.

'All these towns look the same,' said Amar, punching his GPS system in the car. It didn't inspire much confidence to have my guide basically admit to being lost. I grabbed the binoculars and peered out of the window across the desert towards a nearby settlement. I could make out the minarets pointing from the roofs, and above a domed building I could see the black flags of ISIS.

'Erm, I think we go around this one. Maybe let's head back the way we came?' I suggested, in as diplomatic a way as possible. What I actually wanted to say was that he was a bloody idiot for driving us across the desert into ISIS territory in a car that was prone to breaking down, but I thought better of it.

Amar had lost face and was sulking by the time a car came past and towed us away, back along the road towards the Tigris. Eventually, though, we found the way to Sharqat, the largest town on this stretch of the river.

'We'll drive as close as we can, but the town centre is still in ISIS hands,' said the soldiers who had towed us. They dropped us off by a stationary military convoy on the outskirts of the town. We'd found where we needed to be, and it was apparent that the battle was just getting started. The thud of mortars shook the ground nearby and I knew instinctively that they were incoming. Nobody seemed to bat an eyelid.

'Is this the Second Brigade?' Amar asked a soldier wearing a bulletproof vest over an otherwise naked torso.

'No, this is the Tenth,' said the man, who was dripping with sweat in the late morning sun.

Amar looked surprised. 'Right, Wood, we're in luck. These boys are the spearhead unit, we must have bypassed the Second. They are right at the front of the whole divisional assault. See that digger over there?' He pointed down the street. 'That is the point vehicle. Literally everything to the south of him is Daesh.'

They were as ragtag a unit as the men the day before, carrying whatever guns they could get their hands on and driving whatever vehicles worked. Nearby a young soldier in jeans and a cap was busy configuring his phone into a hand-held control pad. At his feet was a small white drone with an inbuilt camera.

'What's he using that for?' I asked.

'Looking for the enemy, I suppose,' said Amar.

I walked over and looked at the screen, as the lad sprang the drone into action and it buzzed into the air. He sent it up two hundred metres and then forward over the digger. From there he flew it higher and sent it first to the left and then to the right and into the distance above the town, until we couldn't see it anymore. I squinted at the screen. It was hard to see all that much, as the sun was reflecting off the monitor, but I could make out the aerial cityscape and what looked like motorbikes zipping around between the alleyways.

The young man looked at me and winked. 'Daesh,' he said, with a mischievous grin.

A tank behind us clunked and lurched forward and followed behind the digger until it came parallel, and then it loosed off a succession of rounds, smashing some houses down the road to pieces. Whoever was on the receiving end was now blown to smithereens. I looked off to the right down a side street. Men in black uniforms with the Iraqi flag on their arms and wearing the latest Kevlar helmets were stacking up outside gates and kicking doors down.

'They're the Iraqi special police units. They're not Hashd,' said Amar. 'They're Sunni, not Shi'a. They go in so they can deal with their own people.'

I asked him what he meant. 'ISIS are Sunni, so the government sends in Sunni troops first, to try and stop it from escalating into a fight between Shi'a and Sunni.' It occurred to me that this was not how it had worked out in Mosul, where Shi'a militias had frequently been the ones to capture ISIS, holding kangaroo courts and impromptu public executions.

Without any direction, the crowd of soldiers and the drone operator slowly edged forward. They followed the tank, which was only a hundred metres ahead of us by now. Amar led the way until we were level with the tank. The digger, just in front, was busy shoving mangled cars out of the way, and I could see that only twenty metres ahead was the town centre in the form of a roundabout. In the middle of it was a flagpole and there, the black flag of ISIS hung limply. Around the edge of the circle were four more identical flags, all surrounded by dangling wires and the debris of war.

'Be careful,' said Amar. 'They're probably rigged to blow.' At this point Amar and I were in front of the digger. As the tank stopped firing, it was eerily quiet. Somehow we'd found ourselves not only on the front line, but in front of the point vehicle. Standing there under the flags of ISIS, I suddenly felt very vulnerable.

Some soldiers came forward and, using their bayonets, started digging around in the soil of the roundabout to make sure there were no booby traps or IEDs. As they got to each flag, they ripped them down one by one and waved them around in joyous victory. They cheered and whooped in delight and soon all the soldiers came forward, along with the bearded imams and white-turbaned sheikhs who had been watching the advance from the side-lines. Everyone wanted a photograph with the ISIS flags, to prove that they had been a part of this final battle.

One of the sheikhs pulled out a green flag of the Shi'a brigades and gave it to a soldier to hoist up the pole, while a special police commander did the same. Soon two flags fluttered side by side above Sharqat – that of the Hashd and that of Iraq. It made me realise that even after ISIS was gone, the contest between Iraq as a nation state and its tribal and religious sectarianism would remain. How could there ever be unity in this divided nation?

It was a question I was left to ponder as we left Sharqat the next day to rejoin the main highway south towards Tikrit. Although we had left the front line behind, the horrors of war were still all too apparent.

'They call this the road of death,' said Amar, cracking into yet another can of Coke, before throwing it out of the window. I could see why. For over two hundred kilometres, the road was flanked by nothing but annihilation.

Entire towns were deserted and abandoned. Death and destruction was everywhere: strafed ruins, bunkers, bombed-out schools and burnt-out cars. Crumbling holes in the road and craters in the sand marked explosions, and the scrawl of graffiti painted on the walls told us whose territory we were passing through. The buildings were held together by the spidery remains of interior metal girders, their doors blown off and the steel contorted.

We passed untended fields with lank stalks of dry, brittle wheat, dehydrated by the piercing heat, and rotting palm fronds lay scattered on the barren earth, russet with decay. The scarred carcasses of pick-ups and detritus of war sat amid pockmarked shrapnel glinting in the dusty sunlight.

Every few miles there was a checkpoint, where we'd be stopped by soldiers. Most of them wore black uniforms and balaclavas

covering their faces. It was becoming harder to tell the difference
between the good guys and the bad guys the further south we got,
but for the first hour or so things were fine. Amar told them he
was with the Hashd and they let us pass without even asking for
identification, but the closer we got to Tikrit, the more intense
became the stares and the more questions were asked.

We crossed the bridge to the east side of the Tigris, where
Saddam Hussein's former presidential compound loomed in its
ruins. Amar pointed to a field on the banks of the river.

'That's where Daesh butchered seventeen hundred Iraqi
soldiers.'

'One thousand seven hundred?' I repeated, not quite believing
my ears, and then I remembered. 'This must be Camp Spiecher?'

Amar nodded solemnly.

'Back in the summer of 2014, when ISIS were rolling the place
up, they came down here from Mosul. The beasts rounded up the
whole cadet force, some of them were just kids. They were
teenagers and lads in their early twenties training to join the air
force. ISIS separated all the Shi'a students from the Sunni and
took them down there.' He pointed to a cliff by the river. 'That's
where they shot them, one by one in the head, so that their
bodies just fell into a grave. Most of the students weren't even
blindfolded, they knew they didn't stand a chance as they watched
their friends getting slaughtered. Seventeen hundred boys.'

It was the single biggest mass execution that ISIS had
committed, but of course there had been many more. In Sinjar,
they had massacred over five thousand people over the course of
a few months. In Mosul they'd killed hundreds, too, mainly Shi'a
again, so it wasn't hard to see why Amar and the Hashd were so
determined to take their revenge.

'This war is sectarian,' said Amar. 'It's not just about ISIS. It's all about the conflict between Sunni and Shi'a. I don't see how this will ever go away. A lot of the people who joined ISIS were the same mercenaries who were in al-Qaeda fighting with bin Laden. And guess where they came from? Most of them were soldiers in the Iraqi army, who had to throw away their uniforms when they lost to the Americans and our military was abolished; what do you expect to happen when you destroy a country and you don't let them have an army?'

He went on, 'If you try and dismantle the military, then all you're left with are a lot of hot-blooded young men with nothing to do. Of course they're going to fight. Most of the time they don't even know who or what they're fighting for, but sooner or later they'll get their hands on a gun and join a cause. Call them gangsters, mafia, criminals, tribes, ISIS or whatever, they're all the same. They're just gangs of young men looking for a fight.' He shook his head. 'That fucker Rumsfeld has a lot to answer for.'

'But there's no fucking excuse for this sort of shit.' He flicked his head back at the execution site, as we rumbled over the bridge and entered the dusty suburbs of Tikrit. The wide, deserted streets were punctuated with rubble and we passed the mournful remnants of a once busy city.

There was another checkpoint at an intersection of the road. I could tell that Amar looked nervous this time, as we pulled over next to a machine-gun position.

'What's up?' I asked.

'Shhh, be quiet,' he said, glaring at me.

I noticed that the flags were unlike the ones I'd seen before at the Hashd roadblocks.

A soldier came up to the window and looked inside the car.

'Passport,' he growled.

I handed mine over. For once Amar didn't mention the Hashd or show them his military ID. He just handed over his Iraqi passport.

'We're journalists,' he said to the man, who grunted and walked away with the passports and began talking on his radio.

Amar leant back and whispered to me, 'These are the Mahdi Army. Muqtada al-Sadr's lot. They're no friends of the Hashd.'

There are something like thirty militias in Iraq, some of them numbering up to fifty thousand fighters, but none were as feared as the Mahdi Army, which claimed to be one of the biggest paramilitary organisations in the country. They were similar to the Hashd in that they were a mainly Shi'a group, but they were led by a militant cleric called Muqtada al–Sadr, who notoriously rose up and fought against US occupation during the mid-2000s. They were known for being some of the most violent killers of coalition troops and operated their own 'death squads'.

These were the same men who had detonated bombs and set traps to kill British and American soldiers only a few years ago. Now they were manning checkpoints as part of Iraq's efforts to bring in the various insurgent and militia groups under Baghdad's control. Despite having a similar outlook to the Hashd in some respects, if they'd known Amar had worked for the Americans, then who knows what trouble we might be in. The soldier returned with our passports.

'Get out,' he said with a snarl, opening the door.

Amar and I got out of the car and stood still. I hadn't seen him look this nervous before and all kinds of scenarios ran through my mind. These were the sort of people for whom the law meant little, and killing a foreigner, especially a Brit, was nothing to them. Amar took out his cigarettes and offered one to the fighter. The man took it without thanks and lit it, the flames briefly lighting up his grizzled face.

Amar gripped the man by the arm and gently pulled him away from me and whispered something to him in Arabic. The man listened in silence. I desperately wanted to know what was going on. I hated being at the mercy of Amar, this unfathomable character for whom violence and intrigue was a way of life. But I knew better than to interrupt a man like this when he was at work. There are different ways of dealing with men with guns, but usually the best way is to let them be in control; to be calm and show them you're not a threat.

So I waited. And waited and waited. I watched as Amar alternated between pleas and jokes, until at last, half an hour later, he returned with our passports and got into the car without a word. He didn't even look me in the eye. I followed suit, and Amar drove in silence.

I wanted to ask what had happened, how he'd got us out of trouble, but there was no point. Amar was an enigma and he would never give away his secrets. I wanted more than anything to try to understand this man, for whom Iraq was home. It was a country he seemed to both love and hate at the same time.

The sun was low in the sky, and soon it would be dark. Baghdad was still a couple of hours away, but there was a place that I wanted to see first. Amar reluctantly agreed to make a short detour into one of the outlying villages.

'It's around here somewhere,' I said, following the course of a map I'd found on the internet. My hunt was for the last hiding place of Saddam Hussein. I'd passed through Tikrit with Alex fifteen years before, when Saddam was still in hiding, and while there was something quite dark about looking for such a grisly place, I felt that his capture was such a pivotal moment in world events that had shaped my life that his hideout was worthy of inspection.

Saddam Hussein was discovered in a tunnel, concealed in a back garden in the winter of 2003, eight months after his regime had been toppled by the Americans. Somehow, he'd evaded capture for the best part of a year, growing a beard and blending in as a peasant.

It was an undignified end for a man who once owned fifty golden palaces, as well as a collection of superyachts and private planes. I remembered watching on the news how he'd been unceremoniously dragged out of the ground by American Special Forces, before being taken away for a show trial and subsequent execution.

We pulled over to ask a local farmer where the spot could be. He pointed to some waste ground to the side of the lane, overgrown with eucalyptus and palm trees.

'You've got five minutes,' said Amar. 'I don't want to be here when it gets dark. This place gives me the creeps, and it's these sorts of places where terrorists make home-made bombs.'

I got out of the car and squeezed through the barbed-wire fence and some bushes. I found the tunnel almost immediately. It was nothing to look at, other than a hole in the ground, filled with discarded litter. But it was what it symbolised that mattered. I'd passed through this place in August 2003, when Saddam was still hiding. I remembered how almost every Iraqi I met was convinced that the Americans had spirited him away to live in opulent exile as part of their great conspiracy. I doubt anyone would have believed at the time that he was dug in under a vegetable patch, buried like a rat.

His hiding sparked one of the largest manhunts in history, and the Second Iraq War, itself arguably one of the most controversial in recent history, went on to shape the politics of the Middle East for the last fifteen years. And this is where it ended for the man at the top of America's most wanted list.

'*Yalla.* Come on!' shouted Amar from outside the garden. 'It's time to go.'

I left the place and got back in the car just as the sun set behind the palm trees. We drove on in silence to the south, as the shadows engulfed the river and the ancient walls of Samarrah faded into the desert beyond. The twirling minaret of the great mosque marked a once fabled land. Now, like everything else in Iraq, it was covered in filth and at risk of collapse.

We arrived in the city late and went straight to the Hotel Baghdad, a shabby place for shady-looking businessmen. The bell boy helped carry my body armour and helmet out of the car and slumped it up against the reception desk.

'You've come from the north?' he asked. I nodded, and in the hope that I wouldn't need it again, I left it there.

Amar was irritable from all the questioning and roadblocks – there had been seventeen on the way in to the capital – so after we'd got the room keys, he just walked off without so much as saying goodnight.

I was tired too, and I needed a bit of a break from Amar, so I took the lift to the seventeenth floor and made my way through a fire escape onto the roof. I looked across the road towards the Palestine Hotel, where I'd stayed thirteen years ago that fateful summer. If it wasn't for those naïve travels, I thought to myself, that had got me addicted to life on the road in the first place, then maybe I wouldn't be here now. I wondered for a while whether that was a good thing or not.

From the roof, I could see the meander in the Tigris and on

the far side the glimmer of lights from the green zone. Nowadays it was quiet. There were still plenty of Iraqi army on the streets, but no Americans these days, and while there were still regular bombings and terror attacks, it wasn't as dangerous as before. I thought about the last few decades and how Iraq had sat centre stage in world affairs, all because George Bush Jr. had a bee in his bonnet about succeeding where his father had failed. Saddam Hussein was a bastard, yes. But there were plenty of other bastards around.

Now it was Syria's turn to be meddled with. Six years of war had reduced that country to ruins, too.

I looked out across the blinking cityscape, as car horns sounded and the roar of motorbikes rattled through the streets. It seemed little had changed in the years since I was here last. In the distance, I saw a stream of red tracer fire dart across the sky. It was so far away, I couldn't hear the gunfire and it was impossible to know if it was belligerent force, or simply a wedding with a few too many guns. Nothing was beyond the realms of possibility in Iraq, and everything was normal.

It was that normalisation of violence that made the place so bizarre, terrifying and alluring at the same time. Amar was only one of a multitude who had clearly suffered from the stress of living in a war zone. I'm no psychologist, but this was a man with mental health problems. How could you not suffer from PTSD, if you had grown up in a war zone for the last fifteen years and went around chasing gunfights for a living.

I reached my room and realised I was exhausted. I'd been in overdrive for a whole week, on the road and weaving through a strange world of war, barely sleeping and in a state of constant emotional excitement. The next few days promised more stable turf in the Shi'a heartlands of southern Iraq, but as I fell into a fitful sleep, I was still on edge.

I may have passed my first test, but I already knew it wouldn't be the last.

7

The Land Between the Two Rivers

I will set up my name in the place where the names of famous men are written, and where no man's name is written yet, I will raise a monument to the gods.

The Epic of Gilgamesh

Leaving Baghdad, we followed the eastern branch of the Euphrates River, arriving at the town of Hilla the next morning at around ten a.m. With its dusty streets and concrete roundabouts and shops selling car tyres, it would have been quite unremarkable, were it not for one thing. This was the site of the most famous city of the ancient world.

Babylon. It's a name that evokes images of despot kings and hanging gardens, Alexander the Great and riches beyond imagination. This Bronze-Age metropolis's name literally means the Gate of God, and for centuries it was considered the very heart of civilisation.

I'd been excited to see the place since reading about the exploits of Alexander as a child. Amar didn't share my enthusiasm.

'There's nothing here. It's just a pile of old bricks,' he grunted.

I didn't care. I wanted to see what was left of the city that used to be the biggest in the world. An old man who served as the guard let me in for a small fee. We entered the complex, hidden behind the palms and thorny acacia trees, through an arch that looked new despite its Akkadian heritage.

'Saddam rebuilt it all,' said Mohammed the guide.

He led the way up some stairs onto a platform, where we could see the extent of the refurbished walls. They stretched out for a mile towards the river, surrounded by crumbling mounds.

Mohammed pointed down towards the new-looking ramparts. 'He did this. He built these walls in the 1980s on top of the original ones two and a half thousand years old.'

'They look quite nice,' said Amar.

I shook my head at the barbaric philistinism.

Amar laughed. 'Iraqis don't give a shit about ruins. They want to see big walls and shiny things. It's how Arabs think.'

Mohammed led the way down the steps, past reliefs of the animal gods, until we reached an archway. I looked at the bricks closely. You could tell the ones above a certain height weren't very old, even though they were of the same clay and earth that Nebuchadnezzar II must have used. The original ones had the name of the Babylonian king stamped on them and the construction date, which apparently said 605 BC. The newer ones had some modern Arabic script.

'What does it say?' I asked.

'Well, when Saddam came here and saw the old writing, he suggested the new bricks should have his own name on them.'

In the reign of the victorious Saddam Hussein, the President of the Republic, may God keep him, the guardian of the great Iraq and the renovator of its renaissance and the builder of its great civilisation, the rebuilding of the great city of Babylon was done in 1987.

'The problem was nobody knew what the original palace looked like, so most of this is guesswork,' said Mohammed.

'Like this arch.' He pointed up at the huge doorway. 'No one really knows how high they were, or how high the original walls were, for that matter. But because it was Saddam, the builders decided they needed to be really big. It was all done by Sudanese immigrants. All the Iraqis were off fighting Iran at the time, and they had to rush to get it done in time for the 1987 arts festival.'

I thought back to my own school nativity play in 1987, when I was only six, and the three kings from the East, bearing gifts of gold, frankincense and myrrh. I never imagined at the time that I'd be standing on the walls of Babylon in the footsteps of kings and dictators.

We wandered through the deserted palace. The only other living things were pigeons, who had taken roost in the garish columns. I supposed there was at least something to celebrate in the fact that in recreating the palace, for all its vulgarity, perhaps Saddam had preserved the site for future generations. Looters were less likely to come and rob a place with such high walls and security guards. If it were left as a pile of crumbling bricks, then in all likelihood it would have been built on by villagers or trampled by soldiers.

Mohammed led me outside around the walls to a patch of waste ground covered in litter, where a barbed-wire fence marked the perimeter of the archaeological site.

'That's where the river used to come.'

He pointed to a small wadi filled with palms. Plastic bags fluttered from their fronds and they were caked in a thick layer of grime from the dust kicked up from a nearby road. I looked across to the far side of the wadi, now dry after centuries of irrigation and redirecting of the river. One of Saddam's palaces loomed on top of the cliff. It was now empty, apart from a few Iraqi troops who were using it as their headquarters.

Mohammed stood looking sullen. 'And this,' he said with a sigh, 'is where the hanging gardens used to be.' I looked around at the acacia scrub and the empty bottles and the piles of baked goat shit and wondered if Alexander the Great would have seen this future as dystopian.

'I can show you where he died, if you like?' said Mohammed.

We walked through another arch and back into the adobe maze, following a narrow corridor, and then into the open courtyard at the centre of the complex.

'Right here,' he said, pointing at the floor. 'They say he was poisoned.'

Standing in the middle of Saddam's folly of Nebuchadnezzar's palace, in the spot that Alexander the Great perished after conquering the known world, was a surreal feeling. After seeing such devastation myself, it was a stark reminder that this land had always been a magnet for conquerors, despots and invaders. The latest strife was merely yet another iteration of an age-old struggle between East and West. And Iraq, now as then, lies on that geographical fault-line.

The *casus belli* may have changed since the days of the ancient kings, but the geography remains more or less the same. Nebuchadnezzar was a local Assyrian who wanted to expand an empire westwards to the Mediterranean, but he was conquered by Cyrus, a Persian from the East, whose empire was in turn defeated by Alexander from the West. These conquerors came from both sides, drawn to the allure of the fertile crescent and the riches it contained, as well as its strategic importance in both overland trade along the Silk Road and its position on the Gulf.

More recently, of course, it's the allure of oil that brings in the armies from abroad, and religion provides a decent enough excuse. Ostensibly, the latest sectarian fighting can be boiled down to the divide between the Sunni majority and the Shi'a minority. Nationalism has increasingly played second fiddle to religious loyalty, as dictators are toppled and identity is called into question.

It took around three hours to drive to the outskirts of Nasiriya and it was already late afternoon. Amar wanted to get to the town and find a hotel. Fair enough, but I wondered if he was using the pretence of needing to report in with the police to justify his own idleness. We'd fallen into a routine of a constant psychological battle, and I felt I was having to fight the man's ego on a daily basis. There was no use in arguing or stamping feet, because he would use his trump card of 'security'.

So I had to explain my motives for wanting to see this or that, and try to convince him how much it would benefit Iraq and him personally to be seen to be helping me. If that didn't work, I'd end up bargaining with him. 'Let me see the Sumerian ruins and you can have half an hour extra in bed,' and that sort of thing. It was like dealing with a toddler at times, and with each passing day I was less inclined to spend time with him, and yet I knew my life was ultimately in his hands.

Anyway, eventually I persuaded Amar to take a short detour to visit Eridu. I'd already stayed in Erbil and seen Babylon, and both can lay claim to being among the first ever cities. Further on in my journey, I hoped to visit Jericho and Damascus, too, arguably the oldest continually inhabited settlements in the world. But Eridu was a place apart.

The city was founded sometime in the fifty-fourth century BC and was the southernmost of a cluster of Sumerian towns based around mud-brick temples. It was here that the first kings were said to have lived.

A German archaeologist in the early twentieth century discovered a clay tablet written in cuneiform, the first recorded written language, in what was then southern Mesopotamia. On it is the first piece of history ever written.

After the kingship descended from heaven, the kingship was in Eridu.

It was said that there were eight kings who ruled before the great flood. While historians debate the reality of the deluge, there are remarkable similarities between the statements made in the 'Sumerian Kings list' and the book of Genesis. Although a word of warning, some of the dates are a little improbable. The tablet continues by listing the lengths of the reigns of these early kings.

In Eridu, Alulim became king; he ruled for 28,800 years, which even by biblical standards is a rather long time.

The list goes on and on to recount the name and epithet of each successive ruler, and after the flood, the life span of these ancient demi-gods seems to get progressively shorter. Etana, 'The Shepherd-King', lived for a mere 1,500 years; and Aga of Kish, 'Son of En-me-barage-si', had a pitiful 325-year sovereignty. By the time Sargon of Akkad came along in 2270 BC, kingships had reduced to a more palatable forty years, presumably as people got to grips with basic mathematics.

But in spite of the artistic licence when it came to data recording on behalf of the royal line, these stone tablets were useful in dating these early civilisations and we now know that Eridu, and its nearby sister city of Ur, do indeed date back at least five and a half thousand years to the very limit of history. It was here on the edge of the swampland between the two great rivers, the Euphrates and the Tigris, that the earliest organised societies were founded after the first agricultural revolution. It was on this spot that prehistory suddenly (in the grand scheme of things) got written down. And, as they say . . . the rest is history.

We parked the car at the end of the dust track, where an Iraqi soldier pointed to the hill. Nearby in the gravel mounds were the remains of an old firing range and a burnt-out tank that dated to the Gulf War. The hill was the only remains of the oldest city in the world and because it was the only hill for miles round, it had been used by soldiers as a look-out point for centuries.

I walked out across the sand towards the monument. There was no one around, no fences or signs, only millions of ancient crumbling bricks of mud. I climbed up to the top of the mound. All around were shards of ancient pottery dating back at least four thousand years, but some of it may have been earlier, perhaps seven thousand years old. It was quite mind-boggling. But it wasn't just pottery that lay abandoned. Many of the bricks and lumps of clay, on closer inspection, were covered in cuneiform symbols – the earliest writing. The place had, of course, been excavated over the last hundred years by archaeologists, but only three or four times, their work usually interrupted by Iraq's seemingly insolvable problem – war.

Now Eridu was merely another lump of dust in the desert, unprotected and unloved. I hope that one day it might be guarded; after all, this was where it all began.

Amar shrugged. 'There's a war on, we've got bigger fish to fry,' he said. 'Speaking of which, I'm hungry, yalla. Let's get to Nasiriya.'

The desert appeared to change into a thousand colours as we drove east. There were reds and oranges and purples. Long shadows were cast by invisible ridges and I spotted an eagle soaring overhead scouting for rats. Near to the ruins of an old shepherd's hut, I saw some camels. They were the first I'd seen on the journey and I felt a shiver of excitement. They represented t h e natural form of the desert, and against a backdrop of melancholy, for some reason they embodied hope. As the sun set over the sand flats, we reached the edge of the town in time for the call to prayer, which echoed across the streets.

We ate binni, a type of barbell fish, on the banks of the Euphrates, at a little roadside restaurant. It's a bottom feeder and tasted earthy, but I was glad to be given something different. It was the first dish we'd had that wasn't meat and rice and it came as a welcome change. I looked across as fishermen in little motorboats sped out into the darkness to lay their nets for the evening.

'They're Marsh Arabs,' said Amar, pulling a bone from his teeth.

I'd read about these people in Thesiger's famous book, *The Marsh Arabs,* but I'd assumed that their culture had long vanished.

'Didn't Saddam Hussein wipe them out? I thought he drained the marshes,' I said to Amar.

'I think there's still a few left. The marshes are coming back,' he replied.

I suggested we travelled east to see if we could meet some and found Amar surprisingly willing.

'Fine,' he said. 'But I'm not sleeping outside with the mosquitoes.'

We compromised and agreed that we'd go towards Chibayish in the central marshes, south of Amara, and find a place to stay for the night before it got too late.

Jassim was a jolly man, with a kind smile and passionate positivity that shone through his sparkling eyes, that were only magnified by his little reading glasses.

'Of course, you can stay here.' He grabbed Amar by the arm and slapped him across the back in friendly encouragement, motioning for us to follow him into his house on the banks of a canal.

We'd asked around for a hotel and been uniformly told not to bother, instead to search for the man who knew the marshes like no other. Chibayish was a small town nestled on a strip of dry land between two great lakes, but it was dark and we could see nothing of the swamps at this time. Only the green light of the mosque reflected off the water and a few lanterns twinkling in the distance, a reminder of the fishermen who spend their nights out looking for a catch.

Jassim worked for an Iraqi environmental agency and his job was to protect and restore the marshes.

'I've been here all my life. I was here in 1991 when that monster Saddam drained the marshes. He wanted to flush out all opposition and the people here hated him, so he punished them by killing off their home. Ninety per cent of the marshes were gone. People have lived here since the beginning of time, and then one man could do so much damage,' he said mournfully.

'So what exactly is left?' I asked, eager to see for myself what remained of this unique environment.

'Get some rest,' he said, smiling. He showed us to his spare rooms and began puffing the pillows. I looked around the house; it was like a museum, full of wooden oars and reeds and trad-itional clothes pinned to the walls. 'I can take you out in the morning at first light, and you'll see the real beauty of the marshes and a side of Iraq you could never imagine.'

We woke at four a.m. to walk down to the canal in the dark. The streets were quiet, apart from a few scavenging feral dogs, which were rummaging around among the piles of rubbish. The canal was filled with litter and a layer of scum floated on its surface, reflecting the moonlight in glinting flashes of foam.

Abu Haider was waiting on a boat. It was a small wooden thing, big enough for only three or four people. He was at the back next to an outboard motor, but held a large punting stick across his lap. He stood to shake hands as Amar and I climbed aboard with Jassim. Abu Haider was a Marsh Arab.

'He is our boat man. His family have lived in these swamps for thousands of years,' said Jassim. 'We call them the *Ma'dān.*'

Abu Haider, in his long black shirt and black-and-white keffiyeh, looked like a wise old man. The wrinkles around his eyes and creases on his face testified to a lifetime of laughter and he looked incredibly happy for a man who had been awake at four to come and get us.

'Yalla,' he said, with a wink. 'Let's go.'

He stood and began to punt with the eight-foot-long pole, pushing us along the canal until it opened up to the lake. As we glided out onto the placid water, I felt an immediate sense of peace and calm. The first glow of light was beginning to appear on the flat horizon, as the sun pushed up above the reeds. It wasn't long before we had gone far enough out to be in the deeper waters, and Abu Haider pulled the rip-cord on the outboard motor, which spluttered into life, disturbing the otherwise serene silence.

We sped across the lake and soon found ourselves zipping in among narrow channels between the high reeds, some of which reached three or four metres high. As the sunlight filtered through, the scale of the swampland became apparent. In gaps between the papyrus, I could see for miles around the utter flatness of the bogs. Only distant plumes of smoke interrupted the pure morning atmosphere, indicating the faraway villages. A kingfisher buzzed in front of our boat, as if to remind us that nature reigned here and we were but visitors.

'All of this was completely dry fifteen years ago,' said Jassim. 'After Saddam drained it, all the local people had to leave. The reeds turned to dust and it was just desert. You wouldn't believe what it looked like.'

He was right, I couldn't imagine it any other way.

'When the British and Americans came in 2003 and got rid of him, we started to try to bring the water back.'

'How did you do that?' I asked.

'We had to dig canals from the Euphrates and redirect the water. Now it's being rejuvenated. We've got them back to just over half of their original levels.'

Suddenly there was a rustling to our left and two metres away I saw the startled figure of a warthog snorting on the bank, before it scuttled off into the bushes.

'Luckily the wildlife is returning slowly, too,' said Jassim.

We sped through the channels before coming to an abrupt stop, as the boat lurched forward. Abu Haider pointed ahead. I could see why he'd hit the brakes. Just in front, I could see the dark black mounds of something moving in the water. There were dozens of them, like vast boulders, but they were alive.

'Buffalo,' said Amar. Jassim smiled.

There was a grunt, but apart from that they ignored us as they swam from one side of the bank to the other, and then one by one they clambered out of the water and lolled themselves into the reeds, munching away on the verdant leaves.

'They belong to the Ma'dān,' said Jassim.

Once the buffalo had passed, we carried on for another

forty-five minutes, deeper into the swamp, as the sun burst above the horizon and the whole world seemed to glow a perfect deep orange. Abu Haider began to chant. It was rhythmic and hypnotic.

'It's their song,' said Jassim.

It was beautiful, I thought. Jassim joined in and added his own lyrics in Arabic.

'What's it about?' I asked.

Jassim smiled. 'It's a poem, about the same things all poems are about. Love and sadness. I used to come into these marshes when I was a boy, even though my family were land dwellers. I used to like coming in here on the boats. It's where I met my first woman.' He laughed with a roar. 'I used to come here in the evenings and make love to her in the reeds.'

The marsh opened out before us and the reeds gave way to what appeared to be flat islands, spreading as far as the eye could see. In the shallow waters were dozens of buffalo wallowing in the mud and yet more grazing on the banks. Ahead I could make out the silhouette of a settlement. A few little shacks made entirely of reeds, bundled together like thatch. It appeared that the inhabitants were already awake and a man waved from the entrance to the house.

'We call the houses *mudhif*,' said Jassim, excited to show me the village.

I could smell the burning of dung well before we disembarked. Abu Haider brought the canoe to a halt, punting us in the final few metres to a grassy bank, where we all jumped out. It was like entering another world, or at least being transported back in time to the Middle Ages.

'You can see why we consider the Ma'dān to be the descendants of the Sumerians.' My guide patted Abu Haider on the back. He led us along a buffalo track towards one of the mudhif, where a woman was squatting next to a buffalo, milking it in the entrance. Her husband walked forward and embraced Jassim and Abu Haider, hugging and kissing them on both cheeks.

I looked up and noticed that on the top of every house was a flag or two. There were lots of green and yellow ones and some had images of the Imam Ali. Jassim must have seen me looking at the flags.

'We're all Shi'a Muslims here, the people are very proud,' he said. 'But even though they can be warriors when they need to be, like when they rose up against Saddam, they are really a peaceful people. All they want to do is be left alone, and to farm and fish and look after the buffaloes.'

The man invited us into the hut, which was semi-circular and reminded me of a grassy barracks. Inside it was decorated with rugs and carpets and pictures hung from the walls.

'Would you like to try the milk?' asked Jassim.

'Sure,' I said, without thinking.

Naturally, the woman outside brought in a pottery urn full of the steaming fresh milk, straight from the buffalo's udder, and placed it down in front of me.

'Drink up,' he said.

I gulped down the frothy warm liquid, trying to ignore the bits of floating matter and thick strands of hair that had fallen into the pot.

'Delicious, isn't it?' said Jassim in earnest. Amar snorted and asked for tea instead.

'You know, the Ma'dān believe in magic,' said Jassim, peering over his glasses.

'I bet they need to, living in this place,' said Amar.

Jassim ignored him, and carried on. 'They call the spirits

Djinns. Like in English you call them Genies. They can take the form of humans or animals,' he whispered, as more tea was passed around.

'They believe in these giant snakes. Sometimes covered in hair, and others are like dragons with big legs and claws. They eat buffaloes and children. Of course, they are stories meant to keep the kids from wandering off into the swamps and getting lost.'

We spent the day exploring the marshes. Going in the boat, watching as the men and women alike would set about with scythes and knives to cut reeds down for fodder for the buffalo and thatch for the roofs. It was a life unchanged in millennia. In the afternoon, we took the boat to Abu Haider's house. He lived on a floating island of compressed reeds right in the middle of the marsh. The reeds themselves acted as camouflage and I asked Abu Haider about his life, as Jassim translated.

'My wife and I have lived here our whole lives, until Saddam came and set fire to our island. We were forced to go and live in the city. My sons worked as labourers in Baghdad, but what could I do? I'm an old man and all I can do is fish and look after the buffalo. My wife makes nice baskets, but nobody in the city wants them.'

His wife, Salwa, came and sat down next to us. She wore a black *abaya*, a full-length robe, and a headscarf, but her face was unveiled. She must have been in her late forties, a good decade or two younger than Abu Haider. Her face was fun and her eyes glistened. She put a soft hand on her husband's shoulder and they sat next to each other, like a teenage couple very much in love. It was heart-warming to see such affection against a backdrop of what would be considered extreme poverty anywhere in the world.

In the marshes there are no schools, no hospitals, no roads or cars, and the only food is what people catch or make themselves. Such isolation and lack of comfort would strike horror into most people, but for them it was a *raison d'être*. Their way of life depended entirely on their remoteness.

'Now we have come back, we want to stay. We've been here for the last ten years and now we just want to be left alone,' said Abu Haider.

My time in Iraq was almost at an end, and the next day I said goodbye to Jassim back at the canal, after Abu Haider dropped us on dry land. Amar and I continued east, following the road through the lakes until we reached al-Qurnah at the confluence of the two great rivers. It is here that the Tigris meets the Euphrates, the place that the Garden of Eden was supposed to have been located – now marked by a few picnic tables and a gaudy concrete pavilion. We stayed for lunch and I swam in the brown waters of the river, much to the disapproval of Amar. By now I'd grown so tired of his irritability that I didn't even bother talking to him.

We reached Basra that afternoon and spent the night in a dismal grey hotel. I felt as though I'd seen the very best and the very worst of Iraq. I'd seen some truly awful things, and dealing with the petulance of Amar had certainly added to the challenge of traversing a war zone, and yet, for all his flaws, he'd done his job and got me out the other side.

Tomorrow I'd leave Iraq behind and enter the Gulf to cross into Kuwait, where I knew a very different world would await.

8

Searching for Treasure

But, Commander of the Faithful, there is a proverb that says 'the more one has, the more one wants.'

Tales of the Arabian Nights

With the Shatt al-Arab canal behind us, we drove through Basra city and over the bridge towards Az Zubayr and the Safwan border crossing point. The sand spread out on both sides. To the east, about twenty miles away, lay Iran, and to the west was Saudi Arabia, and little but desert for eight hundred miles all the way to the Holy Land – my ultimate destination. From here, that eight hundred miles was tantalisingly close, but it may as well have been on the far side of the moon. Saudi Arabia was for the time being off-limits, and so my plan was to continue south, following the coastline of the peninsula and, in doing so, discover more of the Arabia of my imagination.

Amar drove me to the desolate border with Kuwait in silence. He was having one of his familiar strops. When we reached the final checkpoint and pulled to a halt, it was time to pay him his wages. He snatched the dollars from my hand and threw them back in my lap.

'It's not enough,' he said, shaking his head. He didn't look me in the eye.

'What do you mean? It's what we agreed.'

'Lev, I've worked hard.'

'I'm not disputing that,' I said, 'but it's a good wage. Twice as much as I've ever paid a guide before, plus expenses.' I was shocked that I'd also added in some extra for a tip.

'The tip is the drivers' wages,' he said angrily.

'No, I'm paying you a lump sum. What you pay the drivers is not my business.'

I was getting pissed off myself now. We'd already agreed that for a healthy daily rate he would cover all expenses and now he was just chancing his luck.

'You know, Lev, I didn't have to take you to the war zone. I risked my life for you, so you could go and see the front line. I've taken you to places that no foreigner is ever allowed to see. Not CNN, not Fox, not the BBC and certainly not Channel fucking Four. I need this money to feed my family.'

Feed his family, my arse. The bastard lived in Atlanta.

It was the oldest trick in the book, first acting disappointed, then getting angry and making demands, and then trying to make me feel guilty. I'd heard it a thousand times with every street hawker I'd ever encountered. He seemed to have no qualms about lying through his teeth and in the end I gave up, resigned to paying him an extra day's pay. That was his intention all along, and after much gnashing of teeth, outright threats and head-shaking, he walked away all smiles, promising to stay friends for life.

'Add me on Facebook,' he said, driving off in a cloud of dust. I felt disappointed that he was willing to go through all that for a few hundred dollars, but I decided he must need the money more than I did, so what the hell.

I was glad to see the back of him, if I'm honest. Grabbing my rucksack, I waved him goodbye nonetheless and walked across the border, stamping out through immigration and into Kuwait.

I hitched a lift to Kuwait City with an old man called Suleiman Hussein, who wore a red-and-white checked keffiyeh and a black rope headband, or *agal*, which kept the thing in place. He didn't speak English, but with a combination of sign language and my having got to grips with at least a few words of Arabic, he understood that I wanted to go to Kuwait City. The motorway cut through the desert like a steel blade and the heat shimmered off its silver surface. I was both relieved and excited to be in a new country, and even though I knew the Gulf was likely to be different to what I had experienced so far, I wasn't quite prepared for how much of a contrast it actually presented.

We drove through the desert, which was pockmarked with oil wells. The horizon billowed with plumes of natural gas steaming out of tall pipes, and great metal pumpjacks stuck up out of the bland horizon at awkward angles. These nodding donkeys with their vast hammerhead weights hung heavy in the moody sky, ready to pivot and bore down through the greying sand, deep into the earth's crust. A camel lolloped through the rough dry scrub, led by a herder. They danced with the tumbleweed and climbed over chunky pipelines that criss-crossed the barren ground. The landscape was still scarred from the oil fires lit by retreating Iraqi forces after they invaded Kuwait, burnt and polluted by the flames that had raged for ten months.

When oil reserves were discovered across the region in the first half of the twentieth century, it changed the face of the Gulf forever. The economy was revolutionised; no longer restricted to pearling and nomadic grazing, these little states, tied as protectorates to Britain, started drilling for 'black gold' and began exporting it to the West. The money soon poured in. As cars became commonplace and the world grew dependent on oil, the Gulf grew more and more powerful.

Kuwait was no different; oil dollars set it on the path to independence from the British Empire. By the 1950s, it was the largest exporter in the region and was attracting workers from all over the world. The Gulf was suddenly yanked into modernity – world-class architects flocked in to create shiny new cities made up of high-rise buildings. In Kuwait it heralded a golden era, where economic expansion led to development, urbanisation and a dramatic overhaul of culture and traditions.

Oil changed everything for Arabia; these young nations, once so accustomed to the will of imperial powers, could now hold the world to ransom and begin to shape the Middle East for themselves – or at least that was the plan. The new Gulf nations formed the Organisation of the Petroleum Exporting Countries (OPEC), which was intended to stabilise and raise global oil prices and resist pressure from American and European companies, who were lowering prices. When the Americans supported Israel against the Arabs in the 1973 Yom Kippur War, OPEC called an embargo on oil sales to multiple countries, including the US, which resulted in a crisis all across the world.

OPEC found itself a global arbiter and in its power was the fate of countries and governments on the other side of the world. When the Arab–Israeli war ended, prices soared and the incomes for Middle Eastern countries shot up. By 1975, in only two years, Iraq's income had multiplied by fourteen times. Good for them, but less good for the United States.

By the end of the 1970s, US oil production had peaked and had already begun its decline. The US and Europe needed a new fuel supply, and where better than the Middle East? The only problem, of course, was Russia, who also wanted their oil.

Soon enough the global powers sketched out their battle plans for access to oil fields and pipelines, in a bid to influence and control the world's energy supply. When the 1979 Iranian revolution happened, and the US embassy was overrun, the United States decided to back the Saudis, and the theatre of the next thirty-five years was written.

The Iran–Iraq War, the proxy war between Iran and Saudi Arabia in Yemen and, of course, the two Gulf Wars against Saddam Hussein (who had control over one-fifth of the world's discovered reserves), were all arguably down to the price of the black stuff.

I wasn't used to good roads that were not scarred with bomb craters and potholes, so it wasn't long before I dozed off in the passenger seat of Suleiman's 4x4 as it glided along the highway, lulled into a peaceful snooze for an hour or so. I only woke when the sound of his engine growled to a halt. I rubbed my eyes and looked through the dirty window. It appeared that I'd been transported back into the twenty-first century and another reality altogether.

I peered up at the imposing pillars of glass and steel. Huge skyscrapers in all manner of shapes and sizes punctured the sky in a palette of grey and silver, casting long shadows across the capital. The new Arabs had constructed all kinds of geometric contortions: pearly fins spiralled upwards like leaves curling in the heat, and giant needle towers skewered golf balls in the sky. Concrete arteries weaved between them – snaking highways that led from one air-conditioning unit to the next.

A change in colour and style of a roadside wall indicated the end of one sprawling mansion estate and the start of the next, everything else was locked away, out of sight. Spectres flickered from behind blacked-out car windows and the pavements were deserted. The heat was oppressive; it bled through the cracks in the taxi and made the tarmac shimmer. Few people walked here, certainly not the Arabs.

I said goodbye to Suleiman and darted across the road, hopping over the central reservation to try to get to the city centre. I walked past the mosque and into the market, hauling my rucksack through the narrow lanes. Down here in the shadows, I found the pedestrians. The patchwork of faces in the market were more cosmopolitan than they'd been in Iraq; for decades Kuwait had attracted economic migrants, and here they were. Indians and Pakistanis, Egyptians and Syrians, all jostling for jobs.

The souk, although not an old one, was still a chaotic maze of streets, where everything seemed jumbled together: metalwork side by side with textiles, fruits and vegetables assembled in alluring pyramids, which gave way to rows upon rows of televisions; woven baskets, filled to bursting with nuts, dates and spices, sat opposite a treasure trove of gleaming yellow gold. It got busier as the light faded and the heat gave way to a balmy evening and I escaped the clamour.

Down in the port, dusk fell as I passed the dhows moored cheek by jowl on the dock. They swayed with the tide, harpoon-shaped bows lined up for a hazy muted sunset, their Indian sailors busy repairing nets and loading boxes.

'Where are you from?' said a man in a white *kandura*, the body-length shirt that most Gulf Arabs wear. He also wore a plain white keffiyeh on his head.

I looked at the taxi driver touting for business outside McDonald's. 'The UK,' I said.

'Ah, British. I like the British. British and Kuwait is friend. God save the Queen.' He stood to attention and saluted. He had a big smile across his face. 'You like Kuwait?'

'I've only just arrived,' I said.

'Where do you want to go?'

'A hotel, please.'

Faisel Abu Abdel led me to his taxi, an orange estate car, so rusty that it looked like it would fall apart at any moment.

'Five-star luxury.' He beamed, opening the door for me.

I sat down and heard a clunk as something fell off the bottom of the seat.

'So, you're a traveller?' he asked, with a genuine interest. 'You want to know more about Arabs?'

I told him that I did.

'You know, these days we have two great strengths here in the Gulf. Well, three if you include Islam, but we won't talk about religion. The first is oil, but that won't last forever. The other is our language. To understand the Arabs, first you've got to understand Arabic. We don't have good universities anymore, we are not educated, we don't invent things, but we do have our language. Do you know what makes it so special?'

Before I could contemplate an answer, he carried on regardless.

'It's a complicated language. We don't talk about things like they are really there, you know? It's not like English, where you say what you mean. Our sentences are poems, like a philosophy, it means you have to guess, make your own decisions about the meanings. Each word can have many meanings. I could say to you the word *asa,* and this can mean both advance and retreat – imagine the confusion that can make.'

I said that I guessed it would. Although I thought to myself that in many ways English was rather similar. Few people actually say what they mean.

'And we have created many words for what is important to us. Like camel, there are a hundred words for camel. A camel that drinks daily, or every three days, or very little, or all the time, or is very easily scared, a camel that eats everything it sees, or a camel that is a good leader. We like camels,' he said with a smile.

'You know why else our language is good for us?' He looked at me in the rear-view mirror.

'I don't,' I told him.

'I can make friendship with everyone. When an Arab from Lebanon gets in my taxi, I can talk to him, or an Omani, I can speak to him also, and even if a Moroccan gets in my taxi, I can understand him and take him where he needs to go.'

Faisel had a point. In spite of the almost thirty dialects across the peninsula and beyond, with a handle on the Arabic language, you could just about make yourself understood from Algeria to Iraq. And while lofty academics debate whether Arabic is one language or many – surely a potent obstacle that the region doesn't need – most Arabs will say that they speak a single language and that they understand one another.

I couldn't help thinking that in a region rife with division, it was this shared understanding and a unifying language that was the biggest hope for peace.

The next day was a Friday, the Islamic day of rest, and so there was little to do but sit around the hotel pool and watch the city from the rooftop. I was still trying to process the stark difference between Iraq and Kuwait. I listened as the call to prayer brought out the people and they went in their droves to the Friday mosque. I thought back to sitting on the rooftop in Baghdad, watching a stream of gunfire erupt in the distance. That was unimaginable here. All the offices and shops were closed. I think if it weren't a Friday, then I probably would have been in a rush to move straight on, but it gave me a reason to stay for a little while and digest the goings on of the last couple of weeks.

As I sat at the poolside bar whiling away the afternoon, I watched the widescreen TV that hung above the counter. It had been showing football all morning, but the waiter flicked over to the news. There were reports that the Shi'as in Iraq were poised to attack the Kurds over their occupation of Kirkuk, following them liberating it from ISIS. In the referendum last week, the Kurds had voted overwhelmingly for independence, but the Iraqi government had declared it not binding. The international community had turned their back on the Kurds yet again and the whole thing had died a death. As Omer had predicted at the beginning of our journey in Kurdistan, the clashes were about to begin.

Iraq had given the Peshmerga a deadline to withdraw, and it was looming: tension was building and the Shi'a militias were assembling to take the town. And it wasn't just any old Shi'a militias; it would be the Hashd who were most likely to retake Kirkuk, given their location after the Hawija offensive. It was strange to think that the same troops I'd been following were about to attack the Kurds, the people whom I'd grown to respect perhaps the most in this divided region.

I'd spent a lot of time with Omer and Amar and now they were looking set to become mortal enemies. By the sounds of it, they would be at war by next week. I'd seen the rationale from both sides and it occurred to me that there was little on which to base right or wrong in this battle, and it was impossible to know who to trust, or who to believe. I was beginning to realise that separating the good guys from the bad guys was going to be harder than I thought.

I knew that I'd need to keep my wits about me if I wanted to make it around Arabia without getting on the wrong side of history.

Bahrain is a tiny island nation, only ten miles wide and thirty miles long, lying off the coast of Saudi Arabia and Qatar. I was looking forward to stopping over there on my way to the Emirates.

I'd been trying to get a visa for Saudi Arabia for months, but I'd been decidedly ignored. Even pitching up at the embassy in Kuwait had resulted in a polite door slam. They wouldn't even give me a transit visa for the coast. I'd figured that my best chance to get access to at least the west side of Saudi Arabia was to keep trying at the highest diplomatic levels, but to do that I had to tread carefully. That meant not pushing too hard on the east coast, and also avoiding Qatar entirely, since there were escalating tensions between the two countries. Such were the bureaucratic problems, but the long and short of it was that I ended up setting a course for Bahrain.

Apart from having landed at the airport a few times *en route* to the East, I'd never visited the Gulf before and to be honest, I knew very little about its present, but I had managed to read up a bit on its past. The Gulf isn't exactly well known for its ancient culture, but you have only to look at its strategic location in the Arabian (or Persian) Gulf to understand why it has been an important trading centre for thousands of years.

The Dilmun civilisation that flourished in the islands off the Arabian coast was first mentioned in Sumerian cuneiform tablets almost five thousand years ago. They regarded Dilmun as the centre of the universe, the site of worldly creation – a true heaven on earth. Some biblical scholars say that it was here, not in Iraq, that the Garden of Eden should be, and others say that these paradise islands were the first to rise after the great flood.

Whatever grounding there was in these myths, the locals certainly took advantage of their legendary status for their own advancement. The ships used by those early merchants took goods as far as Babylon, Persia and even India. These expert sailors used their prestige as intermediaries to trade in all sorts of wares, from ivory and bone jewellery to pottery, wool, cotton, gold and timber. But there was one thing that people everywhere wanted more than anything else from Bahrain, and that was the famous Gulf pearls.

Successive armies came and went. There were the Persians, then Alexander's Greeks, followed by the armies of Islam and the Portuguese. Then more Persians and Omanis and finally the British, and all of them came in search of these little shiny balls of nacre.

I decided I had better see what all the fuss was about.

'You know they were more valuable than gold,' said Mohamed, the fat sailor, as he grasped my hand and pulled me unceremoniously up the gangplank onto the dhow. It was a traditional wooden boat around sixty feet long. Most of the dhow crews were made up of Tamils and Keralans – shrimp fishermen from India – and I'd seen hundreds of them preparing their nets as I'd walked along the docks, ready for the nightly outing. The weather had been poor the last few days, which meant there'd been a break in the routine and the fishermen were getting restless.

'If they don't go out soon, they'll get very upset,' said my Bahraini guide. 'It's been rough at sea all week and they've missed a few days' wages now.'

'What about you?' I asked. He didn't seem too concerned about the weather.

'I'm not looking for shrimps, my friend. I leave that to the Indians. I only fish for pearls.'

I tried to make myself comfortable on the wooden deck. It was already filled with men who were loading the vessel for our voyage. We'd hoped to take the boat around the coast of Qatar and onwards to the UAE, but I was at the mercy of the Bahraini tourist board and I'd already been stranded for a week in the hotel waiting for a weather window. I'd whiled away the days at the Rotana Hotel in Muharraq, a tiny island north of the capital Manama, swimming in the warm waters of the Gulf and wandering around the old Portuguese fortress.

At night I'd eaten like a king, tucking into the seafood buffet, which came as a welcome change to hummus and flatbread. There was beer and wine, too. Bahrain had its share of bars and nightclubs and I'd sampled a night out or two with some of the expat community, and even found myself drinking with Saudis, who admitted to coming over the border with the sole purpose of getting sloshed. And that applied to the women as well.

So I'd made the error of turning up for my boat trip with a hangover, and that's never a good start.

'Are they really still that valuable?' I said to Mohamed, referring to the pearls he went looking for.

'Oh, yes!' he said, his enormous belly hanging out over his skirt. 'Well, it depends what you mean by valuable, but one of these is worth a lot.' He rummaged in his wallet and produced a little pouch. 'Open your hand,' he said, dropping the contents into my palm. A single tiny pearl rolled around the creases in my skin. It was so light I could barely feel it.

'That's worth two and a half thousand dollars,' said Mohamed, with a glint in his eye. 'I found it a month ago. Shall we see if we can find you one?'

I agreed and put on my best smile. The truth was I was dreading the prospect. I didn't like boats at the best of times. I always got awfully seasick, and the fact that this rickety matchstick was barely out of the water and covered in patches didn't do my nerves much good at all. That compounded by a hangover didn't bode well.

The last of the provisions were hauled on board and we set sail out of the harbour, leaving the shore behind. After an hour we came across the perfect pearl-diving spot. Or so I was told.

'The best oysters grow where the sea is three to five metres deep – that way they get the perfect amount of light. We just dive down and pick them up, watch.'

Mohamed stripped down to his skirts and picked up a net. He jumped off the deck and into the sea, which was so clear you could see the bottom. He smiled and gave me a thumbs-up before somersaulting and diving down. It was amazing that a man so fat could be so agile in the water. After a minute or so, he emerged and gave me another thumbs-up, lobbing the net back onto the deck. He hauled himself up some ladders and flopped onto the wooden floor, like a great hairy sea lion.

'Your turn.' He slapped me on the back, standing up. I thought the sea water might help with the headache and so I stripped down and jumped into the water, which felt as warm as a bath. It wasn't quite as refreshing as I'd hoped for. Using a little wooden nose plug that Mohamed gave to me, I dove down.

Without a mask, everything was blurry, but I held my breath and kept going until I could make out the shape of the sandy sea bed. I saw the outline of some objects that looked like oyster shells to me. I grabbed a handful and put them into my net. I was already out of breath. Five metres is quite deep and by the time you reach the bottom, you're ready to head back up, but pride made me stay for a while longer. I saw nearby another shell, but this was bigger and blacker. Must be a good one, I thought, as I reached out to grab it.

I only realised what it was when it pierced my skin. The needle-like spines stabbed my fingers and sent a shooting pain all the way through my body, until I was almost paralysed. It was a sea urchin, not an oyster. I shot to the surface and gritted my teeth, determined not to show my idiocy to Mohamed, who was already on the deck of the boat, drying himself.

To make matters worse, as I swam back to the dhow, I suddenly found myself surrounded by what on first inspection I took to be plastic bags, but were actually hundreds of little jellyfish. By the time I'd been stung for the third time, I'd given up on hiding my pain and winced my way to the back of the boat, racing up the ladders as quickly as I could, much to the crew's delight.

Mohamed was chuckling to himself. 'They only sting white people,' he said. 'Us brown Arabs are immune.' He winked, sitting down cross-legged over the net.

'Pass me the knife,' he said, pointing at his belt that was lying on the floor. I handed over a little curved blade, which I had been assured had been made in the same style for thousands of years. With a flick of his wrist, he popped open the oysters one by one, and showed me how to use the knife to scour the shell and the flesh for pearls.

'Nothing,' he said, after going through the whole bag. I offered him my meagre winnings and after fishing through some pebbles and a couple of sea snails, he found one tiny oyster the size of a clam.

'You never know.'

He raised his eyebrows and handed me the blade.

I struggled with the muscular seal, and eventually popped it open. I looked around inside, but could see nothing.

'Give it to me.' Mohamed grabbed the little oyster and used his fingers to rummage around the meat.

'Look.' He stared at me, aghast. He handed me back the oyster and there, to my disbelief, right in the middle was a beautiful, shiny white pearl.

For a second my eyes didn't register what I was seeing, and then for a further couple of seconds all sorts of lunacy went through my mind. What's it worth? Do I get to keep it? What can I buy with the money? And then I looked back at Mohamed. His face suddenly creased into wrinkles and his belly jiggled uncontrollably as he burst into laughter.

I realised then what he'd done. The bastard had only gone and planted the one he kept in his wallet.

The whole ship erupted with laughter, and so did I. At least they had a sense of humour.

For two hours, we bobbed and bounced over the waves. This was meant to be the calm season, but it didn't feel like that to me. It was already late afternoon and as the sun grew lower in the sky, the wind picked up and the boat was tossed around in the great Gulf, like a toy in the bathtub. Mohamed said it was best if we drop anchor and get some rest till the morning.

Fat chance of that, I thought to myself, as I rolled around the deck trying to refrain from throwing up. There was next to no space in any case, as every inch of floor was filled with the Bahraini sea men. They didn't appear to do anything really, other than sit around and smoke cigarettes. As the sun set, though, I appreciated their presence.

'They're the entertainment,' said Mohamed.

The sailors arranged themselves in two lines near the stern, in front of the captain's cabin. I was trying to hold myself together and not vomit, while this motley collection of men all in shirts and white skirts began to chant and sing.

'It's a Bahraini tradition,' said Mohamed. 'We've been collecting pearls for over four thousand years. It goes back to the ...'

'Dilmun Empire,' I cut in. 'I know, I've read all about it.'

Mohamed laughed. 'Are you feeling ill?' he said, putting his hand on my shoulder. 'No, I'm fine,' I lied. I suspect I must have been rather pale-faced after the diving.

'Well, you're in luck. These songs fix everything. They will bring good weather for the morning, *inshallah*, and maybe even some pearls.'

I listened to these singers as night fell. While it didn't exactly cure my seasickness, the chanting and their songs gave the night a magical atmosphere. Soon the stars came out and the entire sky was ablaze with them. 'I wish there were as many pearls in the ocean as stars in the sky,' murmured the sailor. 'Then I would be a very rich man.'

'If there were as many pearls in the sky as there were stars, then they wouldn't be worth anything,' I said in retort.

Mohamed just shrugged. 'That is true. But if I owned them all, I could decide how many to sell. Like the oil.' He winked and laughed to himself.

But, of course, it was the oil that destroyed this ancient tradition.

'There's no pearl diving anymore,' he said. 'It's just for the tourists really. All this is just a show.' He flicked his head at the singers and drummers. 'They do it because the Bahraini ministry pays them to come and make you journalists happy. So that you go home and tell the world how amazing Bahrain is and how you found that huge pearl, eh?' He nudged me and winked.

'But you know we need to collect ten thousand oysters to find maybe twenty commercially viable pearls, and by that, I mean ones worth more than a few dollars. The industry was destroyed by the cultured pearls you get in the Pacific, and the fact that everyone in Bahrain now works in oil. Why would anyone want to go and sit on a boat for three days and risk finding nothing?'

I'd come on this journey to try to understand the Middle East, but there was something more. In all honesty, I held a deep regard for the customs and traditions of a region I felt was sacred. I admired the Arabs for their tenacity, and their resistance to modernity. In the desert I sought purity, I wanted to find something real, something authentic. There was something deeply attractive about a culture that kept its traditions and ways of life intact against all odds.

Call it sentimentalism if you will, call it the Western lens if you must, but as travellers we go in search of the extraordinary, the different – not to drive wedges, but to do the opposite. To try to see beyond the pale, and beyond the clothes and stereotypes and labels that we so often assume. The traveller goes in search of an elusive treasure, that of truth, and what defines it.

But now I'd started this journey, I was beginning to wonder what truth really existed after all. So far, the Gulf had shown me only smoke and mirrors.

110

9

Cities of Gold

Travelling – it gives you home in a thousand strange places, then leaves you a stranger in your own land.

Ibn Battutah

It was late morning by the time Sir Bani Yas came into view from the deck of the boat. It was a desert island in the most literal form. Just five miles off the coast of the UAE, this little atoll was my gateway to the Emirates. My plan was to walk across the island before taking another boat on to Abu Dhabi and then Dubai.

This coastline was known to the British colonial administrators as the Trucial Coast – named because of the loose confederation of tribes that made it up. It was a region that until the twentieth century was infamous for piracy, smuggling and the slave trade. Nowadays the tribal affiliations have become slightly more regulated, with borders drawn and nations settled upon.

The United Arab Emirates consists of seven sheikhdoms, which combined in 1971 in order to have a stronger unified force against neighbouring enemies. Abu Dhabi is the largest of these emirates, sitting atop the majority of the land and the majority of the oil; Dubai the best known, with its mega-city a global commercial hub; the smaller emirates of Ajman, Sharjah,

Umm al-Quwain and Ras al-Khaimah sit along the Gulf coast and Fujairah faces out into the Arabian Sea.

I figured that a mini walking expedition of a few days would help me acclimatise to the intense heat of the Gulf. Iraq had been exhausting, but the truth was that most of it had been spent crammed in the back of trucks and, for all its hardships, apart from the couple of days running around the battlefields, it hadn't really given me the chance to explore the place on foot. I was keen to walk, to stretch my legs and feel the sweat pouring down my brow. It makes you feel alive and gives you a sense of achievement, in a way that staring out of a car window can never do.

More than that, I felt as if I needed to test myself against the environment. It had been a while since I'd been in the desert and I knew that what lay ahead could be some of the most brutal and demanding terrain I'd ever encountered. The Empty Quarter Desert and the mountains of Dhofar loomed in my mind. In just a couple of weeks I'd be entering Oman, where my biggest challenge would lie, so whatever practice I could get in now would be not only useful, but essential. I knew all too well the dangers of heat, exhaustion and thirst, so a couple of days getting hot and sweaty now could pay dividends later.

Mustafa was waiting for me in the opulent surroundings of the Anantara resort.

'Welcome, sir.'

I looked around at the luxury hotel, the only one on the island, which serviced the few high-end tourists who ventured beyond the gated communities of the mainland. I took in the traditionally themed lobby, with its boutique shops and butlers in mess kit and huge pieces of aboriginal art. It was truly palatial.

Mustafa was a guide from Morocco, a Berber from the Atlas Mountains, who'd come to the Gulf in search of work fifteen years ago and ended up in the hotel industry.

'But my real love is wildlife. I grew up in the mountains and always wanted to help protect the endangered species. I sometimes think that I love animals more than people,' he said, hoisting a rucksack onto his back.

'This sort of place is all well and good,' he motioned to the beautiful restaurant, where some American tourists were slurping on lobster and steak, 'but the real pleasure is out there.' He pointed out beyond the manicured gardens to the desert beyond. 'That's what life is all about.'

I'd barely taken a moment to appreciate the magnificence of the hotel, before Mustafa was leading us down a track past the staff quarters and beyond some acacia bushes that hid the rubbish bins. We hopped over a fence and my feet landed on the stony gravel that marked the start of my walk.

'You know, we don't normally do walking safaris on the island.' He smiled. 'Most people just want to drive. Arabs are pretty lazy.'

With our backs to the sea, Mustafa led the way down a little slope towards a turquoise lagoon that was trapped by a sand dune. He was clearly excited to be guiding me on foot rather than sat in a jeep, and took great delight in wading through the tepid waters to get to the other side.

We walked up a rocky outcrop and on the far side I saw what we were aiming for. Ten miles distant lay a mountain. It wasn't particularly big, but its looming presence marked the centre of the island, and the point we were hoping to reach by the evening to make camp. But between us were miles of desert, savannah and forest. It seemed like every kind of terrain could be found on this little paradise.

'It wasn't always like this, though,' said Mustafa, as we trekked through a plantation of date palms. 'Until the seventies, it was all empty desert and hardly any trees. It was Sheikh Zayed's idea to bring this to life. He used to have a holiday home over there.' Mustafa pointed to a bay in the distance, where I could make out the abandoned ruins of a palace.

'Then in 1977, he decided to ban all hunting and save the animals. It was basically his own personal zoo and he brought in all sorts of wildlife.'

Mustafa was scouring the gravel for signs of tracks and prints.

'Most Arabs couldn't give a shit about the environment,' he said, shaking his head. 'They throw their litter everywhere and totally ruin the place. You can probably tell, I don't really like Arabs. I'm a Berber and we've always thought they were brutes. Working here, I haven't really changed my mind on that. They're not all bad, though. Sheikh Zayed was different. He had a vision to turn the Emirates into something really special.'

I'd heard of Zayed. It was impossible not to, travelling through the Gulf – his image is everywhere: on posters, billboards and in frames in almost every public space. He was the ruler who had consolidated the tribal powers and pushed for the formation of the United Arab Emirates, not long before discovering huge oil reserves beneath the new country, making him one of the wealthiest people in the world.

'Zayed was a visionary. He was born in the desert as a Bedouin and grew up riding camels. Even when he lived in his palace, he would still go out for weeks in the desert to hunt. Zayed wanted the Emirates to be the best place in the Arab world. And he kind of achieved it, didn't he? I mean look at this place compared to all the other places in the region. They're all screwed.'

Mustafa smiled. He pointed to some faint markings in the sand. 'Hoof prints. Probably gazelle.' He grew suddenly animated.

'If we're lucky, we'll see some oryx soon. They usually hang out on the savannah at the base of the mountain.'

I'd heard about the famous wildlife on the island, but nothing could have quite primed me for the scenes that lay ahead. 'There's thirteen thousand indigenous animals here.' Mustafa grinned.

Sheikh Zayed had declared Sir Bani Yas a no-hunting zone in the 1970s, and with some very expensive irrigation it wasn't long before the island was green, fed by a nine-kilometre underwater pipe from the mainland and some desalination plants. Over the last thirty years, millions of trees have been planted and Zayed set about repopulating the island with animals that needed a safe haven – some of which were already extinct in the wild. Now, under the shade of the palms and acacias, all sorts of beasts roam free.

'In a few years we want to use solar and wind power here, and we even have a no-fishing zone around the island to preserve the sea life,' Mustafa said, as we followed the trail ahead.

We walked for another two hours, beyond the date groves and into the desert. It was brutally hot and my clothes were drenched with sweat. I'd put sun cream on my face in the morning, but now it was streaming into my eyes and stinging them painfully. I'd wanted to push myself and I realised pretty quickly that I'd certainly be doing that. Mustafa looked perfectly happy, however, skipping ahead.

The humidity was over ninety per cent and that meant I was sweating buckets and getting through water rations very rapidly. The deserts I'd been to before were often hot, but usually dry heat, so you don't tend to sweat so much. Here I was literally pouring fluids, and we were only carrying four litres of water, which had to last us till the evening, when we would find a resupply in the mountains.

'Keep up, Lev, we haven't got all day.' Mustafa grinned.

Further ahead, the sandy desert broke into more rocky terrain as we neared the foothills. The trail led through some narrow canyons, which at least afforded some shade from the relentless sun. Mustafa stopped in his tracks.

'There,' he whispered, pointing into some craggy rocks up ahead. I squinted and couldn't see anything.

'Wait till it moves.' Mustafa held a finger to his mouth.

I held my breath in anticipation and then suddenly there was a flash of brown, and I could make out the shape of an enormous ram the size of a small horse. 'That's a urial.'

'A urial?' I said, surprised to see the massive sheep with curled horns. 'Aren't they from Central Asia?'

Mustafa laughed. 'Yes, but it's not just endemic and indigenous species, there's all sorts here. There's rhea, ostriches and giraffes. It's like Jurassic Park.' My Moroccan guide smiled.

The sheep bounded off into the boulders and disappeared. We carried on walking through the gorge and then began scrambling up onto a plateau filled with acacia bushes. It reminded me of an African savannah landscape, the kind I'd seen in Kenya and Tanzania, and I half-expected to see a lion stalking its prey.

'No lions, I'm afraid, but there are a few cheetah and plenty of hyenas and jackals,' said Mustafa. 'There used to be cheetah all across Arabia, but they were hunted to extinction. The same with oryx and ostriches.'

As the day wore on and the water supplies grew low, we ascended the mountain and onto almost the highest point, where we could see views across the island. The orchards and plains spread out below us like a patchwork quilt of greens and browns, and in the far distance you could make out the haze of the Arabian Gulf, glistening like a faraway sea of diamonds.

'It'll be dark soon,' said Mustafa, 'and we're camping down there.' He pointed to a valley of green palms five or six kilometres away. By the time we climbed off the mountain and reached the flat ground, it was already dusk and I was worried we might find ourselves stuck in the open at the mercy of stalking cheetahs.

'Don't worry, they won't hunt us,' said the ever-optimistic Moroccan.

As we crested a small ridge and the plains opened up, I was reassured to see why we wouldn't be the cheetahs' main priority. There, right in front of us, was a scene straight out of *The Lion King*.

Hundreds, if not thousands, of antelope were busy grazing in the golden light of the afternoon. I could make out all sorts of different species. 'They're Arabian sand gazelle,' Mustafa pointed at the biggest group, 'and those are blackbuck.'

I looked to see the slightly bigger beasts with curly horns. There were deer as well, Sri Lankan axis deer with their distinctive white spots, and what I thought to be the common fallow deer, the kind you see in Richmond Park, dozing in the bushes nearby. In among the herds, I saw the most beautiful of all – the muscular black-and-white Arabian oryx with their ramrod straight horns, lolling under the shade of the trees. These magnificent creatures were almost all extinct in the wild apart from here.

Wild Indian peacocks strutted around pecking in between their four-legged cousins, bringing a colourful flash of purple and blue to the party. Some ostriches were busy racing across the savannah in the distance and then, lurching from behind some palm trees came the giants – a pair of beautiful African giraffes, seemingly unconcerned by the ethnic makeup of their companions.

We picked our way through the frenzy and the animals cleared a path, darting away in zigzag dances, but they never ran too far. These beasts had led a charmed life and had never been hunted by humans, and even the timid gazelles thought twice before leaving the comfort of their acacia shade to bolt.

As the sun set behind the mountain and the shadows enveloped the wadis, we entered a little forest where Mustafa had planned for us to camp.

'Not far now,' he said, as we pushed through the trees to find a clearing. We collected some firewood and set up our tents and listened as the sound of the forest grew loud. Bullfrogs and crickets chirped and the last of the birds to roost called their final song, until the crackling of the fire drowned out all else. The blackness surrounding us concealed a sense of wonder and beauty, and it reminded me that on this journey not everything was as it seemed. The secrets of Arabia were all around, hidden just below the surface, if only you searched for them.

The next day we trekked to the pristine white beaches of the coast, and after saying goodbye to Mustafa, I took a boat to the town of Ruwais on the mainland. The scenery couldn't have been more different. I suddenly found myself in a dusty port, walking past industrial sites and huge oil refineries. The road east was hardly appealing. After the greenery and beauty of Bani Yas, I was faced again with the harshness of the desert, scarred with the markings of the modern world: service stations, motorways and grey warehouses.

As I walked along the side of the motorway, I kept my arm outstretched, and on hearing the sound of approaching vehicles, I always turned around to face the traffic head on. I'd learned in years of hitchhiking that the trick to getting a lift was always to look your potential target in the eyes. That way there's a connection, they can't escape and they feel more inclined to stop.

Hitching gets more difficult as you get older. I remembered back to when I was in my early twenties and hitched lifts from England to India. There were some places, like Russia, where it had been difficult, but most of the time people would stop and go well out of their way to look after you. I guess when you're younger, people feel sorry for you and want to help, or perhaps there's a sense of romanticism about being on the road, and it was a familiar tale to be picked up by old travellers wanting to hear a story or two, or to reignite their own sense of adventure by living vicariously.

When you're in your mid-thirties, though, and hitching through a country where there's no real culture of it, it's a bit more tricky.

The cars zipped by, beeping their horns or ignoring me completely. Most of the cars were new; shiny sports cars and big 4x4s screeched past, kicking up dust. These were the only cars driven by the Arabs themselves. You could see them in their white keffiyehs and dark sunglasses, without so much as a glance in my direction, as they roared past at a hundred miles an hour. Then there were the lorries trundling past at a much slower pace, but an equal reluctance to stop for a foreign pedestrian.

Finally, after forty-five minutes of walking in the perilous grit of the emergency lane, a Toyota Corolla taxi pulled over fifty metres ahead. I'd hoped for a free lift, what I considered a 'proper hitch', but I'd already learned that very little comes for free in the Arab world. I ran forward to show a bit of appreciation for him having stopped in any case. The window rolled down and the young man at the wheel invited me to get in.

'Where are you going?' I asked.

'Dubai,' he said.

I'd planned on stopping by Abu Dhabi first, but Dubai was only another hour and a half north-east, and it was where I wanted to get to anyway, so I got in.

'Ahmad at your service,' said the man, who didn't look older than twenty-five.

I asked him where he was from. He wasn't an Arab and must have been one of the eight million immigrant workers who reside in the UAE, keeping the economy afloat.

'I'm from Pakistan, sir,' he said, with a little head-shake. 'From the city of Peshawar. Do you know it?'

I told him that I did, and that I'd visited, at which point his eyes lit up and he was keen to chat.

'Sir, I would love to come to live in your good country. It is my dream to live in London. Do you think you could get me a visa?'

I explained that it was rather more difficult than that.

'Yes, sir, I know. Being an immigrant is a hard life,' he said, with melancholic eyes. 'Especially these days. Nobody wants foreigners anymore. It seems like the world is under a change of management.'

'A change of management?'

'Yes, sir, with Mr Trump in charge, everything is becoming troublesome. I would have liked to study in the great America, but now it is impossible. So I come here in search of employment. But it is hard here also. I am working here now for three years. I am working as a taxi man, but before I was in Abu Dhabi in the building sector. I was working for a big company, but it was very difficult work.'

He shook his head.

'When I arrived, they made me sign a contract in Arabic and took my passport. I couldn't even leave if I wanted to. I had to work seven days a week and it took me six months before I got any money. I worked for more than sixteen hours a day and had to sleep in a tiny, hot room in a low bunk with six other people, there was no fan or air conditioning.'

Ahmad's story was commonplace. Migrant workers were enticed to the Middle East with promises such as green cards and high wages and when they got there, agents often took a cut of their pay and they lived as indentured servants. Living and working conditions could be dire, but with no passports, they had few options but to work without complaint.

'I didn't dare to complain, or they'd take away my sponsorship, and then what would I do? I don't like the Arabs, they are so rude and treat us foreigners like dirt, but the Pakistani agents are even worse, so I was stuck. I waited for my two-year contract to end. That's when I started as a taxi driver, it is better, I have some more freedom and now I can have one day off a week.'

There are something like half a million Pakistanis in the UAE, in addition to the two or three million Indians (the actual figures are pretty sketchy), one million Bangladeshis and hundreds of thousands of Egyptians, Nepalis and Filipinos, not to mention the Russians, Europeans and Brits who fill the majority of the more professional and financial roles. Immigrants make up eighty-five per cent of the population of the UAE, leaving the few Arabs in a sort of ethereal existence. The local Emiratis need the immigrants to make the country work, but as a result, the passing traveller never gets to meet any 'locals'.

The divide was immediately apparent as we drove through the outskirts of Abu Dhabi, with its flashy high-rise buildings and palm-lined corniche. The only Arabs you'd see were in the fancy cars driving to and from the mall.

'Go shopping. That's all they seem to do,' said Ahmad. 'The Arabs, they have jobs in the army and government and run some of the oil businesses, but they are lazy and I never see them do any work.'

It was true that the UAE had outsourced the dangerous and dirty jobs to migrant labourers, as the economy rapidly expanded. Now some ninety-six per cent of the workforce is non-Emirati. As Ahmad had pointed out, the Arabs still held the bulk of the roles in the public sector, maintaining control of the military and government, but a staggering ninety-nine-and-a-half per cent of the private sector was made up of foreign workers.

However, things were slowly changing. 'In the early days it was good,' said Ahmad. 'There was no tax to pay, but now they are saying that we must pay tax.'

It seems that the government has realised the oil isn't going to last forever. The boom years have gone and now the UAE appears to be diversifying its economy, becoming more reliant on sustainability and tourism. But while the gold rush is over, it appears the mentality of the Emiratis has yet to change. 'They think they can just sit back and watch us do all the work? We'll just leave,' said Ahmad, 'and then they'll learn they have to do some work themselves.'

We arrived in Dubai in time for the rush hour. We sat in a queue of 4x4s on a big wide highway with six lanes and a seemingly endless rotation of spaghetti junctions and flyovers. Out of the window were sprawling mansions, endless shopping malls, fat Humvees and glass towers lined up against the sky. In Dubai, it seemed, there was a premium on size. I passed the sparkling base of the Burj Khalifa. Never ones to do things by halves, Dubai created the highest building in the world, so tall it has its own micro climate. We drove past enormous waterparks, indoor ski slopes and vast lawns with immaculate flower beds. It's impossible to imagine that forty years ago, this was a sleepy fishing village that barely made the maps.

Cranes hovered low between the endless hotels, standing by to erect more steel and concrete. Whatever Ahmad thought, the relentless development wasn't over quite yet. Lights blazed from the buildings in all shades and colours, flashing signs that lured my eyes. Nothing much was happening on the streets. Everything seemed to go on behind high walls, tinted car windows and closed doors. We eventually reached the coastline, where the white sand was dotted with sun loungers and leafy palms.

I wanted to get some rest in Dubai, so I'd blagged a few nights in the luxury of the Jumeirah beachside hotel, a five-star resort overlooking the bay, right next to the famous Burj Al Arab 'Sail' Hotel, with its £25,000 a night presidential suite. I wanted to enjoy the beach and make time to catch up with some old university friends. I knew quite a few people who'd made the transition to expat life, and with tax-free status, luxury accommodation, year-round sunshine and a live-in nanny, why not?

I met Griff at his home in one of the wealthy suburbs. His Filipino housemaid opened the door to the five-bedroom mansion. Griff was playing with his two-year-old daughter, while his wife Claire made tea.

'Lev, you old bastard, it's been a while.' He put his daughter on the sofa and gave me a hug.

'Three or four years at least,' I reminded him. I'd served in the army with Griff and he'd since left to come and work in investment banking in Dubai, as a way of earning some money to afford a house in London.

'It's not often the missus lets me out these days.' He slapped me on the back. 'But we can't have you out boozing on your own, can we, Lev?'

He kissed his wife and daughter and we took a taxi to one of Dubai's fancy hotels. It was a Friday and that meant there was only one thing to do.

'Brunch,' said Griff with a wide grin. 'I haven't been to one in a while. Since having a baby, I can't really go out for an all-day session anymore, but they are good fun. It's basically an excuse to eat as much food as you want and drink champagne, well, cheap prosecco at least.'

We'd booked tickets to go to a 1990s-themed brunch at a hotel on the famous Palm – a tree-shaped piece of land built from the sea – now home to hundreds of hotels, resorts and bars. We arrived to find a rather sticky red carpet and a bouncer with a clipboard. We were led to round tables and sat next to total strangers. It reminded me of a gala dinner, except everyone was wearing shorts and gorging themselves on burgers and lobster. There must have been eight hundred people crammed into the room. It was only midday and already most of them were drunk. They were almost all British or Irish, and there wasn't an Arab in sight.

'Isn't it weird, getting pissed in a country where alcohol is illegal?' Griff said, pouring himself an oversized glass of sparkling wine. 'You know, we're meant to have a licence to drink here.

But obviously nobody does.'

'So what happens if you get caught?' I asked. I'd read plenty of reports of British expats and holidaymakers ending up in jail for seemingly minor offences, but I couldn't see how the law actually operated, when almost the entire population is foreign, and a good chunk of them are beer-swilling Brits.

'For the most part, nothing. It's technically illegal to be drunk, but just have a look around later on and you'll see that nobody gives a shit. The problems only really come when the Arabs get involved. There was a guy just last week who was in a bar carrying a pint. He was trying to shuffle past some Emiratis and bumped into one or something, I think he was trying to stop his drink from spilling, and brushed one of the Arabs on his waist or his arse. You know, the usual stuff that happens in a pub on a Friday night. Anyway, the Arabs didn't like it and called the police, who came and arrested the bloke. Now he's in jail and facing charges of indecency. They say he'll get three years in jail. Basically, the rule of thumb is it's okay to get pissed, just don't piss off the Arabs.'

I looked around. In among the piles of sushi and pizza, hundreds of British people, most of them in varying states of undress, were sinking beer by the bucketload as Peter Andre gyrated on the stage, singing 'Mysterious Girl' while showing off a set of remarkably defined abs. It occurred to me that life in the Gulf was far too complicated to try to understand in a week, so better not to bother and simply indulge. When in Rome and all that.

It took about three days to get over that hangover.

I hitched north out of the city, leaving the glitz of Dubai

behind. Huge sand drifts piled up at the side of the motorway as it sliced through the desert. The suburbs and industrial overspill lined the coast to the north, all the way past the airport to Sharjah and beyond to Umm al-Quwain. My lift dropped me off at the side of the road next to an abandoned airstrip that flanked a lagoon. I could just about smell the salty mangroves beyond the haze. He pointed to what looked like a business park half a mile away down a track, and told me that was the best chance of getting another ride onwards to the north.

I decided to take a short cut across the waste ground, since the fence had already been ripped down, so I trampled over the piles of rubbish and broken bottles to what would have been the runway. Signs indicated that it must have been in use until fairly recently. The hangars were up ahead, but what stood out the most was a huge passenger plane simply parked up outside them. The doors had been ripped off and there were holes in the fuselage; as I got closer, I noticed pigeons flying in and out of the broken windows. It was a sorry affair and it looked like the apocalypse had already come here.

Beyond the rusting hulk of the plane, I walked through the hangars. The floor was littered with the remains of humanity: a dusty sofa upturned, papers and files strewn across the floor and bits of wood that had fallen from the rafters. A moth-eaten parachute was draped over some chairs in the corner. I walked into one of the adjacent offices, which still had most of its stationery littered around. There was a faint smell of death and I saw in the corner the rotting corpse of a desert fox.

There were pictures on the walls of certificates. It was a parachute training school for civilians. I saw the dates of the course photographs. The last one seemed to be in 2005. For whatever reason, it had been abandoned and left as it was for the desert to reclaim. Sand had piled up against the walls and there were trees that had already begun to sprout up through the concrete, reminding me that nature always wins.

I carried on beyond the airstrip and rejoined the slip road to the little industrial park next to the lagoon. As I got nearer, I saw a sign for 'Barracuda Wine Shop'. It appeared to be a huge warehouse selling duty-free booze to the wholesalers. It was out of the way, hidden from view by a line of eucalyptus and acacia trees. It was yet another of the dichotomies of the Gulf. In a region known for its strict adherence to Islamic sharia law, there were always exceptions made out of convenience, especially when it came to making money.

I couldn't help but notice that among the queue of foreigners – Brits, Russians and Indians – there were a few Arabs, too. Resplendent in their kandura and keffiyeh, even the Emiratis weren't above pushing a cart load of whisky to the boot of their Land Cruisers. It raised the question, was the image of the Gulf Arab as a strict Muslim really all a façade?

IO

Ghosts and Echoes

You will if you are wise and know the art of travel, let yourself go on the stream of the unknown and accept whatever comes in the spirit in which the gods may offer it.

Freya Stark

The road north grew wilder after it passed Ras al-Khaimah. I'd been travelling for a month and, with the exception of Sir Bani Yas, had yet to see so much as a hill since leaving the Turkish border behind in Syria. Everything had been flat, whether it was the plains of Ninevah, the marshes or the deserts of the Gulf. But that soon changed when I arrived at the Al Jeer border crossing into Oman. It heralded the gateway to the Musandam Peninsula, a finger-like piece of land that juts out into the Strait of Hormuz, a stone's throw away from Iran. I needed to get to the town of Khasab on the coast, and from there my plan was to take the twice-weekly boat around the peninsula towards Muscat.

The mountains ahead marked a new phase of my journey. I was excited to be leaving behind the 'civilisation' of the Gulf and get into the wilderness. I wanted to experience the Arabia of old, and to get a flavour of the reality of rural life in the Middle East. For the most part, I'd had little contact with Arabs in the Gulf, and apart from a few officials, I'd met only foreign expats. I hoped that Oman would finally give me the opportunity to meet the locals.

Welcome to Oman, proclaimed the sign at the remote crossing point, hemmed in by sheer cliffs on the one side and the glistening ocean on the other. There was nobody crossing on foot and being a Friday, there wasn't any commercial traffic either. A solitary lorry up ahead marked the lonely entry into the country that calls itself the 'Jewel of Arabia'.

The immigration official greeted me with a smile, as I handed over my passport.

'Where are you going?' he asked.

'Khasab,' I replied.

He looked at me quizzically. 'Where is your car?'

'I don't have one,' I said.

'How will you get to Khasab?'

I told him that I hoped to hitch a lift or walk.

'Are you crazy?' he said. 'There's no cars this way, it's a Friday, and you can't walk – it's twenty-five kilometres. Where are you from?' he said, and then, remembering he had my passport in my hand, he looked at it.

'Ah, you're British. That explains everything! You're welcome.' He stamped my visa and handed it back, and I walked out onto the fierce heat of the empty road.

The official was right. There were no cars, so I walked, following the road as it wound along the cliff edge, watching as the azure waves bashed against the rocks below, the crashing of the sea being the only sound in this barren land. The soft wind was hot, despite the fact that it came from the sea, and the salty moisture only added to the humidity, making each step exhausting work. Nevertheless, I was happy and excited to be in this enigmatic nation.

The road twisted and turned as it went up and down, contouring the ridges and crags, and keeping the sea to my left was my only guidance as to where I was going. Eventually the road wound down to the beach and flattened out, and I saw my first Omani villages. They were eerily quiet in the afternoon heat. Khasab was still another five or six kilometres away to the north. I could almost make out the minarets at the port in the far distance, obscured by the haze of the afternoon, but I was hot, tired and very sweaty, not to mention hungry and thirsty, so I sat down under the shade of a palm tree to rest for a while.

In the mountains above, I noticed an eagle soar high on the invisible thermals, twirling and gliding; as majestic as the crags themselves. Half hidden in the jagged escarpment I saw the ruins of an ancient fort, standing guard to the high passes of the east. All that seemed missing from this scene of antiquity were the people. They must either be at prayers or at home with their families, I thought. The phrase 'mad dogs and Englishmen' came to mind. I began to doze off and my thirst was replaced by the light-headedness that comes from too much sun. I wrapped my *shemagh* cotton headscarf around my head to try to keep cool and drank the last sips from my water bottle.

After a short while, I heard a car speed past from the way I was heading and screech to a halt. A young Omani man with a neatly trimmed beard wound down the window and said hello. '*Salaam alaikum.*'

'*Wa alaikum as-salaam,*' I replied, 'and unto you peace', noticing that a woman in a black abaya robe was sat next to him. I could just make out her eyes watching me.

'I heard there was an Englishman out walking.'

'Word travels fast,' I said.

'It does here. We don't get too many visitors.' He spoke in

almost perfect English. 'You want a lift to Khasab?'

I said that I would love one. 'But aren't you going the other way?' I asked.

'Wait here, I'll be back,' he said, before screeching off, leaving behind a trail of dust.

That was odd, I thought to myself, wondering if he'd actually come back.

But, true to his word, five minutes later he did return. This time there was no woman.

'Get in,' he said. 'I had to take my wife home first.' I put my rucksack in the boot and got into the passenger seat. I noticed that he'd put a plastic cover over it, which hadn't been there before. No doubt he'd seen how sweaty I was and wanted to keep his car clean.

Making myself as comfortable as I could against the sticky plastic, I enjoyed the fact he blasted the air conditioner on cold in my direction. More to avoid the smell than anything, I supposed.

'I'm Rashid,' said the man, who said he was a student of criminology, but also volunteered for the local police service. 'It's my day off. Don't worry, I won't arrest you,' he said and laughed, as we drove along the road to Khasab port. Rashid insisted on buying me lunch when we arrived. 'You are a visitor in my land and it is my duty and honour to feed you. A guest must never pay.'

After the kerfuffle I'd had with Amar in Iraq, and the endless sales pitches I'd had all along the Gulf so far, I was slightly taken aback by his hospitality, and the fact he'd driven well out of his way to give me a lift and used up his entire afternoon. 'Everyone in Oman is like this, you will see.' Rashid not only paid for my lunch, but insisted on taking me to the port and making all the arrangements for the onward ferry towards Muscat. It's amazing how a simple act of kindness from a stranger can lift your mood.

The ferry, a crusty old vessel, filled with Indian and Bangladeshi merchants and their boxes of goods, left at three in the afternoon. Rashid had sorted me out a passenger ticket with a seat, but I preferred to stand on the outside deck and watch as we left the old port. The boat sounded its horn and we passed the rows of moored dhows, which bobbed in the wake. Soon we were in the open water of the Strait of Hormuz, but never strayed too far from the brown cliffs to our right. The route weaved past fjords, where dolphins frolicked in the waves.

We skirted by Telegraph Island, a barren rock that was once one of the most important British repeater stations on the main submarine telegraphic cable between London and Karachi. It was deemed such an unfortunate posting for the colonial administrators, who complained of the heat and the flies and the lack of shade, that it became synonymous for sending people stir crazy. Being despatched to the desolate channel, with its remote twists and turns, became known as 'going round the bend'.

Fortunately for me it was a brief encounter. The boat journey took only a few hours to reach Shinas on the mainland, and here I hitched a lift down the coast to the capital of the sultanate, Muscat.

I arrived late that evening and got a room at the Intercontinental Hotel. It was already dark, so I thought I'd get some rest before exploring the city and meeting my guide. I asked the receptionist if there was any food available, given that it was already gone ten p.m., and I was directed to the 'Al Ghazal'.

I don't know what I was expecting, but it certainly wasn't an English pub complete with wood panelling, Bass Ale and bags of salt and vinegar crisps. There was fish 'n' chips on the menu and football on the telly; I could have been transported straight back to London, were it not for the patrons being dressed in long white dishdashas and an array of Omani-style headscarves. The Arabs were all drinking beer from pints and leaning on soggy beer mats. It was all quite surreal.

Mahrouqi was waiting for me the next day at an outside table at a café on the promenade overlooking the port. The bay curved around, surrounded by jagged mountains that glowed pink in the morning sun. Above us on the craggy high ground was Muttrah Fort, marking Muscat's ancient city defences towering over the inlet. The coast was lined with old adobe buildings, with deep-set windows and cooling whitewashed walls to stave off the already scorching morning heat. The pattern was broken by the speckled dome of a mosque, its gold tip just visible as it glinted in the light, and next to it an azure minaret against an even bluer sky.

Flocks of squawking gulls competed noisily for scraps below them. A fishing boat chugged in from the open sea and they went mad, flapping and circling and angling for food. In the bay, a few lonely boats were moored, bobbing steadily. Husbands and wives wandered along the corniche, complementary in black and white, their long fabric flapping in the breeze. The place was immaculate; a perfect vision of Arabia.

I'd been on the hunt for a good guide in Oman for a while. I'd learned through good and bad that having a local travel companion can be invaluable. It's not that they necessarily need to navigate the route, one can do that oneself with a bit of planning and a decent online map, but nothing can beat having a local who knows the language and the nuances of native customs, religion and culture. What's more, if you're lucky and they do know the route intimately, then they can show you places that no guidebook can ever take you to.

Amar had been barely tolerable in Iraq, and I'd made my own arrangements in the Gulf, but I knew that in order to get across Oman in the way I chose, across the central sands, I would need to have someone who knew a thing or two about deserts. There were a lot of things to arrange – special permits, camels and provisions – and while I'd crossed deserts before, namely the Sahara, this was a different beast entirely. What lay ahead was the *Rub' al-Khali*, the notorious Empty Quarter.

'*Marhaba*,' he said coldly. Mahrouqi looked like a stern old man. He was fifty-eight and was wearing the traditional clothes of his homeland, a long white dishdasha and a golden Indian-style turban. On his belt he wore a silver curved dagger and if it weren't for the mango smoothie he was slurping through a straw, he would have made a fine prince in the *Tales of the Arabian Nights*.

'Sit,' he said, offering me a chair. I sat down and ordered an orange juice.

'So, you want to cross the Empty Quarter?' he said, peering through thick spectacles. I could tell he was weighing me up.

I told him that I did.

He pulled out a map and laid it across the table. 'This is the route we will take,' he said. 'First we go south from here. I'll drive us to Jebel Akhdar, where we can do an acclimatisation walk. We can climb up the mountains and get you used to the heat.'

It sounded sensible.

'Then we will go to Nizwa, the old town, and you can see the ancient fort and the market. We'll need to stock up on provisions anyway, so it is a good place to stop off. Then we will carry on to Adam, that's my home town. There we will pick up the camels and take them to the edge of the desert, where we will start walking. We will leave in three or four days, when I am ready, and then by the time we get to Adam and set off it'll be a week, and then depending on how fast you can walk it will take another week or so to reach Haima, and then it's to the coast. You'll be at the coast by the end of the month, and then you can go across Dhofar on your own.'

It seemed like he had it all planned out. On the one hand, it was reassuring; after all, this was a man who'd crossed the Empty Quarter by camel multiple times and was regarded as Oman's foremost camel man. On the other hand, I wondered if I'd get any say in the matter at all. I couldn't abide the thought of this expedition turning into a guided tour, and I knew full well that the best laid plans often fall apart at the first hurdle anyway.

'It is as you like,' said Mahrouqi, with a tilted head. '*Inshallah* we will make it.'

I was hoping to depart straight away, but Mahrouqi said he was busy, so I had to kill a few days before setting off. I used the time to explore Muscat.

I wandered along the corniche past the mosque and the souk, and the rickety, balconied tourist hotels. I was invited to visit the British school and was reminded of the close relationship between the United Kingdom and Oman. Its position on the Trucial Coast had meant that it had been an important strategic foothold for the Empire in the eighteenth and nineteenth centuries, but even before that, Muscat had been a significant draw for traders and invaders alike.

It all started when the Ibadi Imamate arrived from over the

mountains in the eighth century, unifying the disparate and nomadic peoples. For the hundreds of years that followed, Muscat and its outskirts saw the rise and fall of dynasties, as family disputes and warfare rumbled on. But they were facing difficulty. In the west, tribes were earning a fortune from frankincense, but in the east, with difficult access to the trade routes and surrounded by desert, mountains and sea, Muscat was cut off from the rest of the peninsula. Eventually, they abandoned attempts to conquer the dry and barren interior, in favour of exploring the high seas and discovering neighbouring coastlines and islands.

Oman's strategic spot on the corner of the peninsula made it a valuable trading post, but a succession of invading empires ruled Oman and utilised its sea link, taking away all its riches. Finally, in the mid-seventeenth century, the Omani Yarubid dynasty became colonists themselves.

Omani warriors sailed across the Gulf of Aden in dhows and took over a part of what is now Pakistan, as well as vast swathes of East Africa – installing a capital city in Zanzibar. As it built up its overseas territories, the Omani sultanate became an influential power in the slave trade. Villagers were captured from Central Africa and hundreds of thousands were sold as slaves to towns in the Arabian Peninsula and across the whole Middle East.

But with the ban on slavery in the mid-nineteenth century, the Omani economy collapsed. About eighty per cent of the population emigrated to Zanzibar and Britain swept in and claimed Oman's overseas territories. Eventually the two signed a friendship treaty, which gave way to a declaration of independence in the 1950s.

Although the British officially withdrew in the early seventies, the relationship has remained strong – perhaps more so than any other Anglo–Middle Eastern bond – and even today the Sultan of Oman retains a number of British officers on loan from the army to train and serve alongside the Sultan's Armed Forces.

On 19 October, I met Mahrouqi at four a.m. He picked me up in his 4x4 and we drove up into the Al Hajar Mountains. The road wound between the rocky escarpments and terraced villages. In between the bronzed boulders sprang palms and acacia bushes and little rivers that cut narrow gorges through the ancient hills. We walked all day through the wadi, as Mahrouqi bounded from rock to rock in a way that concealed his years. He sang and murmured Omani folk hymns and stopped only to point out the flowers and waterfalls.

There were magical little villages made of mud that seemed as though they hadn't changed in centuries, and their inhabitants walked across the tiered fields tending to flocks of goats. It was the Arabia I'd yearned for. 'It's beautiful, isn't it?' said Mahrouqi, proud of the land of his forefathers. 'But wait till you see the desert. I prefer it there, where it is pure.'

By late afternoon, we'd almost reached the top of the ridgeline at over two thousand metres. Mahrouqi stopped and pointed across the valley. I could see out over the Jebel Akhdar range for miles. The rock burned rose gold in the setting sun and the view was spectacular. I could make out the peak of Jebel Shams, Oman's highest point. Beneath it, sheer precipices of jagged, bronze limestone descended into the valley below. The wadi seemed to go on forever.

The sun dropped out of sight and Mahrouqi was eager to set up camp before it got dark. 'It'll be freezing tonight,' he said. So we made a small fire and he brewed a pot of sweet chai, which went some way to alleviating the chill. I realised it was the first time on the journey that I had actually felt cold.

Mahrouqi had come prepared for the altitude and was

hunkered down in a thick blanket, whereas I had only a thin cotton sleeping liner, which did nothing to protect against the whistling wind. So I ended up wrapping my roll mat around me and shivering throughout the night.

The following morning, we descended from Jebel Akhdar to Nizwa, the last major town before the start of the dunes. It was a green city, filled with date palms and bisected by a great river. It used to be the old capital of Oman in the seventh century when Islam arrived, and later on in the sixteenth century, Nizwa Fort was built, one of the most impressive in the whole peninsula, to defend against marauding tribes. In its heyday, it was a centre of learning and scholarship, earning it the title, 'The Courtyard of Islam'.

Nizwa was considered to be the main stopping-off point for the camel trains crossing the Empty Quarter, before reaching the Sultanate of Oman and the coast to the north of the mountains. As such it was an important trading centre.

Ibn Battutah came to Nizwa in 1329 and said of the place:

It is a fertile land with rivers, trees, orchards, palm plantations, and all kinds of fruit. We reached the city of Nizwa, considered to be the main city in this country. Here, people usually eat in the mosques, where each one brings whatever food he has to eat in the mosque courtyard. Everybody shares the food and these people are helpful and courageous.

But given its remoteness and susceptibility to lawlessness, it was inevitable that when oil was discovered in the desert, Nizwa formed its own opposition groups against Muscat, and became a rebel stronghold that kept away even the hardiest of travellers. Wilfred Thesiger, that most stoic of British explorers, who travelled through Oman in 1948, was forced to avoid Nizwa altogether, warned by his Bedouin guides that he would certainly be killed by the fanatics if he attempted to visit.

These days it was at peace. Although I wouldn't call it quiet. It was a Friday morning and that meant that it was market day. People had travelled from all over Oman to visit the famous souk and haggle for their goods.

I followed the flow of merchants through the ancient gates into the walled city and into the old marketplace, where cows, sheep and goats were being auctioned off, as well as the odd camel. Bearded men in a rainbow of patterned hand-embroidered hats stood around assessing the livestock from afar. The women wore *niqabs*, full face veils, in a style I'd not seen before, with an adjoining piece of material from between the eyebrows to the middle of the nose. Little boys darted around, teasing the animals. It was a racket and I could only just hear the auctioneer over the din of the nervous bleating.

'Camels are very expensive,' Mahrouqui barked over the noise. 'These ones start at around twenty thousand rial, about forty thousand British pounds, but two years ago, an Omani camel went for over two million rial.'

'That's more than four million pounds,' I spluttered.

'Well, it was a very good camel,' he said, matter of factly. 'Look at how they are inspecting them very carefully, that's how they can tell the value.'

I glanced across to where a remarkably chilled-out camel had three men peering between its legs.

'Anyway, we better get some supplies,' said Mahrouqi. 'This is the last place before we go into the wild.'

We wandered past the crenulated city walls to the pointed archways of the market, where palm leaves hung low. Everywhere sturdy coloured baskets were full to bursting with spices, cereals, dates, fruit and vegetables, and beige pottery was lined up like dominoes.

There were jewellery and hardware stores, where brooms and mops spilled out into the gangway, and the usual tourist tat stalls. I lusted after curved silver *khanjar* knives, famed in this region, and some of which were going for a whopping ten thousand dollars.

We bought some batteries and solar-powered lights, we got matches and firewood and bartered for blankets. Then we needed food. We bought chickens and rice, dates and vegetables. I'd learned that the best fruit to survive the conditions of the desert was oranges. Bananas went black and shrivelled, apples got battered and bruised; only oranges could do the job, and when you're hot, thirsty and tired, nothing is more refreshing. I bought an entire sack of them.

From Nizwa we drove to Adam, sixty kilometres to the south, and reached Mahrouqi's house by early afternoon.

The mountains were a hazy blur in the distance and everything to the south and west was a seemingly endless expanse of flat sand. Mahrouqi lived on a farm on the edge of the desert. It was quite a big house, surrounded by a concrete wall that hemmed in his allotment and garden. There were thatched sheds filled with straw for the animals and outbuildings, too, and everywhere hung goatskins and water bladders, nets and tools.

It was a ramshackle compound, but inside the house it was modern, with a games room and a billiards table. Outside, roosters, sheep and goats roamed freely. The noise from the chicken coop was deafening, but it didn't seem to bother the several lazy dogs that lounged around the garden, or cats lolling on the tops of walls. It was a veritable petting zoo of beasts. After a lunch of rice and chicken, Mahrouqi took me to help get the camels from the backyard, where they were sectioned off in little enclosures.

'They're a bit small, aren't they?' I said. I'd bought camels before in Sudan and knew that in order to carry enough water, they'd need to be strong and healthy. These ones looked a bit feeble and one was an infant.

'They're fine,' he snapped. 'When they get into the Empty Quarter, they will be fine.'

I assumed it must be bad form to insult a man's camels, so I apologised, and thought it best to keep my mouth shut and changed the subject.

'Who named it the Empty Quarter?' I asked him.

Mahrouqi sniffed. 'It was named by the great Arabian explorer Ahmad Ibn Majid. It's not just you white men who can be explorers, you know. He called it the *Rub' al-Khali* – Empty Quarter – because it was bare and he found no one living there.'

I'd read somewhere that the origins of the name might actually have been from visiting European explorers, as they tried to map and define the region, but I thought it best not to mention this to Mahrouqi.

He continued, 'The Bedouin just call it *Al-Ramlah*, or "The Sand", because it's the largest desert in the world, the sand goes on and on. But even they won't live there, they stay on the fringes, because it's impossible to survive. They only cross if they really have to. The dunes move in the wind, so all of a sudden you don't know your way. And in some places, there are sinking sands that can swallow you whole.'

I was not filled with confidence that Mahrouqi and his sickly-looking camels were capable of getting us across this dangerous desert wilderness. I knew that modern-day camels were less hardy than in Thesiger's day, and in one of the driest places on earth with zero phone signal, we'd be dependent on them to survive in the wasteland.

It didn't really assuage my fears to see him drag the camels out of the yard and whip them. They grunted and snorted and made the most awful groan, but I put it down to the fact that they really couldn't be bothered to walk across the Empty Quarter, rather than a more general dislike for their master.

Mahrouqi saw me watching. 'When we get to the desert, then they will behave,' he said.

If only I believed him. I felt something licking my hand and looked down to see a little golden dog, with scruffy fur and a needy expression. It was panting in the hot sun.

'That's Snugly,' said Mahrouqi. 'He's coming with us.'

I didn't know what to say. It looked like we'd be a very motley crew for our Empty Quarter crossing.

11

Rub' al-Khali

For years the Empty Quarter had represented to me the final,
unattainable challenge which the desert offered.

Wilfred Thesiger, *Arabian Sands*

We took the camels in a truck to the end of the road that night
and set up camp in a dusty lay-by, as oil lorries trundled by
through the night. The following morning, we loaded the four
animals with our supplies. We had enough food and water to last
and we strapped the blankets and roll mats to the traditional
leather saddles. Loading the camels was a noisy business, as they
roared and snarled when we approached, and especially when
they carried a load, although Mahrouqi assured me this was
quite normal.

Mahrouqi and I were both wearing long dishdashas, which
was the best clothing for the desert once you'd got used to
walking in a long skirt, and on our heads we wore golden
headscarves, topped with black rope to keep them in place. 'You
look like an Omani now,' said Mahrouqi. I couldn't tell if he was
being patronising or not, but I was comfortable and it kept the
sun off.

I wanted to begin the journey on foot, but Mahrouqi said that
he would ride to begin with, so he mounted his beast. Camels
have a rather annoying habit of standing up when you don't

want them to, and when they do get up, it is in the most awkward fashion, first using their hind legs to lean forward, so that when you are in the saddle, you're lurched almost head over heels. It's at that point you realise the need to lean back as far as you can, until the camel pushes back with its inverted knees and stands upright. Mahrouqi used the same noises to control the camel's movement that I'd heard across the Islamic world from Sudan to Afghanistan. *Khrrr, khrrr* from the throat tells the beast to sit down, and then a sort of teeth-sucking noise lets it know that it's time to get up.

We turned our backs on the road and set off into the Empty Quarter, the largest sand desert in the world.

At first the marks of vehicle tracks criss-crossed the flat gravelly plains. 'They're the paths the oil prospectors take,' said Mahrouqi, who was lolling from atop the biggest camel. Behind him trailed the little female. The two other male camels walked behind, as I led them at the end of a long tether. Snugly the little dog followed on behind us, oblivious to the perils ahead.

I looked back at the road, as it melted into the wastes. A distant truck rumbled past. It would be the last we would see of humankind for a while. I suddenly felt rather excited to be entering the desert.

The loose shale was white and crumbled underfoot. We were heading south-west, with the sun gradually rising behind us, warming the sand as the morning progressed. Ahead were the dunes, shimmering in the ferocious heat. They were golden in colour and rose like an impenetrable wall in the far distance.

'We'll be among them before noon,' said my guide.

Here there was no phone signal, and that marks the final frontier when it comes to wilderness in the twenty-first century. The paths petered out as we carried on. Somewhere to the north-west was the Saudi Arabian border, only thirty kilometres away, but it was off-limits still. I was worried that I'd not heard from the embassy, who were dealing with my request for a visa. I had hoped to secure permission to enter the forbidden kingdom before embarking on my journey into the Empty Quarter, but there had been no reply, so now I'd have to wait until I reached the city of Salalah before I could figure out my next steps. But that was still weeks away. All I could do now was concentrate on getting through the desert, and beyond that, Dhofar.

The sand dunes loomed larger as the sun beat down, until it was almost overhead. The going so far had been flat and even though the ground was rough and filled with pebbles and flint, at least it was hard and the camels were happy, covering five or six kilometres an hour comfortably.

By late morning, we were upon the first ridge, which spread out like a vast yellow hedgerow, the dune rising up to sixty or seventy metres high.

'It's enormous,' I said to Mahrouqi.

Mahrouqi snorted. 'These are nothing. The ones on the Saudi border just over there are over a hundred and fifty metres tall.' He pointed to the north. 'And there's one near Salalah that's four hundred and fifty metres.'

'Four hundred and fifty metres?' I exclaimed, hardly imagining a sand dune almost half a kilometre high!

Mahrouqi ignored me and rode off ahead. He began singing to himself. It was an old Bedouin song. The Arabic drone of Mahrouqi's voice drifted across the sands, breaking the silence of the desert. 'It's about the beauty of the Rub' al-Khali and the majesty of the Bedouin women, and about the prowess of the Omanis as sailors,' he said, with effeminate lyricism.

Then just as my ears had grown used to the rhythmic chanting, the tempo changed and a new melody floated backwards. The song sounded familiar, so I walked quicker to catch what it was. It took me some time to decipher Mahrouqi's lyrics, but the tune was unmistakable. There he was, singing along to John Lennon's 'Imagine'.

When the famous explorer Wilfred Thesiger walked across the Empty Quarter Desert in 1947, it was the last time that camels were used out of necessity. With the advent of the oil age and the widespread introduction of cars, the Bedouin that Thesiger had so respected for their traditional way of life adapted quickly to the new form of transport.

Now it was virtually impossible to find a Bedouin guide willing to cross the sands without a Land Cruiser and a cool box in tow, let alone one who had any decent camels that weren't purely for show. Mahrouqi had come good at the last moment, but I wasn't convinced the camels were the best stock, even though I'd paid him good money to source ones that would be used to the hostile conditions.

At first, the camels glided up the steady slope of the dune, but when it got steep, they snorted and whined and we would have to follow the contours around, weaving our way through the great sands. As the sun beat down, the silky grains were hot to touch, and even for a camel it was hard going.

'They're just not used to the soft sands,' he said. Hang on, I thought to myself. He told me yesterday that they'd be fine. It wasn't exactly reassuring, He had only been telling me what I wanted to hear, but we had no option now.

In the Sudan I'd walked with bull camels, but in Arabia the Bedouin have ordinarily used females. The males were normally slaughtered for their meat and occasionally used for pack animals, but rarely were they ridden. Mahrouqi brought a mixture. There were three males and a female, which I found odd because it became quickly apparent that the girl was on heat, meaning that not only were the males all trying to mount her, but she was constantly thrashing about and getting irritable.

'She just needs a good servicing,' said Mahrouqi, 'but she's young and doesn't know what to do.'

Snugly the dog trotted on behind, pausing only when the camels stopped to take shelter in their shadows. I fed the poor thing water from my bottle, which he lapped up in delight. Mahrouqi went ahead in silence. I'd not worked him out at all. Sometimes he would be all smiles and telling me stories of the myths of the desert, sometimes he'd sing, and other times he would storm off in a huff for no reason whatsoever. Now he was just silent.

'A cloud gathers, the rain falls, men live; the cloud disperses without rain, and men and animals die. In the deserts of southern Arabia there is no rhythm to the seasons, no rise and fall of sap, but empty wastes where only the changing temperature marks the passage of the years. It is a bitter, desiccated land which knows nothing of gentleness or ease . . . Men live there because it is the world into which they were born; the life they lead is the life their forefathers led before them; they accept hardships and privations; they know no other way.

Thesiger's words rang true. There was something timeless about life in the desert that, combined with its apparent emptiness, gave it a purity for which I'd yearned. Like Thesiger, I had no desire to travel faster. Walking gave me a respite from the rushing about that so often comes with the build-up to an expedition, and for me, Syria, Iraq and the Gulf had seemed to rustle past in a swift succession of experiences, conversations and glimpses into another world. Here there was no such distraction and there was time to notice the little things, which make you realise that the desert isn't empty after all – the tracks of a hare or a viper, the lifeless roots that emerge from the sand proclaiming a corporeal existence beneath; the shape and colour of the ripples in the dunes, and the weathered flints that glisten like diamonds in a Martian landscape.

The very deliberateness of walking, however contrived, both diminished its monotony and gave a sense of purpose. I didn't know what lay ahead beyond the borders to the west, everything was so uncertain. But for me this was the steady approach I needed to gather my thoughts and prepare myself for the hardships of Yemen and Saudi Arabia beyond that. The Empty Quarter for me symbolised not the final unattainable challenge, but the ascent to a secret world, where an unknown prize might lie.

At around five p.m. we halted, surrounded on all sides by golden dunes rising like mountains. It was perfectly silent and the sun hung low in the sky, casting long shadows from the camels, which crept like tentacles over the gilded waves.

'We make camp here,' said Mahrouqi, stopping on a flat, gravelly plateau. We'd covered over twenty-five kilometres and we were all ready to stop. The female camel in particular was getting petulant and the rope around her neck did nothing to stop her randy protestations. There were a few dry bits of scrub for the camels to chew on, and they preferred here than in the soft dunes. I helped Mahrouqi with unloading the camels, imitating his sounds.

'Khrr, khrr,' I repeated over and over, gently tugging on the rope attached to the camel's neck. In an awkward motion, he rocked down forward and then back until he was sitting. Once his foreleg had been tied, I took off the provisions and we dumped them in a pile. When the saddles were off, we released the camels to graze. 'Don't worry, they won't go far.'

By the time we'd finished unpacking the gear it was almost dark, so we went out in search of brushwood. It's amazing to discover that even in the most barren desert, it is possible to find kindling.

'Look here,' said Mahrouqi, as he bent down over what looked to me like a raised bump in the sand. He dug down with his bare hands and I saw a desiccated root emerge. It was nothing more than a dry twig, I thought.

'No, help me dig deeper,' he said. I scooped away the sand around the edges of the root and as I got deeper, I realised that it went down and down, and as it did it got thicker. Finally, about a foot deep, I felt the base of the root about as thick as an arm. It came away easily and when I pulled it out, there was a good lump of dry wood to use.

'These plants only flower once every few years. Sometimes it won't rain for seven or ten years, but when it does, they come to life.' I almost felt bad burning it, knowing it was alive, and suggested that we left it, but Mahrouqi was having none of it. 'We're burning it,' he said, grabbing it and throwing it into a pile next to the equipment. 'There's plenty, and I need my tea.'

So we made a fire as the sun set and Mahrouqi boiled some water in a tin kettle, then filled it with loose leaf tea and ten spoons of sugar.

A thin sliver of moon rose behind the dark silhouettes of the dunes and a billion stars twinkled in the night sky. The only noise was the crackling of the fire and the occasional shuffling of the camels.

We ate tinned beans with some flatbread and drank the sweet masala chai with a fresh orange for dessert. Mahrouqi threw the orange peel in the direction of the camels, who snaffled it up with their big rubbery lips. Snugly the dog sat apart on a little hillock watching out into the blackness. Sometimes he'd bark if he saw a rabbit or a fox.

'I met Kissinger in 1985,' said Mahrouqi, as we gazed at the flickering flames.

'Kissinger?' I said. 'Henry Kissinger?' wondering why my guide had met the former US Secretary of State.

'No, Wilfred.'

'Ah, you mean Thesiger?' I said, understanding now.

'Yes. Kissinger. He was a tall man with a strong face. The Bedouin liked him. You know they had an Arabic name for him? They called him Mubarak-bin-London.' Mahrouqi grinned. 'But by then he was an old man. He came back and met with the sultan and visited some of the places he'd been to before, in fact he came this way. We are following the same route that Kissinger took in the 1940s. But, of course, he wasn't happy. By then everything had changed. The roads had been built and oil discovered, and the towns were growing bigger and all the Bedouin had swapped their camels for cars. It's a shame.' The flames licked the edges of Mahrouqi's dishdasha and reflected in his glasses, and his weathered skin shone a deep red.

'I prefer life in the desert,' he carried on as I listened, trying to understand the man who had agreed to come with me. 'I don't like the city. The boys drive too fast and kill themselves, and nobody has any time to enjoy life anymore. Oman is a good place, it's certainly better than the savage countries that surround it, but even here everyone is rushing around and nobody is happy.'

He looked at me. 'I lived in England once,' he said. I was surprised.

'Yes. I lived in Chorleywood. I used to be a health and safety officer with the fire service. But there nobody is happy either. You have these nice houses and fancy cars, but nobody has time to do anything. That's why I like being on my own. That's why I like the desert and that's why I came with you on this trip.'

There was a deep sadness in his bloodshot eyes and I suspected that his melancholy ran deeper than a nostalgic lament for the past, but I empathised with a large part of what he said.

In the preface to his immortal book, Thesiger wrote that his return to Arabia was 'the final disillusionment.' I dared not think what he would make of places like Dubai and Abu Dhabi these days. But even here on the fringes of the Empty Quarter, that sense of purity was already being lost. Even the mighty sands couldn't conceal the fresh tracks of 4x4s and the scars of oil stations that littered the desert.

'The discovery of oil ruined them. It was the worst thing that could have happened,' said Wilfred Thesiger in his final interview. Thesiger held the Arabs in such high regard mainly because he himself was searching for a sense of purity that he found nowhere else but in the sands. Thesiger spent five years in southern Arabia and crossed the Empty Quarter twice, in 1945–6 and 1947–8, travelling on foot and by camel with only a select few Bedouin guides of the Rashid and Bait Kathir tribe.

It's no wonder he is known to posterity as the last great explorer. Thesiger's observations are viewed as archaic these days, and I doubt many Arabs would agree with his sentiments about oil. But for the Old Etonian and Oxford boxing blue, it was a person's character that counted, not his wealth.

Thesiger was a man of contradictions. For a man who despised civilisation so much, he was the epitome of grandeur. He himself hailed from an aristocratic military family. His grandfather was Lord Chelmsford, Commander of the British Imperial Army in Zululand, and his father was the Consul-General in Addis Ababa, in what is now Ethiopia. Thesiger grew up in Africa shooting lions, and his sense of adventure was only fuelled at the outbreak of the Second World War, where he signed up to the Special Operations Executive and then became a founding member of the elite SAS. He was never one to settle down, and never married or had children. After the war, he spent decades travelling in the wilderness, searching for answers among the most remote communities in the world. He lived among the Marsh Arabs and Kurds of Iraq and spent much time photographing the tribes of Iran, Afghanistan and Pakistan. But none of those places moved him as much as the deserts of Arabia.

The philosophy of the desert was simple. For the Bedouin, the sands, as they called the interior of the peninsula, were a place of hardship and foreboding, to be crossed only when needs must. It was a place of danger and hostility, yet also a refuge. It was an escape from the endless blood feuds of the villages and the creeping rules that governed on the coasts and in the towns, and these men-only journeys made by the caravans were often an escape from the monotony of family life.

The desert was a place where life must be lived to its fullest. As a result, the sands provided a sanctuary where unwritten rules directed the behaviour of those who dared enter them. In a place so full of hardship, the principles of generosity and benevolence were omnipotent. Even a sworn enemy must be welcomed as a guest if he asked for hospitality, and treated as a member of the family. It was a way of life to which Thesiger aspired.

There was one particular story that summed up his experiences. A month had passed since Thesiger had eaten meat when he crossed the sands from Liwa to Salalah, and his party was on the verge of starvation, when one day, his Bedouin guide Musallim jumped off his camel and caught a hare. After they made camp, they all threw their remaining flour into a pot and sat around watching hungrily as it was cooked over the open fire into a stew. Just when it was ready to be eaten, one of the men, bin Kabina, suddenly looked up and saw three unfamiliar Arabs cresting a sand dune.

'God, guests,' Thesiger's companions groaned.

Thesiger recounted what happened next.

We greeted them and asked the news, made coffee for them, and then Musallim and Bin Kabina dished up the hare and the bread and set it before them, saying with every appearance of sincerity that they were our guests, that God had brought them, that today was a blessed day, and a number of similar remarks. They asked us to join them but we refused, repeating that they were our guests. I hoped that I did not look as murderous as I felt while I joined the others in assuring them that God had brought them on this auspicious occasion.

Despite relishing hardship and physical challenge, I think, for Thesiger, the true appeal lay in the inner journey. He looked to the desert for answers in life's dilemmas and found them in the people he met. In the Bedouin, he discovered the traits he aspired to the most: courage, generosity, loyalty and stoic determination – the same values drilled into him at public school. He was a man who aspired to fit in on the one hand, and yet couldn't bring himself to do so with his own people. He looked for a transformation.

In his own words:

No man can live this life and emerge unchanged. He will carry, however faint, the imprint of the desert, the brand which marks the nomad; and he will have within him the yearning to return, weak or insistent according to his nature. For this cruel land can cast a spell which no temperate clime can match.

Thesiger's background might seem outdated and old-fashioned. Even at the time he was regarded as a bit of a Victorian throwback, and yet when you read his motivations and get to the core of his ideals, they seem more aligned to those of a modern, new age traveller. He should probably be regarded as the first hippy, rather than the last Victorian.

For Thesiger, the sands represented a threshold into another world and another age, now lost forever. The Empty Quarter was the final frontier in the age of earthly exploration, and he wanted to be the man who finally pushed himself to the very limits of human endurance, even if he did do it in rags and tweed. The dangers he encountered only served to add spice to his adventures. Salim bin Ghabaisha, his guide, described Thesiger fifty years after their travels together as 'loyal, generous, and afraid of nothing'.

His dangers involved warring tribes, roaming bandits and getting arrested by the Saudis. It seemed to me that you have only to look at the newspapers and read about southern Arabia to realise that, in that respect at least, little had changed.

We woke at dawn to the sound of a camel's fart. Mahrouqi had just finished praying and the cold chill of the morning cut through my blanket like a knife. 'Get up,' he said waving at me. Snugly was wagging his tail, glad to be getting going again.

I looked at my phone and checked the map. There was still a hundred kilometres to go to the next village of Haima, where we might be able to follow a road south to Hasik, and another three hundred kilometres beyond that to Dhofar. We aimed to walk thirty kilometres a day, perhaps forty if we were lucky, but really my fate was entirely in Mahrouqi's fickle hands, and the hooves of his capricious camels.

After breakfast we cleaned the pots using only sand in the old Bedouin way, which gave them a scoured sparkle. 'We can't waste water,' Mahrouqi reminded me. Looking out across the seemingly empty sands, I needed no reminder.

As Mahrouqi fixed up the camels, I noticed the tracks of all sorts of beasts around us. The paw prints of foxes and slithery patterns of snakes that had paid us a curious visit during the night. I was sure that Snugly must have seen them and barked, but I hadn't heard a thing. It was the best night's sleep I'd had on the journey so far.

'Have you got a pin?' enquired Mahrouqi, as he was loading the saddles.

'What kind of a pin?'

'A safety pin.'

I thought I might have in my first aid kit, so I rummaged around until I found one and handed it to him, wondering what on earth he wanted a pin for.

He unclipped the sharp end and grabbed the female camel by the snout and jammed the pin straight through her nose, until it pierced the nostril right through. She let out a loud groan.

'What are you doing?' I asked in alarm.

'Giving her a nose ring. She's being very naughty,' he said in a mutter. Mahrouqi then untied the rope from her neck and placed it in a loop, and using a piece of string, tied the rope end to end so that he could pull her by the nostril. 'It will make it easier to control.'

As we set off, the camel refused to move, even with Mahrouqi's rather barbaric methods, and soon he resorted to beating her with a whip until she headbutted him right on his forehead. It was his turn to yelp, although I couldn't help thinking that he deserved it.

For the next two days, Mahrouqi was in a strop. He set a course to the south, over more dunes and across flat gravelly plains. He wasn't one to use a map and kept insisting he knew where he was going. 'I've been this way before. I don't need one of those stupid phones.'

While I admired his sense of adventure, I knew for a fact that he was going the wrong way, given that I could see on my phone and compass which direction we ought to be going. I wasn't in any rush to get to Haima, but I knew that our water supplies would only last for three days and so we couldn't take any unnecessary risks.

He ended up riding on ahead regardless and we didn't speak for the rest of the day. He was irritable and I could tell he was getting tired. He began beating the camels with more frequency and when I asked him to stop, he'd tell me that I had no idea about camels. I told him that I'd crossed the Sahara and bought three of my own when I walked the Nile.

'Sudanese camels are different. I am a great traveller and you are nothing,' was his only retort and he punched his camel in the skull to prove a point. I liked him less and less as the days went on.

'If you don't like my ways, then I will leave,' he snapped. 'I'll ride off and leave you and you can find your own way out of the desert.'

He carried on without even looking me in the eye.

'I'll take all my water and you can see if you can survive then.'

I knew his intimidations were empty, but the fact he was threatening to abandon me in the middle of the Empty Quarter to die of thirst was foreboding. I forced myself to be the bigger man and massage his ego a little.

Whenever he was tired, he would stop to pray. I didn't have any problem with him praying, and in Oman like most of the peninsula, the devout Muslims would perform the *Salah* five times a day. But they were meant to be done at certain times and I was sure he was using it as an excuse to stop walking. One day, I'm pretty sure he fell asleep halfway through his prostrations.

I reminded myself that he was fifty-eight and not as fit as he probably used to be, and in all likelihood he was getting tired and hungry, too. We'd been living on a diet of pasta and tinned vegetables, and the oranges were fast running out. Our water supplies were low and my feet were aching after miles of walking through the soft sands in unrelenting sun, where the temperature in the day was always over forty degrees. There was no shade and the sand would get in your boots and you would have to stop every mile to pour it out. I'd got raging blisters and sores from my rucksack and my lips were cracked from the scorching winds. The romance of the desert was beginning to wear off a little.

I'd come to the desert, like Thesiger, in search of a dream; of purity and authenticity. And instead I'd found brutality, cruelty and complexity. Mahrouqi was an enigma, and the desert itself was not half as pure as it seemed at first glance.

After a few days, we rounded another ridge and on the far side saw some trails in the sand. They were old 4x4 tracks that didn't seem to lead anywhere. Mahrouqi stopped on top of the ridge and pointed to the far distance. 'That's an oil station.' I peered through the heat haze and could just make out a thin black column of smoke that rose into the deep blue sky. 'It's five kilometres away. We will go to it and find a road leading to Haima,' he said, pushing on before I could even reply.

I looked at the map. It was actually nearer twenty kilometres away, but I'd learned that it was pointless to argue and knew it would take a full afternoon of walking to get there, so I followed on behind. The dunes dissipated into stony, arid plains and soon they were just a memory. After an exhausting eight-hour walk in silence, we arrived when it was already dark and slept on the edge of the station compound, near to a rubbish pit full of half-burnt plastic bottles.

Even though I'd found Mahrouqi hard to get along with, and he'd threatened me and ruined my own romantic notions of what life in the desert is like, he had probably done me a favour. His prickly demeanour and capricious nature reminded me that things aren't always as they seem. I'd seen the desert in a way that it is no longer seen. People simply don't cross deserts on camels anymore; why would they? And yet, for all its hardships and disappointments, I had caught a glimpse of what had formed the mentality of Arabia in the first place and for that I was glad.

We reached Haima, where we handed over the camels to Mahrouqi's son Farhad, who took them back to his house on a truck. We continued on south towards the coast, leaving the wilderness behind. Now the desert was criss-crossed with roads and tracks and oil stations; pumps and jacks and electricity pylons. The flatness became broken at first by rolling undulations, pockmarked by wadis and low scrub, and soon acacia trees sprang from the creeks of the barren wastes, until the Arabian Sea finally came into view on the horizon.

I said goodbye to Mahrouqi on the coastal road at Hasik, and he drove off to the north-east, towards Muscat. I hauled my rucksack onto my back, waving to his car as he sped off into the distance. I don't know which of us was more glad to see the back of the other. I stood there, alone, at the side of the road and looked up to the east. Looming in the distance I saw the outline of the craggy peaks of the Al-Qarah range, which appeared as a vast ridge shrouded in grey mist.

It was the start of the Dhofar mountains. After the flatness of the desert, and the monotony of the endless sands, I was excited to be almost among them. But I also knew that on the far side would mark the beginning of the biggest ordeal of the journey, Yemen.

12

The Mountains of Dhofar

Far are the shades of Arabia,
Where the Princes ride at noon,
'Mid the verdurous vales and thickets,
Under the ghost of the moon;
And so dark is that vaulted purple
Flowers in the forest rise
And toss into blossom 'gainst the phantom stars
Pale in the noonday skies.

Walter de la Mare

When the three wise men came from the East bearing gifts for the baby Jesus in Bethlehem, Mary and Joseph would have been rather pleased to receive their presents. The gold would have proven handy to pay for some decent accommodation and the myrrh useful to anoint the newborn infant, but the frankincense was perhaps even more valuable. Weight for weight, it was worth more than gold and was not only widely lauded as a priestly air freshener, but also reputed to have healing properties.

Two thousand years ago, as Jesus was being welcomed into the world by these mysterious visitors, Dhofar was at the heart of the lucrative frankincense trade. For millennia it had been used as a valuable currency between the roaming Bedouin tribes. The Boswellia tree, from which it comes, evolved in the unique

biosphere of the misty mountain plateau and its sheer inaccess-
ibility accounted for its worth.

As such, Dhofar was the source of the greatest trade route in
the Middle East. This precious resin was exported through what
is now Yemen, Saudi Arabia and up towards the Holy Land. The
prized cargo was carried in caravans, mainly by camel, but also
on donkeys, mules or in baskets on the heads of slaves. The
traders were often vulnerable to looting by bandits or being
heavily taxed for passing through foreign territory. Centuries of
a booming frankincense trade made the towns and cities along
the route wealthy and powerful. Demand grew as far away as
India and Europe, and ports were built on the coast of Dhofar
to ship the prized incense over the waves.

Frankincense became a revered symbol of the utmost holiness
and a staple part of religious rituals in churches or temples. It
was a key substance to mask the rotting odour when embalming
bodies and the white smoke that appears when it's burned was
believed to reach heaven. Christian priests have been walking
down the nave swinging their smoking thuribles ever since and
to this day the Catholic Church buys frankincense by the basket
load. The trees themselves grow in the mountains of Yemen and
Somalia, too, but the Omanis have always claimed that their sap
is the finest.

Hadi al-Hikmani knew these mountains better than
anyone else. He was a man my own age who worked for the
Oman Ministry of Environment and Climate Affairs,
preserving leopards and other endangered species, and there
wasn't a track or trail in these mountains that he didn't
know. I'd been introduced to Hadi through a friend in the
army, who ran a business in Muscat, and he came
recommended as the region's expert.

Hadi was waiting at the foot of the mountain in a dusty car park with six camels.

'*Salaam alaikum*, Lev,' he said. I looked at my new guide. After the problems I'd had with Amar and Mahrouqi, I was nervous that he might be another eccentric, but as I shook his hand, I saw he had a wide smile and a kind round face. I knew instinctively that I was in luck.

'Ready for an adventure?' he said, with genuine excitement. I smiled back.

'Come and meet the boys.' He led me over to the camels and on the far side, four men were busy stuffing water bottles and rations into hessian sacks.

'This is Salim Suhail,' said Hadi. An old man, who looked to be in his sixties or seventies, stood to attention in a sarong and green check shirt and shook my hand with a firm grip, afterwards touching his chest.

'And this is Ali Saïd, his cousin.'

A slightly younger man, who looked to be fifty or so, with a grey stubble that matched his turban and smiling through perfectly white, shiny teeth, grasped my hand and pulled me towards his face. For a second, I thought he was going to kiss me on the lips and in a slightly awkward fashion, I did the most English thing possible and puckered up in reluctant expectation. Fortunately, he was just gracing me with the typical Omani greeting, a touching of noses.

Next to him were two much younger men, in their twenties. 'This is Saïd Suhail and Saïd Salim.'

Saïd number one, resplendent in a full maroon outfit, wore a pair of stylish aviator sunglasses and brandished a huge hunting rifle. The other Saïd said nothing and just held his hand on his heart. These were the sons of the older men.

'It's to protect against wolves and hyenas,' said Saïd in Arabic, as he saw me eyeing up the rifle. As I walked away to sort out my own bags, Hadi whispered in a conspiratorial fashion, 'It's actually to protect against the smugglers.'

Of all the men, only Hadi wasn't wearing the traditional dress of the Jebali people, that being a wrap-around skirt, a bit like a sarong, with a long-sleeved check shirt, military-style waistcoat and an ammunition belt with a long, curved dagger stuck down the front. Despite having been born in a cave in the mountains, Hadi was a modern man. He had been to the city and even studied in England for a while.

When everything was loaded up, we set off from the road towards the looming cliffs. From here they looked almost impenetrable.

'There's only two ways up,' said Hadi, 'and both are off-limits. But I have special permission.' The escarpments rose sharply; a steep climb lay ahead and even though I could not see a path, Hadi assured me there was one that wound up through the valleys and into the rocky cliffs ahead. I had no idea how on earth the camels would manage it. After the ones Mahrouqi had brought for the Empty Quarter, I was feeling a bit pessimistic.

Hadi laughed when I told him. 'Ha! The man clearly had no idea what he was doing. And you haven't seen our camels. They're proper camels, the ships of the mountains, never mind the desert, not like those town camels he had for show. These can carry a hundred and fifty kilograms and will still fly up these cliffs. Don't worry about that.'

I watched with amazement. Hadi was right. These animals barely needed any encouragement; they were carrying twice the weight of Mahrouqi's camels and travelled at twice the speed, without so much as a groan. Their padded feet seemed to glide

LEVISON WOOD

right over the jagged rocks, and they weaved between the enormous boulders with ease.

The narrow footpath led to the base of the cliff, where under the shade of an acacia tree, a group of soldiers marked the entrance to the jebel. They wore a mixture of orange and black camouflage uniforms.

'They're the Oman army,' said Hadi, as we neared the machine-gun position, flanked by sandbags. The soldiers in orange turbans, with futuristic-looking rifles, seemed surprised to see us. 'Wait here,' said Hadi, as he went ahead to greet the soldiers. I noticed two more soldiers get up and shake hands with my new guide. They looked different, though; these two wore flip flops and green headscarves. Hadi waved me and the camel men over and we approached with caution.

'These are the *Firqat*,' said Hadi, introducing me to the two irregular fighters. 'They're the local tribal militia. They've guarded these hills since the war.'

'Why are they here?' I asked, wondering why they were needed.

'To protect against smugglers,' said Hadi. 'Somalis come by boat and sneak into the jebel to harvest the frankincense illegally, and they usually come armed. And as you know, Yemen isn't far away. The sultan has been careful to make sure these passes are guarded against insurgents after what happened last time.'

'You mean the rebellion?' I said, recalling my military history. I remembered from my army days, studying all about the Dhofar insurrection in the 1970s, where the SAS were involved in flushing out the terrorists from these very mountains.

Hadi smiled. 'You could call it that, I suppose. We prefer to say uprising. Anyway, that was a long time ago, before you and I were born.' He slapped me on the back and waved to the soldiers, as we passed under the barrier and followed the trail that led up into the craggy valley. 'Let's go.'

The sun was beating down and by mid-morning the temperature was almost forty degrees Celsius. The path became narrower and narrower as it climbed, until it was nothing more than a thin footpath that zigzagged between the bronze-coloured boulders. The camels lumbered on unperturbed and I watched in astonishment as they climbed. I was sweating like a pig following in Saïd's footsteps. He was wearing a full-face balaclava and not an inch of his skin was showing. 'To stop the sun,' he said, pointing at the blazing orb above that had burned the mountains to a crisp.

He was a decade my junior and the heat didn't seem to bother him as much as the prospect of getting a suntan. He skipped along with his rifle across his shoulders like a crucifix. I kept my eyes fixed firmly on his feet ahead, making sure to watch my step. One false move and a slip would mean disaster. The cliff fell away to the right with a hundred-metre drop and it was only two feet wide.

Suddenly there was a loud rumble up above. Hadi shouted, 'Watch out!' I looked in dread; one of the lead camels must have stumbled on the loose shale and sent a boulder crashing down the cliffside. I saw it bounce with horrifying violence across the footpath in front of us and down into the crevasse below. That was close, I thought to myself.

'You okay?' shouted Hadi, as he and Salim came running over.

'Fine,' I said, relieved not to have been crushed by the rock, but in reality, acutely conscious of the new dangers the mountains presented.

I noticed for the first time that Salim, the old man, was carrying a full-length broadsword in a silver scabbard.

'What on earth is that for?' I asked. 'Don't tell me Salim is going battling smugglers with a bloody sword? Or even leopards for that matter.'

Hadi chuckled. 'No, of course not. It's for killing injured camels.'

'Do the camels ever fall?' I asked, now slightly concerned I'd end up with a tonne-weight beast falling on my head. 'I thought you said they can fly up the cliffs.'

Hadi laughed. 'I told you, they're the ships of the mountains. They rarely fall.'

'Rarely?'

'Well, it does happen sometimes, of course, but not very often. If it does, the camel driver gets blamed and they never live it down. Camels are expensive, you know.'

I knew that much alright.

'There was this one guy thirty years ago that my father told me about, when I was five years old. He was leading the camels along this very same ridge, and his camel slipped down a cliff and was killed. It took the men three days to carve it up and carry the meat down to the village. None of it went to waste, but the camel driver was so ashamed, he left the village forever. People still talk about him to this day.'

We carried on up the gorge for another few hours and as we got higher, the brown, arid rocks began to sprout vegetation. Palms, acacias and thickets of long pampas grass erupted from the crags, and even little streams appeared in the precipices. It was the dry season, so most of the wadis were empty, but colourful stains were left from the trickles of ancient waterfalls in the limestone bluffs. With the ascent, more and more trees and bushes clustered around, so at last we could get some shade from the unrelenting sun.

At around noon, we came upon a cave in the sandstone. 'We'll stop here for a break and take some lunch,' suggested Hadi.

At once the camel men unloaded the beasts with rapid efficiency, and within five minutes, the camels were stripped bare and left to roam in the thickets and munch on the thorn bushes. The two young Jebelis gathered some brush from the trees and built a little fire to brew the tea, and all the while they sang songs of the mountains. The serenity was only once broken by the distant braying of a donkey.

The camels' ears all pricked at once and Saïd stood up to look up the wadi, gripping his rifle.

'It might be a Somali smuggler,' whispered Hadi. 'They use donkeys to carry frankincense off the mountain.' He shrugged his shoulders. 'Or it might be a feral one, descended from the pack animals of the nomads who used to live up here.' I looked around and could hardly imagine anyone actually living in this sublime yet brutal environment.

'Our families all lived up here till twenty or thirty years ago,' said Hadi. 'I was born in a cave not far from here.' He smiled, proud of his tribal heritage, which seemed at odds with his word-perfect English and the British accent he'd picked up at university. 'Now, of course, everyone has moved down to the villages or cities, or where there's a phone signal.'

I had noticed that all the men had mobile phones, which they tucked in next to their daggers, both amounting to the same thing. They had their practical uses, but more importantly they were status symbols. Saïd came and sat next to me, resting his rifle across his lap and pulling out the latest Samsung from his ammunition belt to show me. He smiled. 'Are you on Instagram?' he asked. 'Add me.'

That afternoon we carried on climbing for another few hours and settled in another cave by around five p.m. We weren't quite to the top of the mountain yet, and there was another five or six days of walking along the ridge still left, so I was content to let Hadi and his men lead the way and sleep wherever nature would allow.

The following morning, we continued the ascent, climbing up a steep ridge until we crested onto the plateau. 'Look,' said Hadi. '*Luban.*'

'What's Luban?' I asked.

'Frankincense,' he said excitedly, and walked off the main trail and grasped the tiny leaves of a nearby gnarled tree. I noticed that its trunk and branches were scarred with knife cuts and the oozing sap had collected in solidified gum, dripping down the bark like a melting candle. 'That's the frankincense right there,' said Hadi, breaking off the hard, yellow crust. 'It's worth over fifty dollars a kilogram. Not bad for a bit of gum, eh? The problem is, the Somalis come and steal it all from us. It's theft. And then they have the cheek to sell it as Somali or Yemeni brand.'

At that moment I heard an ear-splitting noise in the distance. It was the familiar whirr of a helicopter rotor getting closer and closer. 'Quick, let's move,' said Hadi, 'we don't want the army thinking we're bandits.' He motioned for us to leave the tree alone and carry on down into a gully and out of sight. I saw three helicopters soar past overhead and disappear behind a far ridge to the north. Luckily, we hadn't been spotted. 'They're probably on a mission, dropping troops off or resupplying the Firqat.'

That afternoon we found a deep ravine in which to camp for the night. We'd gone from sea level to well over a thousand metres in the space of two days and as we'd climbed higher the temperature had cooled, which had made walking in the day more pleasant, but it meant that it could get very cold at night. 'It'll be out of the wind at least,' said Hadi, pointing to the dry river bed. 'We shouldn't camp on the top, as the camels won't have anything to eat and we'd get blown off, plus we'd get spotted by the army.'

After the gruelling day's climbing, we were all glad to rest and in the absence of a cave, we spread our roll mats out on the bare stones and watched as the sun faded behind the mountain, and the stars came out. It was a perfectly clear night and even with a full moon, which lit the plateau brightly, we were still treated to a magical night sky.

Ali, who didn't speak a word of English, and had been singing his usual Jebali songs, must have noticed me admiring his Arabian nights. Suddenly, out of nowhere, he broke into a rendition of 'Twinkle, twinkle, little star . . .'

With his lullaby ringing in my ears, I wrapped my blanket tight around me. The breeze around my face was pleasant and I felt inordinately happy. I fell into a deep slumber, not caring about the hard, cold stone underneath me.

I dreamt I was walking through the Empty Quarter again. The sand was deep and I struggled to walk. I lifted my legs higher and higher, but the sand just got deeper. It rubbed at my ankles and I could feel my skin wearing away. It was hot and the sun beat down on me, searing into the back of my neck. My throat was cracked and dry and I was desperate for water. In the distance I saw a shimmering lake, sparkling in the hot desert sun, but with every step it slipped further away.

Suddenly the heavens opened and rain cascaded from the sky. It fell heavily, turning the sand into mud, and soon I could hear the slapping sound of waves as the desert around me flooded. Water! That source of life, which I hadn't seen, apart from the salty depths of the Arabian Sea – and that didn't count – was now all around, even in my mouth. I was getting wetter and wetter. But what on earth was happening?

Drip, drip, drip. I could feel the water splashing onto my face and I could hear it sploshing onto the rocks around me. I rolled over onto my front. It was the early hours of the morning and even if my dream was a reality, I had no intention of waking up.

'Wake up,' mumbled Hadi, and began shaking my shoulder. 'Lev, wake up.'

I grunted and rolled over. It wasn't a dream after all, although I could hardly believe it. I'd been travelling now for almost two months and had not even so much as seen a cloud, and now it appeared to be raining. 'It's only water,' I mumbled, squinting into the darkness to see Hadi's shadowy figure above me. 'No, we need to move,' he said. 'There could be a flash flood.'

My brain suddenly engaged. I didn't need to be told twice. I'd been in a flash flood before in the Himalayas and it had been one of the most terrifying experiences I'd encountered. I jumped out of my sleeping bag and automatically started rolling it up into its stuff sack. In the blackness I could hear Ali, the Saïds and Salim as well; they were all up and busily trying to herd up the camels.

'Quickly,' shouted Hadi. Pools of water were already beginning to form from the rain drops in the hard-baked earth, and I knew that every second would count. If it had been raining upstream already for a few hours, then a torrent of water and deadfall could fill this channel in minutes. I looked up at the sheer cliff walls, which in the darkness would have been impossible to scale.

'Yalla!' shouted Ali. 'Yalla, yalla,' Saïd repeated. 'Let's go!'

We shuffled off through the thicket, as thorns from the acacia trees scratched our arms and faces. All the camel men shone the lights from their phones on the rocky trail, which weaved around the river bed and up a gravelly embankment. We walked and walked through the blackness, until I could sense we were on higher ground, although the storm clouds had obscured the moon and stars so that all around there was nothing but an eerie mist. After twenty minutes of stumbling about in the rain, Hadi stopped at the entrance to a cave.

'We'll stay here,' he said. The boys tied the camels on long ropes to the trees nearest the entrance and unloaded the gear again, spreading it out under the shelter of the overhanging rocks, while we took off our sodden shirts and laid them out on the boulders. I was tired, wet and cold. It was pointless making a fire now to dry off, I thought; best to get at least an hour or so sleep before the dawn came. Hadi was in agreement.

So we flopped down where we stood, onto the dry sand of the cave floor. It was a primeval existence we were now living. Walking and sitting, eating and sleeping. Nothing else seemed to be of concern. We'd move when we needed to and stop wherever we wanted. Time seemed to stand still and only survival and the basic comforts mattered. I drifted off back into a deep sleep, but this time I dreamt of nothing.

The next day, the clouds had cleared to reveal a deep cobalt sky and the sun had returned with a vengeance. Ali and Salim were already up and had made tea and porridge. I knew it was time to leave when they began to sing their morning song, which seemed to cheer up the camels and get them ready for the day's walk. We emerged from the cave and followed the trail out of the wadi and onto the flat scrubland of the top of the plateau. We passed the isolated frankincense trees, all of them scarred with the scratches made by the illegal harvesters. Despite the best efforts of the Sultan's Army, as I looked out across the vast escarpment, filled with crags and valleys and gorges all hidden from view, I knew that the task of protecting the resource was almost impossible.

Hadi led our caravan on foot, while Saïd played around with his camel. Sometimes he'd stand on its back and drive the beast while surfing it, imploring me to take photos. The majestic camel didn't mind at all and seemed to love its owner, nuzzling Saïd and resting its drooling lips on its master's shoulders whenever we stopped. Saïd would always pretend to kiss it and never failed to give it a hug. I thought how different these gentlemen were to Mahrouqi and his poor creatures.

Hadi stopped abruptly and turned around, beckoning me to come over quickly. He squatted down at the side of the trail and pointed at some prints in the sand. 'It's an Arabian leopard.' He grinned and shunted to a rock nearby. 'And this is the scat.' He picked up a twisted, dry piece of excrement. He looked so excited. 'He's been here recently, perhaps just yesterday. It makes me so happy to know they are still here.'

The trail led south to the point at which we reached the very brink of the cliff top and for the next two days we skirted the edge of the mile-high escarpment. For the first time, I could see clear views of the Arabian Sea from above. It glistened a bright turquoise and in the far distance, ten miles away, the tiny dots of fishing boats and oil tankers signified that the port of Salalah wasn't far away.

Also for the first time we got a phone signal, with uninterrupted line of sight to the west, and at that moment everyone's phones buzzed incessantly as a stream of text messages and emails flooded in. The primordial dream was broken, as Hadi, Saïd, Salim and Ali all spent the next hour with their noses buried into Facebook updates and stern messages from their wives. Ali had two, so he took a bit longer than the others.

But in spite of the banes of the twenty-first century, we were treated to one of the most beautiful views I had ever seen. Stretched out for twenty kilometres, the ridge appeared as a layered painting, with every pastel colour dissipating in the afternoon sunshine so that the cliffs disappeared altogether, but not before inviting us all to stand in awe at the spectacle of such sublimity before us. The Jebalis prayed on their rugs and only a soaring eagle, with its circular ascent, dared to defy the grandeur of the cliffs.

I was happy. Not only had I somehow managed to get across the Empty Quarter of Oman, but also ascend its most feared and imposing mountains and traverse the notorious Dhofar ridge. Looking down, Hadi pointed to a trail that zigzagged down the mountain to a faraway village.

'That's Mirbat,' he said. 'We'll pass it tomorrow and maybe you can meet my father, Musalam. He fought in these mountains.' I glanced at Hadi and knew why he had called the Dhofar rebellion an uprising. Hadi smiled.

'Yes, he was a rebel. He fought against the Sultan and the British. He fought against your SAS. And survived to tell the tale.'

The final night on the mountain, we slept in the acacia forest that ringed the top of the escarpment. There was a full moon, which lit the cliffs and gave the frankincense trees an ethereal glow. As the Jebali camel men prayed in unison, the song of devotion floated out across the land; its only competition was the cooing of an owl and the far-off howl of a wolf.

On the road to Mirbat, we stopped off in a village to drop off the camels and say goodbye to Ali, Salim, Saïd and Saïd. Hadi's father was waiting at the foot of the mountain in a 4x4. Despite the fact he was wearing kohl round his eyes and was well into his sixties, he looked like a hard man. He wore a dagger on his belt and a green turban over a greying head. He gripped all of our hands with a firm shake and hugged his son with nose touching. He insisted we stay for lunch, as he'd killed a goat to celebrate our successful walk, and he gave me the brains and eyeballs as a special treat.

Hadi came as far as the main road and we said goodbye. 'Here I must leave you to carry on alone.' He told me he needed to be back at university the following week. 'And in any case,' he said, 'you wouldn't catch me going to Yemen.' With a hug, I waved off the jolly mountain man and he went back into the hills.

I hitched a lift to the coast and stopped off in the port town of Mirbat, once famous for its old fort, which a small detachment of British SAS soldiers had defended against a much larger force of communist fighters from the mountains in 1975. It was a decisive battle that settled the sultan in power once and for all, and to this day Oman remains a peaceful, safe place to visit, unified in spite of its fractured history.

The same could not be said for what lay a few miles to the west. Yemen, a place so fractured and divided after years of war, lay terrifyingly close. I still had no idea how I was going to get through it, since it was impossible to get a visa. Foreigners were banned; even aid workers and journalists had all been kicked out. The Saudi army controlled most of the borders and their allies – the UAE – had invaded the island of Socotra and were hell bent on taking over all the ports.

Al-Qaeda ruled the roost in the mountains, and the Shi'a Houthis, a rebel force sponsored by Hezbollah and Iran, were in control of the capital. War ravaged the frontier, hospitals were being bombed and millions had been forced into poverty and starvation; and to make matters worse, a cholera epidemic had broken out in the interior. It wasn't somewhere I was going to enter lightly and I knew that the only place to get up-to-date information would be in the city of Salalah.

I hitched a ride with a passing melon-seller, following the main road as it wound westward along the lush coastline. The scrub gave way to vibrant orchards, towering coconut palms, thick plantations of bananas and meadows of sugar cane. Even outside of the monsoon season, the place was green and lush, and I could only imagine how beautiful it must be during the *khareef*, as the Omanis called the monsoon. The golden beach stretched out to the south, it was a steamy paradise, and for a moment I felt like I'd suddenly been teleported from Arabia into the humid jungles of south India.

Perhaps it was because everywhere I looked there were men in sarongs: Keralans, Tamils and Goans, tropical imports, like the coconuts they sold, in a foreign land. The beachside road was lined with ancient ruins – vestiges from the ancient frankincense trade – and palm-thatch shacks, where mangoes, sweet potatoes and alien-looking jack fruit were sold.

For a moment I put the ordeal ahead out of my mind and simply enjoyed the unexpected delights of Salalah. I was happy to have got this far, to have crossed some of the most brutal terrain I'd ever encountered and to have navigated the complexities and contradictions of the Arabs I'd met, which was perhaps a greater accomplishment in some respects.

But there was another reason to feel content. Here, under the shade of a coconut tree, a hundred miles east of the Yemen border, I had reached the halfway point of my journey.

13

Into the Forgotten Land

A foreigner should be well-behaved.
Yemeni proverb

I spent several days in Salalah making inquiries into how to get into Yemen. I called everyone I knew, and pulled in favours from friends in the army, security contractors and NGO workers, and the team back home were working around the clock to try to find someone who could get me in.

Most leads went nowhere. Almost everyone said it was impossible. Almost everyone said I'd be killed, or at least kidnapped. There was only one man who said it could be done. 'John' was a former British army officer, who'd negotiated some deals with the rebel tribes of eastern Yemen in recent years, and through my network of contacts, I'd somehow been given his number. I knew nothing about him, or his business, but I rang him anyway, and asked if he thought it would be possible to at least enter.

'Yes, mate, you can get in. I can put you in touch with a Somali bloke who knows the sultan. It'll cost, but not too much, as they'd be glad of the publicity in that part of the country. They haven't had any foreign journalists in years. I can get you into Al Mahra, but stay out of the Hadhramaut, it's swarming with al-Qaeda.'

I listened as the words swirled around my mind. 'Somali ...
Sultan ... Hadhramaut ... al-Qaeda.' It all seemed very dangerous
and surreal. I knew it was risky, but I also knew that I couldn't
give up without trying. Yemen was the forgotten land, hidden
from the world by a veil of ignorance and uncaring. I needed to
go there, to see for myself what it was like and what the people
wanted, and to hell with the naysayers.

'Okay,' I said. 'When can you make it happen?'

'Abshir will come to your hotel tomorrow night. Be on
standby. In the meantime, do not talk to anyone in Salalah about
your plans. There are spies everywhere.'

I waited in the courtyard of the hotel, a sprawling complex
on the outskirts of the town, near to the airport. It was charmless
and modern, with an air-conditioned shopping mall and cinema
complex attached, and I was eager to get out of the place.

The courtyard was bustling with men, almost all of them
dressed in pristine white dishdashas, and either small white hats
or the colourful pashmina turbans worn by most Omanis. I
scanned the seats of the coffee shop, which was full of Arabs
holding business meetings, smoking shishas, or just drinking tea
and talking into their cell phones.

In the midst of it, I noticed two men looking around shiftily.
They were dressed identically in their white robes, but the
taller of the men was dark-skinned and looked distinctively
African. It must be him, I thought to myself. I walked over and
looked him in the eye. He smiled and stood up without
introducing himself.

'You are John's friend?' said the man, inviting me to take a
seat. I didn't wish to undermine our relationship by saying that
I didn't know John from Adam, so gave a knowing nod.

'I'm Abshir,' said the hulking Somali in fluent English. 'And

T. E. Lawrence.

The author aged 21
with Alex Coutselous
in Petra, 2003.

Erbil Citadel at the heart of Iraqi Kurdistan.

Omer 'Chomani' negotiating access through Kurdish and Iraqi checkpoints.

Al-Nuri Mosque, Mosul where the Caliphate was announced in 2014. It was destroyed by ISIS when the Iraqi army started to retake the city.

Two suspected ISIS fighters are captured by the Hashd during the Hawija offensive.

Sharqat town centre being liberated from ISIS rule.

Abu Tahseen 'The Hawk Eye', Iraq's most famous sniper.

The new walls of Babylon, thanks to Saddam Hussein.

Abu Haider in the Iraqi Marshes.

Sir Bani Yas Island, UAE. Home to some of the most famous
Arabian wildlife including the Oryx.

Dubai, a very modern oasis.

Locals in traditional Omani dress
gather under the walls of Nizwa.

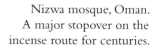

Nizwa mosque, Oman.
A major stopover on the
incense route for centuries.

Mahrouqi leading his camels into the Rub Al Khali – the Empty Quarter Desert.

The Dhofar ridge. Susceptible to the annual monsoon, these mountains
are the perfect conditions for Frankincense to flourish.

Displaced people
from Aden seek
refuge in Al Mahra,
Eastern Yemen.

My Somali guide
'Abshir' in Qishn,
Yemen.

MSV Sarina Al Saraj, my
dhow across the Arabian Sea
from Oman to Somalia.

Under armed escort in Somaliland, the Horn of Africa.

Ancient villages hidden away in Saudi Arabia's Asir Mountains.

The flower tribe of Habala in Saudi Arabia. The traditions remain strong among this remote tribe despite the onset of modernity.

The Oasis town of Al Ula, Saudi Arabia. A stopover for pilgrims and camel caravans, and gateway to the Hejaz.

One of the trains T. E. Lawrence blew up in 1917 on the now defunct Hejaz railway.

Mishael, my Bedouin guide in Jordan.

Petra, Jordan. One of the regions most popular tourist destinations, made famous in the 1989 movie *Indiana Jones and the Last Crusade*.

Church of the Nativity, Bethlehem, Christmas Eve, 2017.

The infamous wall inside the West Bank dividing Bethlehem in two. It is daubed with graffiti and political statements.

A sign in the West Bank warns Israelis not to enter Palestinian areas.

Palestinian protestors in Jericho burn tyres in protest at the US president's decision to move the US embassy from Tel Aviv to Jerusalem.

Dome of the Rock – the Al Aksa Mosque, Jerusalem. The centre of the Abrahamic religions.

Tel Aviv, a world apart from the nearby political strife. On the shores of the Mediterranean it's known for its beach clubs and restaurants.

Zaatari Camp, Jordan.
Home to over 80,000
Syrian refugees. I was
invited as a guest of
UNICEF.

Welcome to Syria.
The roadside billboard
depicts the regional
allies of Bashar al-Assad.

The Temple of Baal,
Palmyra in Syria.
Destroyed by ISIS.

Homs, Syria. This town lay under
siege for three years and lies in ruins.

Hayat and Nada (*right*) my
guide in Syria standing amid
the ruins of Homs.

The Hakmati of
Damascus telling
stories from the
Arabian Nights.

Leaving Hezbollah territory. Hadi, walking over the Lebanon mountains from the Bekaa valley.

Byblos, Lebanon on the shores of the Mediterranean. One of the oldest cities in the world.

Photograph of the author.

this is Sayeed. He's from Al Mahra in Yemen.' The other man was skinny, but had a good smile and noble features. I immediately felt as though I could trust them both, which was unusual given the circumstances, but I knew I had to take John's word as gospel in the absence of any other options.

'So, what do you want?' asked Abshir, ordering me a coffee.

'I want to go to Yemen.'

'Why?' said Sayeed.

Why indeed, I thought to myself. It was a good question. The truth was that I felt as if I couldn't ignore Yemen. For me, it represented the ultimate frontier, a land shrouded in mystery; and as a traveller, in spite of the apparent dangers, the allure was just too much. But of course, all of that was a bit of a mouthful.

Keep it simple.

'I'm writing a book about Arabia, and the Arabs came from Yemen.'

This made the man smile. 'You are correct. You can't travel all the way around Arabia without visiting Yemen. You would be most welcome.'

Abshir explained that the situation was 'fluid', which I imagine was a bit of an understatement. 'Look,' he said, 'we won't use any names or passports. If you want to go, I can get us across the border, but we will need to meet the sultan of Al Mahra. If anyone asks, you're a journalist writing about the tribes and culture, and nothing to do with the politics, okay?'

I assured him that was my interest anyway.

'Good.' He seemed relieved. 'I don't know how far I can get you. The Hadhramaut region is off-limits, but we could try the coastal road to Aden, but after that you're on your own, as I can't get you through Houthi territory.'

It sounded like a good start at least. I had no idea what I'd do once I was in, but one step at a time. Better to get in for a bit and see something rather than nothing, so I agreed to pay him a fee for his vehicle and for him to come along as a guide. And then, almost as an afterthought, I remembered that I should probably figure out what on earth a Somali was doing smuggling people into Yemen in the first place.

Abshir smiled. 'I do business.'

Best not ask *too* many questions, I thought, and left it at that.

The following morning we left at dawn. Driving along the road, we left Salalah behind and with it the morning glow of the streetlights and campfires of the Indians making their brew. The road wound up over undulating hills, until soon we were back in the mountains, flanked by vast cliffs, and to the north the bluffs disappeared into the mist that engulfed the upper reaches of the great forests of acacia and groves of frankincense. Abshir had advised me to try to blend in, so I'd come dressed in my best impersonation of a Yemeni – beige Kashmir turban, black skirt and a green check shirt. My beard was two months old now, and with a deep suntan, I looked in the mirror and could barely recognise myself.

Abshir laughed. 'You'll fit in better than me.'

We rounded a bend and the road took a downhill turn towards a forested ridge. 'That's the border there.' Abshir pointed towards a ramshackle checkpoint, where some military vehicles and a few lorries were parked up. We pulled up alongside them. 'Wait here,' said Abshir, as he got out and whispered something to the border guards. He came back five minutes later and got back into the car. We drove around the queue of lorries and a soldier lifted up the barrier and we drove through and out the other side.

'Is that it?' I said, astonished. 'No passports or anything?'

'That's it,' he said. 'No stamps here. We won't use names either. From now on, you simply don't exist.' He looked serious. 'We'll meet our escort over there.'

Abshir pulled over at the side of the road in a lay-by under the shade of a big tree, where three vehicles were waiting to travel with us in convoy. They were all 4x4s and rough-looking men with machine-guns and radios milled about smoking cigarettes and chewing *khat* leaves. We didn't hang around. A fat soldier got into our vehicle and squeezed in next to me, resting a rusty AK-47 into the footwell. He didn't take his sunglasses off and looked rather like a hamster, since his mouth was full of mushed-up khat. The lead jeep roared off, and Abshir followed on. Sayeed looked around and grinned. '*Marhaba*. Welcome to Yemen.'

As the road wound back down towards the coast, I felt as if I'd arrived in another world. If I thought Salalah resembled the south of India, here in the aftermath of the *khareef*, you could be forgiven for thinking you'd been transported into the rainforests of Central Africa. The whole mountainside was covered in a thick, green jungle and colossal baobab trees reached from the canopy high into the sky. Only rising columns of smoke coming out of the forest indicated that it was inhabited at all.

'They're the Mehri people,' said Sayeed. 'The same Jebalis you were with in Oman, but here they never left the mountains – they still live like cavemen.'

We took a mud track into the mist and passed by little huts that seemed to be dug into the hills themselves and were covered in grass, so that they were almost completely camouflaged, and

LEVISON WOOD

looked like the kind of mounds from which you'd expect to find Bilbo Baggins emerging in *The Hobbit*.

Eventually we veered off out of the forest and towards the coastal road, where dramatic cliffs fell away into crashing azure waves, and the glint of the ocean gave the place the feel of a lost world, forgotten by outsiders and yet magnificent in its beauty and isolation. As we speeded along in our convoy towards the west, the mountains to the north grew further away, until we were driving parallel to the pristine, flat beach.

To the right, wild palms were dotted across the plain, alongside fields of alfalfa. Dolphins danced in the shallows and further along I saw men spreading dried silverfish across the sand to dry in the sun, while seagulls hovered above the beach, waiting for the opportunity to steal a free lunch. A solitary man stood idly throwing pebbles from a slingshot to deter the winged thieves.

'We're going to Al Ghaydah,' said Abshir. 'It's another hundred kilometres away, though, so let's stop for a break, it's been a long day.'

I agreed; my legs were cramping up from being stuck next to the fat soldier, who was spilling over onto my side of the seat. Abshir got on the radio and in Arabic he told the lead vehicle to stop. We drove on a little further, until we passed an old deserted village and found a little glade of palm trees nearby that gave some shelter from the sun. I saw some dark-skinned children playing football on the beach and asked Abshir where they were from.

'They look like coastal blacks,' he said, without a hint of racism in his tone. 'They're the descendants of Africans who've lived in Yemen for generations. But they might be Ethiopians or Somali refugees as well. Who knows, everyone here is a blend anyway. Nobody cares about skin colour in Yemen, that's why I love it so much.'

As we got out of the car and stretched our legs, I noticed some of the soldiers who were accompanying us. They came in all shapes and sizes and looked remarkably different. Some were dark-skinned with African features, others had more traditional Arabic features, with Semitic noses and high cheekbones; some were tall, others short and squat; but to a man they all had their cheeks filled with khat, the green mulch that seemed to be ubiquitous on this side of the border.

Khat is a narcotic that's chewed widely across Yemen and East Africa. Its effect is mild stimulation akin to several cups of coffee, but it's very addictive, and you can't go far in this country without finding men chomping on the stuff. The problem, of course, is that it has become so popular that farmers don't bother growing any real crops, which has led to starvation, economic stagnation and mass poverty.

At its closest point, Yemen is a mere eighteen miles away from Djibouti. Since ancient times, Yemen has had close relations with the Horn of Africa. The mountains of Yemen and the Ethiopian highlands have been intertwined in each other's history and culture since the time of the Queen of Sheba.

It's easy to see how those early tribes made the journey across the narrow straits in little boats, island-hopping across the Red Sea, across a smaller distance than the English Channel. It's no wonder that there are so many similarities in the people you encounter – and the wars in Somalia, Eritrea and Yemen itself have resulted in mass migrations in both directions.

I noticed some rustling in the bushes nearby. 'Look,' said Sayeed, 'refugees from the west.'

Fifty metres away, I saw a group of people huddled together under a baobab tree. I walked over and was immediately greeted by some children, who ran to me and began tugging at my trousers and chanting something in Arabic.

'*Musaeada, musaeada,*' they cried.

Sayeed followed me and translated. 'They're asking for help,' he said. 'These children look like they're from Aden, or maybe the west coast, let's go and ask the adults.'

We walked over to the group. There were three men in turbans sitting glumly in silence and several women, some in black niqabs and others in colourful long dresses. They had dark mysterious features, but an overwhelming sadness in their eyes. One of the older women told me her story.

'We've come from Hudaydah to escape the fighting,' she said, staring into my eyes with an anger I'd rarely seen before. 'The Saudis are killing us. Our children are dying.' She grabbed a nearby infant, who was naked apart from a pair of dirty pants. Snot dribbled across his face and flies covered his body. His stomach was distended and he looked like the kind of famished child you see in the charity adverts.

'Look, look at my son,' she said, holding him out in front of her. 'We've lost everything. This is all we have left.' She pointed at a small pile of clothes and pots. 'We have no food and no money.'

'Where are you going?' I asked, assuming they must have a plan.

'We have nowhere to go. This tree is our home. We came to Al Mahra, because we heard the people are friendly and we will come to no harm, but they are poor, too, so we can't expect anything.'

The civil war in Yemen had been raging for six long years, barely noticed by the outside world. In the Arab Spring, authoritarian president Ali Abdullah Saleh was forced to relinquish power to his rival, Abdrabbuh Mansour Hadi. But Saleh went on to form an alliance with his former enemies the Houthis, and began co-ordinating attacks on the new government, eventually claiming the capital Sana'a for themselves.

The Saudi-led coalition, sponsored by the West, had taken it upon themselves to fight the Houthi rebels in an attempt to try to restore the Hadi government, and in doing so curb Iranian influence in the country. But like everything else in the region, it wasn't quite as simple as that. On the one hand it was a battle between Sunni and Shi'a, but also an official government versus a rebel force with foreign sponsorship.

There were lots of outsiders meddling with the affairs of the lawless state. The UAE were busy invading the ports, while Saudi troops massed on the northern borders, using Houthi missiles aimed at Riyadh as an excuse to carpet bomb the mountains; there were US Special Forces supporting the dubious Sunni alliance and conducting raids against high-level opposition targets; all the while Russian, Chinese and Lebanese proxies were backing the usurpers with money, drugs and weapons.

On top of that, al-Qaeda ruled the roost along the south coast and in the mountains of the Hadhramaut, a somewhat inevitable result of the old tribes forming a fanatical alliance against any outside interference; and finally there was the Southern Transitional Council – another loose collection of tribes, who ultimately wanted autonomy and to return to the good old days when Yemen was split in two. The Yemenis had found themselves caught in the middle of a bloody sectarian fight and they are ultimately the ones who had suffered.

'Yalla,' said Abshir, 'Time to go.' There was nothing to do for these poor people, except give them a handful of dollars and wish them luck. 'They're the lucky ones,' said Sayeed as we walked away. 'The ones who are stuck behind are getting bombed and dying of cholera.'

Al Ghaydah appeared on the horizon. Whitewashed shacks and adobe walls with rustic minarets signalled the suburbs of the little town, which sprawled on the west bank of a dry river bed a mile away from the sea. We went via the beach first, as the soldiers said they wanted to go shopping. We pulled over next to a little harbour, where wooden fishing boats bobbed in the waves. Somalis were wading in, carrying enormous swordfish and dumping them in wheelbarrows, ready to take to the market. All sorts of fish were drying on the floor around the ramshackle huts, including tiny hammerhead sharks that had been spliced down the middle and now looked like cardboard replicas. The Africans looked shifty when I began to take photographs.

'Who are you?' screamed one. Abshir went over and spoke Somali to the man, who changed his demeanour immediately. 'Please sir, go and tell the world what is happening here. We are so poor, and need the help of the white people.'

Some kids nearby were playing table football in the shade of a garage, spinning the little handles with joy. But our soldiers weren't interested in fish or football. They'd come for one thing only – khat.

The Somalis were the dealers here and handed out plastic bags filled with sticks for twenty dollars a go.

'That's obscene,' I said. Abshir nodded.

'It is two days' wages here. A bag like that will only last an afternoon. It's all these people have to do, eat khat, get high and sleep.'

But the soldiers didn't care. They handed over their money and immediately began munching on the little shoots as if they were the tastiest treats to be found.

Sayeed handed me one. It looked like a wilting sprig and its leaves were covered in a thin film of dirt. 'What do I do with that?' I asked.

'Pull off the good leaves,' he said, plucking the smallest, greenest leaves from the top of the stem, 'and chew on them. Don't swallow it. Just chew it up into a ball and keep it in your cheeks. You'll feel the effects after a few minutes.'

I took the vile shrub and thought about chewing it, but as I looked at the others and saw how bits of vegetation got stuck in their teeth and their dazed, bloodshot eyes – I politely declined, using the excuse that I had a bad stomach.

Content with their purchase, the soldiers rallied with bloodshot eyes and we got back into the ragged convoy to drive into town: It was almost dark by the time we got there, and the streets were bustling with all sorts of people. It had the feel of a frontier town: lawless and desperate. We were a hundred miles from the front line with al-Qaeda in the Arabian Peninsula and yet life went on. There were shops selling wedding dresses next to restaurants selling sweetmeats and cows' entrails. As we rounded a corner going towards the hotel, I noticed a shop selling an array of assault rifles and ammunition belts.

Abshir grinned. 'Do you want a Kalashnikov? You can get one for a hundred dollars. I know the owner, he'll give you a discount.'

'I think I'm okay thanks,' I said.

The convoy pulled over in a side street. There were dozens of Toyota pick-up trucks parked outside of a hotel. Some were brown, others beige and yet more covered in military camouflage pattern. The hotel was lit with green and blue fairy lights and the bricks were painted a vile shade of pink.

I looked up and saw it had four floors. The sign above the door welcomed visitors in English to experience 'three star deluxe'.

I grabbed my bags and followed Abshir and Sayeed inside. Our hosts, with their machine-guns and belts, still chewing their khat, followed on behind. Perhaps I was expecting to stay in some sort of traditional Yemeni home, or maybe even camp in the wilds, but no, we'd been brought to the swankiest hotel in town.

The reception room was filled with cheap pleather sofas and Perspex coffee tables. The marble floor was covered in cigarette butts and phlegm, where the guests had deposited the remains of their khat onto the floor. The walls had gaudy posters of Swiss cottages plastered all over them, next to tatty pictures of Mecca, and in the corner was a rather surprising Christmas tree with a plastic fairy on the top. I was just getting used to the bizarre accommodation when Abshir motioned for me to follow on.

'The sultan will see us shortly,' he said. 'He's taken over this hotel just for you.'

'What do you mean?' I said.

'You're a journalist, the first foreigner they've met in a long time. And you're here to tell his story. So just be grateful.'

'Okay.'

I walked up the filthy stairs to the fourth floor, where I found a basic single room waiting for me. The bed was lumpy and the sheets filled with the burn holes of cigarettes, but I didn't care. I was in Yemen, and about to meet a king.

Sayeed led the way. He'd got changed into his best white dishdasha, as had Abshir. I hadn't brought any formal wear, so I felt somewhat self-conscious in my sarong and cheap shirt, although since everyone else was in a turban, I kept mine on. We went down a floor to a meeting room and suddenly I found myself in a conference of rebels.

There were about twenty men lounging around the edges of the room on cushions. Most of them had formidable daggers tucked into their belts; some had pistols in holsters and several had laid out their AKs at their feet. There were dozens of grenades lying on the coffee tables and at least one man had brought a rocket launcher to the tea party. They all stood up when we entered. I was presented first to the sultan.

'This is Sultan Abdullah bin Essa,' said Sayeed, introducing his chief. 'Son of Sultan Essa bin Ali Al Afrar, who was the last king of Mahra and Socotra.'

The sultan smiled. He was a fifty-five-year-old, benevolent-looking man in a long robe and a khaki Kashmir turban, the same as mine. 'Welcome. Please sit down,' he said gravely. 'You are from England, I hear?' he went on.

'I am,' I told him.

'Well then, please listen. I have gathered the tribes and ordered them here to Al Ghaydah. Look around. We are the Al Mahra people and I represent them at the Southern Transitional Council.'

A man walked in with a tray of food. It was a steaming pile of BBQ goat with the skull sat neatly on top of the meat and offal. Placing it carefully on the floor at the sultan's feet, he walked away gingerly. The sultan gestured for me to dig in. I looked around at the cluster of militia men and warlords. Half of them wore camo jackets over their shirts and I imagined that this was probably no different to the al-Qaeda conferences that were happening only a hundred miles away in the villages of the Hadhramaut.

I ate a chunk of liver, washed down with sweet black tea.

'We are in a state of emergency. We have always had autonomy here in the East and we are not interested in the affairs of the West. We do not support the Houthis, nor do we give any assistance to al-Qaeda. We just want to be left alone, but those brutes the Saudis are threatening to invade. The Emiratis already have – they have occupied my homeland, Socotra, and they are planning to take over all the ports until we give in. I do not plan on that happening. We will resist, and fight if we must.' He stared at me over his glasses, looking like a disappointed headmaster.

'Please tell your government to stop supporting the enemy. Saudi Arabia is killing innocent people. They are sending teams of their barbarian Salafis to try and convert the people to their medieval mentality. We are a civilised, peaceful people, who simply want to be left alone. We have already been betrayed by Britain once. We used to admire your great kingdom and were happy serving under your queen. Our people used to be friends. We were happy to be part of your empire until 1967, but we do not want to be part of the Saudi empire now. Their methods are brutish. They kill without mercy. Did you know the UAE are torturing people and throwing our leaders out of helicopters? Helicopters that were supplied by your government.'

He took a sip of tea and then smiled. 'Now ... how may I help you?'

I promised to pass on the message and explained that I was on a journey trying to get around the Arabian Peninsula, but thought it prudent not to mention that I wanted to get to Saudi Arabia. Instead, I told him I wanted to travel west towards Aden and from there I'd make another plan. The truth was, there was no real plan. I just knew that I'd have to take each day as it came in a place like this. The sultan stroked his chin.

'I can only guarantee your safety as far as Sayhut. After that you're into the Hadhramaut, and the road to Aden isn't safe. I can't authorise that, I'm sorry.'

I stayed silent. I wanted to explain to him that I'd done this sort of thing before, crossing war zones and dealing with rebels. Abshir must have read my mind and I guess he wanted to earn his keep with me.

'Sultan,' he said, placing his hand on the king's arm. 'This Englishman was a soldier.' Abshir looked at me with a glint in his eye. I hadn't told him that and had no idea how he'd found out, but I suppose he'd done his research on me.

'And he has already been across Iraq and Syria. He is very experienced, and simply wants to go to Aden.'

The sultan looked at me and back at Abshir and then back at me. He didn't blink in almost a minute, as he stared in silence.

'This isn't Iraq. This isn't Syria. This is Yemen, we are in the middle of a civil war and if you fall into the hands of the enemy, then you will be executed. And that reflects badly on me as a host. But since you insist, I will think about it, and I will speak to the tribes in the Hadhramaut. I will speak to al-Qaeda and see whether they might let you pass. Until then you may explore my lands and go as far west as Qishn.'

With that, Abshir nodded. It was time to leave and so we went upstairs to our rooms and went to bed.

The next day we set off after breakfast along the coast, in one of the military vehicles out of Al Ghaydah. We passed the port of Nishtun and spent the morning exploring the ancient town of

Qishn with its historic white fortress. These days it was little more than an empty village, but the beauty of its architecture betrayed a glorious past, filled with stories of kings who adorned the pages of *One Thousand and One Arabian Nights*. The mountains guarded the crumbling walls, and palm groves flanked meadows filled with camels and cows.

It was a scene of perfect serenity and it was hard to imagine the horrors of a war that seemed so far away, and yet in fact raged on in the mountains beyond. I thought of the remote tribes I could meet and the incredible history of places like Shibam, with its famous mud skyscrapers, which was hidden in the valleys of the Hadhramaut. Freya Stark, the English explorer, had described it as the 'Manhattan of the desert' and the most enchanting view she had ever encountered.

'Do you think we'll be allowed to carry on, Abshir?' I asked my guide.

'Honestly,' he said, 'I think you'd be crazy to go any further. If you do, then I can't go with you. But let's see what the sultan says later on.'

That night we drove back to Al Ghaydah at the sultan's request. 'He has summoned us back,' said Abshir. 'He has something he wishes to tell us.' It sounded ominous, but I had no choice. I was entirely at the mercy of the sultan and for now at least, I had to backtrack to the main town and find out what his decision might be.

The sultan was waiting for us, sitting on his cushions in the same spot that we had left him. There was a queue of men waiting to meet him. Abshir told me they would come from all over Al

Mahra to get his advice, to settle family disputes, to pay taxes and even ask to borrow money. They went in one by one, like children waiting to have a private lesson from their teacher. Abshir ushered me to the front of the queue. Sultan Abdullah stood up and hugged me.

'Did you enjoy Qishn?' he said. 'It is my ancestral home. The fortress has been the home of the bin Afrar for centuries.'

I told him that I had.

He gestured for me to sit next to him and poured me some yellow Arabic coffee.

Another man entered the room and closed the door behind him. He was a huge hulk of a man, with deep creases in his weathered face. The sultan stood up and hugged him, too.

'This is Colonel Ali Salim Al Hareysi,' said the sultan. 'He is my finest warrior.'

The colonel gripped my hand and sat next to me. 'You can call me Mr H.'

Abshir whispered in my ear. 'They call him the Lion of the Desert, he's the most feared man in Eastern Yemen.'

'British?' The colonel raised his eyebrows. 'We don't get many British here. It's a shame you're not American. We want to ask the CIA for some money, since we're the only ones stopping al-Qaeda. You Brits don't have any money to give do you? I look after the borders and make sure no undesirables get in.' He pointed at me. 'You're lucky you're not an undesirable.' He grinned, flashing gold teeth. 'But we're expecting war soon. If the Saudis come, or those bastards from the UAE, then I will defend these mountains to the death.'

I couldn't tell whether he was saying these things for effect, or whether he actually meant it.

The sultan stepped in.

'I have some bad news for you. Mr H will explain.'

The colonel, or Mr H, took out his phone and showed me a website. It was an online news article from the Yemen national newspaper. It was in Arabic, but Abshir translated.

'It says that a British spy is known to be operating in Eastern Yemen and he is trying to convince the Al Mahra government to cede to Oman and separate from the rest of the country.'

I shook my head. 'I'd be surprised if that was true,' I said. 'Do you know who he is?' I asked Mr H.

The colonel laughed. 'Ha! They are referring to you.'

'Oh shit,' I said.

'Yes. The newspaper is sponsored by the Saudi barbarians, and they put this kind of thing in, so they have an excuse to invade. Luckily, they don't know your name, but they know you are here. They have spies everywhere, and I've had reports from my men that if they find out that this conference is happening, then they will cause problems.'

'What kind of problems?' I said, although I really didn't need to ask. If the Saudis found out that I'd been in Yemen illegally, then they would almost certainly ban me from Saudi Arabia and my journey would be over.

The sultan put a hand on my shoulder. 'We can't stay here any longer. Now that the Saudis are interested in you, we are all in danger. If they find out that me and the Colonel are in this hotel, then they might send a missile from their drones and kill us all. We need to leave, we need to go to Oman tomorrow and I will take you there personally.'

14

Pirate Waters

*I wish longingly to fare homeward and see the day of my returning. And
if some god shall wreck me in the wine-dark deep, even so I will endure.*
                                                    Homer, *The Odyssey*

On the morning of 10 November, we left Al Ghaydah in a
convoy of four pick-up trucks with the sultan in the lead. He'd
decided that the safest thing to do was leave the country for a
few days himself and go to the safety of Oman, where he would
meet some diplomats who might be able to help in negotiations
with the Saudis, who had by now issued an ultimatum: accept
the UAE troops willingly in the ports and on the borders, or else
prepare to be invaded.

We left after breakfast. The drivers were bleary eyed after a full
day of khat-chewing the day before. They knew they had to get
their fill, as they couldn't take any across the border to Oman,
where it was illegal.

I got into the back seat of one of the cars and sat next to
Abshir and Sayeed. Both of them seemed to be relieved to be
going back to Oman; even Sayeed, who was Mahri himself,
preferred the calm streets of Salalah to the constant edge of
living in a rebel hideout. We took the same road as we had
entered on, first driving out across the dry river bed and following
the coast to the east. We passed the African fishermen, who sat

around on the beach oblivious to the political machinations going on all around. For them it was one and the same. As long as there were fish to catch, they didn't care who stood around on the borders.

Soon the country became more undulating and the mountains closed in from the north. The road wound upwards, following the jagged cliffs around and zigzagging up and down over the precipices above a glistening ocean. I saw dolphins in the bay and wondered if they were the same ones I'd seen on the way in. We passed the dusty villages hemmed in by palm glades and waterfalls and I couldn't help but think that I was leaving paradise. I had no idea what lay ahead, or was it behind?

I'd lost my sense of purpose now. For two months I'd been moving forward, driven by a singular urge to explore Arabia, whatever that may mean. But for me, it had necessitated movement. By moving I was able to compare, to contrast and to draw parallels. Getting stuck in one place meant a loss of momentum and with that the prospect of getting stuck in one narrative, learning only one side of the story – the risk of becoming drawn in too far.

But there was something else, too. I was only halfway. I knew that what lay ahead could be the most difficult part of the journey. Now I'd been defeated by Yemen, what did that mean? What were my options? I had no idea how I would complete the journey I'd set out to do. It might sound dramatic, and perhaps a little petulant, but I couldn't just fly home and give up. There was more at stake than merely the loss of pride of not having completed the expedition.

I'd given up everything for this. I'd set out on my ultimate journey against all the odds. I'd done it with no external funding or official commission. There was no TV deal, only the backing of a couple of good friends, and I had a duty, to them as much as myself, to finish the job. I'd set out to learn about Arabia and the people who lived there, and I hadn't even seen the half of it yet.

I dreamt of seeing the Hejaz, Petra, Jerusalem and Damascus. I'd promised myself the prize of standing on the shores of the Mediterranean at Byblos, in the ruins of antiquity, looking out west towards a Europe I'd left behind so long ago, and south towards the Nile, where this long journey began all those years before.

And in any case, what did I have to go back to? This was my life, my work and my passion. I'd lost my girlfriend: she'd left me, finally fed up with my wanderings. I had no job, no ties apart from my parents, and nothing but the prospect of a drizzly winter in London. No. I had to find a way to carry on.

We continued into the mountains and into the mist of the forest. By the time we reached the border post, it was already dark and it had started to rain. The Omani border force, quite content to let us depart illegally into Yemen, weren't quite so happy to see us come back, especially in a convoy filled with armed rebels and in the company of an exiled king.

It took three hours of standing around in the rain and hard negotiations and persuasion on the part of Abshir, Sayeed and the sultan himself to convince the Omani officer in command that our intentions were innocent. We sent one of the cars back filled with all the guns and had to somehow cram all the tribal chiefs and their bodyguards into three pick-up trucks. By ten p.m., however, we had left the mountains behind and arrived back in Salalah, cold, wet and tired, but at least we were alive.

I said goodbye to the sultan in the lobby of his hotel. He'd offered to pay for my stay there, but I didn't want to be a burden any longer, and anyway he had an important job to do, trying to negotiate a peace deal with the coalition. And from a selfish perspective, he was a wanted man, and I didn't think it was wise to be staying in the same hotel while I myself was trying to figure out a way of getting around Yemen.

I found myself a room in the same hotel I'd left the last time I was here, and arranged to meet Abshir the following day to see about a plan. That night I passed out and slept better than I had done in weeks.

The following morning, I gathered my thoughts and stared at a map. I followed the coastline from Salalah round to the west. That was the way I'd driven into Yemen, all the way to Al Ghaydah, and then on to Qishn, four hundred kilometres away. I looked at the coastline: Mukalla, Aden and then the narrow straits where Djibouti is but a stone's throw away. I followed the course of the Red Sea. The first port inside Saudi Arabia was Jazan. I knew instinctively that was where I needed to get to, somehow.

For now, though, there was no way of entering the secretive kingdom. I'd applied months ago for a Saudi visa, and been told that they don't issue tourist visas. I'd tried applying for a journalist visa. They didn't do them either. A business visa? Not a chance unless you work in oil, it seems. I'd tried everything. I'd pulled some strings and asked the British Embassy in Riyadh to see if they could help. I was met with a dubious, bureaucratic throat-clearing. I'd even managed to get a personal introduction from a very senior member of the royal family, but that had also disappeared into the vortex of the diplomatic service.

I was told I might have to fly back to London, but there was one more option – apparently the Saudi Embassy in Djibouti was a bit more, how do we say, flexible on these sorts of matters.

I saw on the news that there were the rumblings of war between Saudi Arabia and Iran – if that happened, then I knew my journey was completely over.

When you're on an expedition, there's nothing worse than getting held up somewhere. Danger, jeopardy and general excitement are all fine; part and parcel of the journey itself. But getting bogged down by bureaucracy and paperwork is torment. When momentum is lost, it's hard to get it back again.

I looked at Djibouti on the map. The tiny country lodged in between Ethiopia, Eritrea and Somalia could be the key to the puzzle. For now, it seemed my only hope was to find a way to get there. It was as good a plan as any.

'A *dhow*?' Abshir laughed. 'Nobody goes on a dhow,' he said, when I met him later in the afternoon the following day.

'But there's hundreds of them in the harbour. Somebody must use them,' I said.

'Yes, of course, fishermen. And some of them take cargo to Africa or Iran or India.'

'Well, that would be perfect,' I said, with a sudden glimmer of hope.

'No, no. It's impossible. They're run by war lords and Somalis.'

'You're a Somali.'

'That's exactly why I'm telling you not to even think about a dhow. You'd be a sitting duck, floating on a matchbox in the middle of the Gulf of Aden in the most pirate-infested waters in the world. They'd have a field day if they caught you.'

'But how would they know I'm on it? I'd just blend in with the fishermen.'

Abshir looked serious and shook his head.

'No, no. I tell you what, why don't you look into a proper ship? Cargo ships and oil tankers sometimes pass by Salalah on their way to the Red Sea. Maybe you could hitch a ride on one of those?'

It seemed like a reasonable idea, I thought.

'I'll ask my people and you ask yours,' he said.

For the next few days, I sat in my hotel room staring into the screen of my laptop; scouring the internet for contacts. I tried calling and emailing all the main shipping companies and drew on all my contacts from the military who worked in maritime security. Most of them ignored me and even with those who picked up, the answer was always the same. No.

'You won't be insured,' said Maersk.

'We can't stop in the Red Sea,' said the captain of the *Braemar*.

'We don't pick up in Salalah,' said the chief of Affinity Tankers.

Orient Marine came back with a rather polite, 'Human loads don't suit us.'

After days of trying and being hung up on, I did find one company willing to do the journey, but they insisted I'd need an armed escort and outlying boats to protect against pirates. The only catch was that it would cost one hundred and twenty thousand pounds for the privilege.

I was back to square one. To make matters worse, I was rapidly running out of money, and my Oman visa was due to expire in a couple of days. I needed an answer fast. I called Abshir.

'Any joy?' I said hopefully, although I expected the worst.

'All the big companies say no. They just aren't willing to take a foreigner on board.'

'Yes, I know, that's the response I got.'

'But there is one option,' he said.

I suddenly got a tingle down my spine.

'There's a guy at the port. His name is Aladdin, and . . .'

'Let me guess, a magic bloody carpet?' I butted in.

'No,' said Abshir. 'It won't be that comfortable.'

'Well, what is it?'

'There's a boat, although I don't know how big it is. It's leaving in a couple of days.'

'Great,' I said. 'How much?'

'They'll take you for free, as long as you pay for your own food, and maybe chip in for the fuel. It'll take five or six days.'

I was ecstatic. 'What's the catch?' I said.

'Meet me at the port and I'll explain.' He hung up. I was glad he was willing to help me. He didn't have to, but he sounded somewhat embarrassed after failing to see me off in Yemen. He was a fixer after all and had a reputation to maintain like everyone else.

I took a taxi and parked up outside the gates of the commercial harbour. It being a strategic facility, no one without a pass was allowed in, so I sat there under the shade of a palm tree waiting for Abshir.

True to his word, ten minutes later he pulled up in a white Toyota Land Cruiser. On top of it was a flashing orange light attached to a coiled wire, and on the dashboard lay an orange hi-vis vest. Abshir was sitting in the passenger seat. The driver was another African with glowing teeth.

'This is Aladdin,' said Abshir, winding down the window.

'At your service, mate,' interjected the driver.

The man, who was clearly a Somali, also had the unmistakable accent of an African who'd spent a fair amount of time in London. He didn't get out of the car and the interaction felt like something tantamount to a dodgy drug deal.

'So, you want a boat, eh?' he said, in a menacing whisper.

'Yes, I want to go to Djibouti.'

'Nah,' he muttered. 'No boats to Djibouti,' he added, shaking his head. I looked at Abshir, who just shrugged.

'Well then, where do the boats go?' I was beginning to lose patience. This guy was meant to be the one in the know.

Aladdin smiled. 'There's one boat and it leaves tomorrow to Bosaso.'

'Bosaso?' I said. 'Where on earth is that?'

I looked at the map on my phone and followed the coast south along from Djibouti. The next port along was Berbera in Somaliland. I kept swiping. Another three hundred miles to the east lay Bosaso, in the heart of Puntland, Somalia.

'Somalia,' I said, out loud.

'Yep.' He beamed.

'Puntland. Isn't it one of the most dangerous parts of Somalia?' I asked.

'Yep.' He grinned again. 'But it's the only boat. The next one to Berbera might be in a week, or even a month.'

I looked at Abshir. He shrugged again.

'Do you want it or not?' He looked over his shoulder. Aladdin clearly worked at the port, but I suspected it wasn't his position to be smuggling white men onto boats bound for Somalia.

I sighed.

'I'll take it.'

Aladdin winked at me. 'I'll see you tomorrow.'

'You're doing what?' said Richard, my contact at the maritime security agency. I thought I better check in. 'That's off the fucking Richter scale. You do know that is the most pirated route in the whole Arabian Sea? You're mad.'

'I don't have a choice.' I said.

'Take a bloody plane.'

'You know me better than that.'

'Well then, at least let the Royal Navy know, just in case you get nabbed.'

'I'll do that.'

I knew it was a risky move. I'd be uninsured, travelling at the mercy of the Somalis, and for all I knew, they could be pirates themselves. Maybe they'd steal my stuff and throw me overboard? No, no, I'm worth more to them alive. Perhaps they'd sell me to their cousins? All sorts of anxieties scrabbled through my mind, as I packed my bags and stocked up with provisions for the impending voyage. I finally settled myself with the hopeful thought that at least if I was travelling on a pirate ship, there was probably less likelihood of getting kidnapped, especially if I gave them a decent tip up front.

The next day I arrived back at the port at two p.m., as directed by Aladdin. Abshir was also waiting for me to say goodbye.

'Good luck, Lev. When you get to Somalia, don't hang around in Bosaso. Get yourself to Hargeisa as quickly as you can, it's safer there.'

'Are you sure you don't want to come?' I said. Abshir had been good to me and helped me way beyond any expectations, and I knew I'd miss him.

He chuckled. 'No, no. You won't catch me going back there. And anyway, I don't think I'm welcome.' He winked. 'I'll see you in London when you finish.' With that, he waved goodbye and got into his car and drove off, leaving me with Aladdin.

'Come on, mate, I can't be seen here with a white man. The boss will think I'm up to no good. Follow me.'

He led me in between some shipping containers and into a little office. He looked around.

'Quick, nobody is here. Passport,' he said. I handed him mine and out of a dusty drawer he pulled out a rubber stamp. He pressed it firmly into an ink pad and stamped me out of Oman.

'There you go. Immigration done, let's go before anyone sees us.'

We sneaked out and walked quickly across the yard. We walked to the harbour itself, where the tiny fishing boats were dwarfed by enormous oil tankers and naval vessels.

'There she is,' said Aladdin, pointing ahead to where the tiniest wooden dhow was being loaded up.

'Are you for real?'

I looked on in astonishment at the rickety little vessel, which couldn't have been more than sixty feet in length. A dozen Indians were busy hurling cardboard boxes onto the deck.

'That's the boat? It's not fit for an ocean crossing.'

'Well, that's your only option,' said Aladdin. 'It leaves at dusk.' He gave me a dirty slip of paper written in Arabic, which I assumed to be my boarding permit, and he walked away.

There's no turning back now, I thought to myself. *Inshallah.* It's God's will. I'd convinced myself there was no choice in the matter, that I was here because of fate. I'd asked for a dhow and now I'd got one. Be careful what you wish for.

Resigned, I followed my destiny and walked up the plank, and climbed over the rigging onto the port side of the boat. The Indians looked at me with an impassive glare. I tried to introduce myself, but they didn't speak a word of English.

I looked around at my reluctant hosts. For the most part they seemed inclined to ignore me, but I was determined to get them on side from the outset, so I got stuck in helping them carry the boxes, which they seemed to appreciate. None of them wore shoes, so I took mine off as well. Eventually one of the men came up and insisted I sat down in the captain's cabin. Through a mixture of sign language and repetition I understood him to be the captain and that his name was Mr Hussain.

'Gujarati.' He pointed to his chest.

'English.' I pointed to mine.

We shook hands.

'Ingleesh, ingleesh.' Mr Hussain gave a little head-wobble in the Indian fashion and smiled in a bewildered way.

'No Ingleesh boat.'

I think he was trying to convey that he'd never had any English people on his boat before. In fact, he'd probably never met any Englishmen before in any circumstances, and having one forced upon him by the Somali boat owners must have come as a bit of a surprise.

I counted the men. There wasn't a Somali in sight, but I think there were fifteen Gujaratis in total, although it was difficult to tell, as they kept disappearing into tiny hatches that led to the belly of the boat. There was almost no room at all to sleep. The entire bow was taken up with the boxes that were stacked five high. On closer inspection, I discovered that the valuable cargo was nothing more than thousands of packets of powdered milk.

At sundown, we set sail. Or more specifically, we motored out of the harbour, leaving the bright lights of the port city behind. I was too nervous and excited to sleep much and so I sat on deck as the hot night air breezed past. With each breath we chugged further and further into the night, where the glittering waves appeared to blend seamlessly into the infinite stars of the Arabian sky.

The Indian cook, the youngest member of the crew, took a shine to me and was keen to practise his three or four words of English. He handed me some sweet chai and we watched as the stern bobbed and left a trail of sparkling foam. In the cabin, Mr Hussain sat cross-legged on a cushion, as another of his crew steered using an old wooden wheel that looked like it had been salvaged from a pirate ship. There was a compass glued to the helm and the entire boat was pitch black. Apart from the red glow of the Indians' cheroot cigarettes, there were no torches allowed.

'No light,' whispered the boy. 'Somali pirate.'

He pointed out into the darkness with a wild glare and a flash of yellow teeth.

For four nights and five days we navigated to the south-west. There was more than eight hundred kilometres of open sea between us and the Horn of Africa. We'd average at five knots, something like six-and-a-half miles per hour, but when the wind was strong and blew in the right direction, the crew mustered to the rigging and unleashed a huge patchwork sail, which bolstered our speed, and we managed to cover over two hundred kilometres in twenty-four hours.

For the most part, the sea was calm and we ploughed on. Dolphins followed us occasionally and the men laid fishing lines out to trail, but caught nothing. The Indians rarely spoke to one another, and each had their little tasks, whether making the tea or scrubbing the decks. Cleanliness was important, and Mr Hussain told me off for cutting my toenails on deck. Most of them shaved daily using a cracked mirror and a cut-throat razor, leaving only pencil-thin moustaches. I joined them in their rituals and got rid of my two-month beard.

Going to the toilet was probably the most challenging task. A wooden box had been roped on the side of the boat with a hole cut in the bottom. To answer the call of nature, you had to squat and aim for the hole between your legs and watch the results drop ten feet into the green ocean below. Fish would trail us in eager anticipation of their next feed.

The walls of the cabin were covered in posters of Mecca and the *Kaaba* and yet I never once saw these Muslim sailors pray. They ate in a circle, sat cross-legged on the floor; dishes of rice and sometimes chicken. But most of all they drank tea and smoked their little bidis. Life at sea was dull and monotonous. Often the only noise was the constant crackling of the CB radio. It would sometimes tune in to faraway frequencies and for a second or two I'd be listening to the conversations of Iranian merchants, Saudi sailors and even the familiar tone of a British oil-tanker captain.

The only excitement was when the captain, Mr Hussain, would rush in and listen to the radio for reports of piracy and change direction when they came. For me, the outsider, there was nothing to do but read and think. And when I finished the books I had with me, all I had to do was think, and that is a dangerous thing.

For the first time in a very long time, I was homesick. My thoughts drifted away from Arabia and towards home. It was the middle of November and I imagined how the Christmas lights would be going up in the streets and my friends would be preparing to spend time with their families. I would be missing yet another holiday, missing my parents grow another year older. With each missed birthday and wedding, it was another black mark against me, and soon I'd stop getting the invitations altogether.

I was getting fed up of travelling, truth be told. In the past year I'd been away from home for almost nine months. And in the five years before that, I'd been away at least seven months of the year. The reality was that I'd been on the road pretty much constantly for eight years now, and it just struck me. I missed my ex-girlfriend. I'd thrown away too many perfectly good relationships in favour of the freedom of the road.

I supposed that I'd accepted that as part of my lifestyle, but now I had time to think, it suddenly seemed to sink in. What the hell was I doing? Was it all worth it? I started to wonder about all the things I'd lost and sacrificed because of my own doings, and I realised I was forlorn. Not only that, I was scared stiff. It dawned on me there and then, in the little captain's cabin, that I was leading a very selfish, ridiculous life. There I was in the middle of the Arabian Sea, surrounded by the prospect of kidnap by pirates, or being eaten by sharks. I was lonely and afraid.

15

Footsteps in East Africa

Do what thy manhood bids thee do,
from none but self expect applause.
He noblest lives and noblest dies
who makes and keeps his self-made laws.
Richard Francis Burton

Five days on a boat doesn't sound like a long time, but when you're lying in a pool of your own sweat and the floor is crawling with cockroaches, trust me, it was enough to get a true flavour of life at sea. I knew there was a reason I hadn't joined the Navy. The isolation, the boredom and the sheer inescapability of being stuck on a boat was enough to drive me mad. Waking up each morning and seeing an endless ocean; talk about cabin fever – there was simply no escape.

I think it was on the third day that I came to the realisation I'd had enough. Not just of this journey, but of travelling in general. I decided that this would be my last big expedition – after this, if I survived and made it home, then I was going to settle down, move to the country, and get a dog. I promised myself that my adventuring days were well and truly over.

When we were three hundred kilometres off the Horn, I noticed something strange. For the last few days I'd been aware of the side the sun was rising and setting, and I'd kept a close watch on the stars, but on the penultimate day I happened to glance upon the ship's compass, and it wasn't pointing in the right direction.

'North. What on earth are we doing travelling north when we should be going south-west?' I said to myself out loud. 'Mr Hussain!' I shouted.

The little Gujarati peered in through the open cabin window. He raised his eyebrows. I pointed at the compass and flicked my wrist upwards to indicate that I was confused. He simply copied my gesture and walked away.

Surely we couldn't be going north. To the north was Yemen and I guessed that we must be not far off Mukalla and that meant al-Qaeda territory. I got my own compass out of my bag to double-check. We were definitely going north.

I stepped out of the cabin and over the lounging sailors, who were sleeping on the deck, and into the helm. The only bearded Indian was at the wheel, with Mr Hussain at his side sipping tea in silence.

'Where are we going?' I asked, even though I knew they couldn't speak English. I pointed ahead. 'Yemen,' I said. My concerns couldn't have been more obvious.

Mr Hussain pointed to the port side and said, 'Bosaso.' Yes, I knew that, but why then were we going to the north. There was no way of communicating.

I dashed back to the cabin and dug out my satellite phone and turned it on. I'd been turning it on once a day at six o'clock anyway, to check in with my support team back in the UK, because obviously there was no mobile signal out here. But when it loaded up this time, it beeped and flashed for a solid twenty seconds as a stream of messages came flooding in. Simon and Charlotte back in London had noticed that the boat had changed its course five hours ago, as they'd been following the tracker that I'd hidden in my bag.

They were clearly concerned. Simon had sent a coded message saying that if he hadn't heard from me in two hours, then he was going to inform the Foreign Office and Global Rescue, our security evacuation company. I looked at my watch; that was four hours ago. The problem was that even if I was about to be kidnapped, there was little to be done anyway. The nearest Royal Navy ship was hundreds of miles away and I was way too far out of helicopter range to be rescued.

I tried to call back, but there was no answer. The signal was terrible on the deck of the boat, so I climbed the mast. Eventually I got through to the team.

'You're alive?' said Simon with evident relief. 'We thought there'd been a problem when you changed direction. The FCO are aware, but there's nothing they can do.'

'It's okay,' I told him. At that moment I noticed that we were turning again. 'Hang on,' I told him, 'I think we're heading back on course, the boat seems to be going west again.'

I told him I'd give it another hour and see what happened. I climbed back down the mast and stood next to Mr Hussain, who seemed unconcerned about the situation. He simply pointed towards Africa and repeated, 'Bosaso.' He pointed south and spread his arms. 'Mota dhow.' What could he mean?

'Mota, mota. Dhow, dhow. Big, big.'

It dawned on me that he was trying to say there were big boats in that direction. We must have veered off course to avoid the main shipping lane. It made sense now. Our tiny dhow wouldn't stand a chance if it got beneath one of the 400,000-ton monsters that travel this route.

The next morning, I woke up at first light. The horizon was blood red and our sails were up, flapping in the light wind. A seagull was sitting motionless on top of the crow's nest. Land must be close. I looked beyond the bow into a hazy distance and sure enough, I could trace the faint outline of faraway mountains. There it was, a continent I hadn't thought I'd be seeing on this journey at all. Africa.

It took another six hours before the port of Bosaso came into view. The russet mountains beyond seemed to stretch on infinitely. Bosaso appeared as a crumbling assortment of wood and tin shanties. We were in Africa alright.

We dropped anchor a couple of miles off shore and just stopped. What was going on? Why did we not carry on into the port? I tried to ask the questions, but my Indian captain only shrugged. After an hour, I saw a small rigid inflatable boat zipping towards us. I'd watched *Captain Phillips* and a few other pirate movies, and this was exactly the kind of scene I'd been dreading. 'Mr Hussain. What the fuck is going on?'

The captain stood motionless on the deck, as the bearded man gazed through binoculars at the impending rib. I grabbed them and looked myself. As it got closer, I could make out the figures of three Somali men, their black skin gleaming in the morning sun, and one of them was carrying a machine-gun.

'Who are they?' I asked. The Indians just stood still.

The rib came alongside our dhow and one of the Somalis shouted at the captain. He looked mean and malicious with his little tinted glasses and enormous white teeth. Mr Hussein looked at me and pointed at the tiny boat. I walked slowly to the side of the dhow and looked down. The three Somalis were wearing oversized shirts and shiny trousers.

All sorts of terrifying thoughts ran through my mind. Were they pirates?

One of them shouted at me, 'Come, now!' I looked at Mr Hussain and he wiggled his head in assent. It seems I didn't have much choice in the matter.

I assumed that Aladdin had made arrangements, but he hadn't really told me what they were, other than, 'it will be sorted.' I had to trust that these were the good guys.

I quickly gathered up my kit and stuffed it into my rucksack, careful to make sure my valuables were hidden at the bottom, in case I was searched. I made sure my tracking device was still on as well, and hid that in a secret compartment. There was hardly any time to say goodbye to the crew, but I shook hands with Mr Hussain and wished him luck on his return voyage to India. I didn't envy him the two-week sea crossing, and even though I was being hauled off by unknown men into the lawless heartland of Somalia, I think I preferred that to the prospect of sitting on that boat for another second.

I gave the Somali men on the little speedboat my firmest handshake and biggest smile, and tried to engage them in conversation from the outset, in a bid to ingratiate myself. They looked stern and suspicious and didn't say anything back, other than telling me not to take any photos. We sped away from the dhow and across the bay towards the glinting tin roofs of the city. As we got closer, we zipped past dozens of fishermen in little wooden boats, bobbing around waiting for their day's catch. We turned left and then around a harbour wall into the port itself.

The place was a rubbish tip, piles of garbage lying around and raw sewage dripping into the sea. The whole place stank of shit and rotting fish. As we pulled into a jetty, there were lots of armed men hanging about. Some wore military uniforms, others were in shiny suits and yet more were half-naked, with ammunition belts slung over ripped T-shirts. It was a scene straight out of *Black Hawk Down*. I'd left the perils of the sea behind, only to find myself in the middle of yet another war zone.

'Come. Follow,' said the man with the big teeth and the shiny trousers, as he stepped out of the boat and onto dry land. I hauled my rucksack after him and walked across the dusty shipyard to a shaded veranda that led to some makeshift offices. The sun was beating down and the soldiers were all vying for shelter, in competition with the feral dogs that were covered in sores and pustules.

'Enter,' said the man and pointed to a doorway. I took off my bag and left it at the entrance. The office was bare, apart from some faded government posters advertising the benefits of celibacy to combat AIDS. A large man in a white shirt was sat at a desk chewing on a pen.

He looked me up and down and squinted through thick glasses.

'What are you?' he said.

What am I? That was a good question. What was I indeed?

I thought I'd best keep it simple, given that I didn't have a visa for Somalia, or any paperwork to prove that I was leaving to the north.

'I'm a photographer,' I said. I used that job title when I needed to, since it was suitably vague and explained away the camera and electronics equipment. I didn't want to say writer or journalist, or anything like that, for fear of him asking for my special permits, which inevitably come with a large fee. Plus, I had no idea who this man was.

He looked unimpressed and stared a while longer. I couldn't tell whether he was angry or bemused.

'What are you taking photographs of?' he said.

'Arabia,' I said, instinctively.

He looked even more confused now. 'This isn't Arabia. This is Africa,' he said. 'All the white men come here saying they are this and that, but really they are spies.' He glared. 'I ask again. What are you?'

'A photogra—' I said again, but he cut me off.

'Prove it!' he shouted. 'Take my picture.'

He sat up straight, rearranged his collar and patted down his thin curly hair, as I unslung my camera and began to take his portrait.

'I am the head of customs of the port of Bosaso. You know that place is not safe,' he said, once he'd finished posing. He was smiling now. Phew, I thought, that was a relief. I told him that I'd read the news and I knew that piracy was still rife.

He laughed. 'Pirates!? They are nothing. Just local boys trying to make some money.' He waved his hand dismissively. 'The big dangers are al-Shabaab and al-Qaeda. They are all over the mountains, and even the Islamic State are here now. They are always blowing up the streets and we have all these foreigners coming from Syria and Chechnya. And now last week the Americans started bombing with their planes, too. Here we are stuck in the middle. You cannot stay here. Take a taxi and go north to Djibouti, it is safe there.'

He took my passport and scribbled the words 'transit visa' in Arabic.

I knew what he was saying was sensible. I didn't have any intention of hanging around. At least in Yemen I had half a chance of blending in with my beard and local clothes. Even with a decent suntan, I was sticking out like a sore thumb here and felt acutely self-aware. I was glad that it wasn't pirates that had nabbed me off the boat, but my prospects were hardly any better right now. Puntland had suffered greatly in the Somali civil war and was still one of the most lawless parts of the world. I knew I had to find a way to Djibouti as soon as possible.

'Go with this man, he will help.' And with that the customs man shuffled off. The man with the big teeth led the way through the soldiers on the veranda and found me a nearby car. It was battered and rusty and full of holes, but I liked the look of the driver. Abdul seemed friendly enough and helped me put my bag in the boot. 'Let's go,' he said. 'We have a long drive.'

We set off to the west in the heat of the afternoon towards the mountains of Somaliland.

It felt exciting, surreal, disappointing and terrifying all at once. I was discouraged by having to skirt around Yemen and yet here I was driving hundreds of miles across Somalia on the wrong continent altogether. The scraggy brown peaks seemed to go on forever. For the most part, the road wound through the acacia valleys and barren, dusty scrub. It felt very different from the land I'd left on the other side of the Gulf of Aden. Black faces peered out of patchwork huts made of leftover blankets, bits of plastic and animal skins. Dry river beds cut through the scrub and solitary camels wandered aimlessly in search of a thorny meal.

In the mountains, we stumbled upon Palaeolithic cave paintings: bulls and dogs drawn by bored cavemen. If Yemen was the land that time forgot, this was the land where time had stood still for five thousand years. The nomadic herdsmen reminded me of what Arabia had once been, a life that I had searched for and yet seen only glimpses of in the desert. Here in the bush of Africa, it carried on, unaffected by development or modernity.

I felt incredibly vulnerable, as it dawned on me the extent to which I was at the mercy of some random taxi driver, in the middle of a country known for its violence and anarchy. And it wasn't just these days: 'The Horn' has been keeping travellers on their toes for a very long time. I gave a thought to my childhood explorer hero, Sir Richard Burton.

As I looked out of the window at the brutal landscape, the hot wind blew like the breath of a volcano. I remembered that he passed on this same route in 1855. He'd been on his way back from a visit to the fabled African city of Harar, as part of an expedition sponsored by the Royal Geographical Society. Harar in Ethiopia had never received a European visitor, and Burton was picked as the man for the job.

For those who don't know Burton, he's worth looking into. Raised in Italy and France by Anglo-Irish parents, he was an unruly and angry schoolboy, who allegedly smashed his violin over one teacher's head. At fifteen, he was caught writing passionate letters to prostitutes. By his late teens, he was experimenting with opium. He went to Trinity College, Oxford, in 1840, already sporting an impressive moustache – and within an hour of arriving had challenged another student to a duel for laughing at it.

Nicknamed Ruffian Dick at university, Burton was an impressive-looking chap: over six foot tall with fierce facial features; but he was no brute. He had an inconceivable talent for languages – by the end of his life he would speak twenty-five of them. He was also to become a gifted writer and translator, an acclaimed soldier, diplomat, swordsman and archaeologist – not to mention amateur hypnotist, heroic boozer and translator of the *Kama Sutra* and *Arabian Nights*.

Dusty old Oxford was no place for Dick. So he got himself chucked out for breaking petty rules, joined the infantry and sailed to India instead, where he found himself a job as a spy in the newly conquered area of Sindh – now Pakistan. His job was to collect information on the region's people, culture and geography. Not one to do things by half, he disguised himself as an Indian, and wandered around the streets chatting to unsuspecting locals in flawless Sindhi.

Nothing was taboo for Captain Burton: he smoked opium with addicts, supped *bhang* (a cannabis drink) with holy men and quite openly had affairs with dozens of local women. Then, in an even more risky endeavour, he dived wholeheartedly into the homosexual brothels of Karachi.

His behaviour raised a few military eyebrows, to say the least, and after falling out with his brother officers, Burton quit India with his army reputation in tatters. He returned to Europe and began planning his next dramatic move: a pilgrimage to Mecca. Non-Muslims have always been barred from entering Mecca and over the centuries many curious Christians and Jews who tried to penetrate the sacred city had been impaled, crucified or sold into slavery. But this didn't bother Burton.

In spring 1853, disguised as an itinerant priest, with his skin stained with walnut juice and his penis recently circumcised, he sailed to the Middle East. He travelled first to Medina, before crossing the desert to Mecca itself. The journey was a brutal and violent affair. Bedouin bandits attacked the caravan he was travelling with, killing many of his companions and their camels.

Yet here's the great thing about Burton: he found life in the desert exhilarating and was relieved to leave behind the 'hypocritical politeness and the slavery of civilisation.'

Once inside Mecca, Burton met pilgrims from every nation. He visited every shrine and performed every ritual. He wasn't the first non-Muslim to see Mecca and survive, but none produced such a successful account of their travels and his *Pilgrimage to El-Medinah and Mecca* became an instant bestseller.

Emboldened, Burton now turned to Africa. His goal: to become the first European to visit the forbidden city of Harar, in what was then called Abyssinia. Like Mecca, Harar promised death to the infidel who dared to cross its threshold. Burton could never pass for a local in Africa, so instead he brazenly rode up to its gates alone wearing his British army uniform and simply asked to come in. To his amazement, they agreed and let him have a look around. But Harar was a disappointment – a drab, dusty place with little to see.

On his way back to the coastal town of Berbera, he met up with his three other team members, William Stroyan, G.E. Herne and the infamous explorer John Hanning Speke. They set up camp in the desert and contemplated their next move. That night a raiding party of two hundred Somalis armed with spears and war axes attacked the camp as they slept.

Burton described the assault in his book, *First Footsteps in East Africa*:

> *The enemy swarmed like hornets with shouts and screams intending to terrify, and proving that overwhelming odds were against us: it was by no means easy to avoid in the shades of the night the jobbing of javelins, the long heavy daggers thrown at our legs from under and through the opening of the tent ... The revolvers were used by my companion with*

deadly effect: unfortunately there was but one pair . . .

Stroyan was killed in the unexpected battle. Speke was taken prisoner and tortured (he later escaped, bleeding from several wounds). Herne got away lightly. One Somali warrior threw a spear directly into Burton's face, the blade entering his left cheek, smashing out his back teeth and part of his palate and re-emerging from the right side.

Luckily Burton, too, managed to get away. He made it to a friendly ship berthed in the port and was taken on board by the sailors, who pulled out the spear and stitched him up. Burton was sent home with a souvenir of Africa – a massive, ugly scar that gave his fierce image an even more sinister edge.

Personally, I hoped to escape East Africa without such theatrics.

I was relieved to finally reach the city of Hargeisa. It spread out like a breeze-block jungle, in contrast to the rawness of the surrounding scrub. For a few days I stayed in the compound of the HALO Trust, a landmine clearance charity that had spent years trying to rid the country of these lethal, indiscriminate bombs. I'd made it to Somaliland, the semi-autonomous region in the north-west of the country that has its own language, flag, administration and even armed forces. The people considered themselves to be independent and despaired at the chaos in the rest of Somalia. It was relatively safe here, but I'd arrived in the middle of the local elections, which meant there were whistling crowds on the streets and I'd been advised not to wander around alone, especially at night.

There was no terrorism here, but the aid workers generally

kept themselves to themselves and stayed away from the markets of downtown. I needed to get to Djibouti as soon as possible, if I were to make the Holy Land for Christmas. I was already well behind my schedule, after being forced to leave Yemen and hang around in Oman, so I found a local lad who could speak English and asked him to come with me to the border.

'It's at least two days' drive, maybe three,' said Hersi, an intelligent, smartly dressed young man, who had aspirations to stardom in Hollywood. 'I'm going to be the next Kanye West,' he said, as we piled into a local bus to drive to the market and get some provisions for the journey ahead.

I exchanged a hundred dollars into local currency, which was so devalued I ended up with a brick of worthless notes taking up half my rucksack. I looked around, and no wonder everyone was pushing wheelbarrows about – they were full of bundles of cash. We passed streets full of khat sellers and mobile-phone shops. Donkeys and pigs and mangy dogs ran amok in the cratered alleyways. It was the Africa I knew and loved from my Nile journeys, but now I wanted to get away and carry on with my expedition in Arabia. It all felt alien and incompatible.

We bought some fruit and biscuits and set off in the sweaty bus along with fifteen other Somalis all bound for Borama. We passed dozens of checkpoints and at each one I was called off to be questioned. What was a white man doing on a local bus? Luckily, Hersi charmed my interrogators each time, and four hours later we made it to the next settlement. The next day was more problematic – what was supposed to be five hours' driving ended up being nearer twelve, as the road disintegrated into a dirt track, winding up lethal mountains clad in juniper and dwindling through the gorges, before disappearing altogether in the desert on the far side of the hills.

Apart from a numb arse, the only excitement of the day was spotting occasional antelope grazing in the arid wadis. We skirted the Ethiopian border and then the road wended east towards Jidhi, and then north again for another three hours to the ancient coastal village of Saylac, which we reached after dark. It took another day of negotiating passage through the remote border post at Loyada, where I was subjected to another five hours of questioning by the local policemen. They wanted money, but apart from the brick of useless notes, I had nothing to give them and eventually I was allowed into Djibouti, a country that until now, I would have struggled to place on the map.

Luckily the roads improved once I'd crossed the border. I said goodbye to Hersi and wished him luck in his bid to top the charts, and flagged down a car heading for the city. Djibouti City sits at the entrance to the Red Sea and, like Burton's Harar, came as a disappointment. In Somaliland, I'd heard wonderful tales of a beautiful colonial town, filled with French restaurants, good wine and wide boulevards. Perhaps it was my state of mind, but instead I found filthy streets and crumbling mansions, abandoned by the foreign invaders and left to rot by the locals. The wine was crap and expensive and the food average at best.

I found on the main square a grotty little hotel resembling a prison, where I hunkered down. It had bars on the windows, hard single beds, bare walls and suspicious stains all over the carpet. Perhaps it was a brothel. But I was low on money and couldn't afford the next best option, which was a resort on the beach, so I resigned myself in anticipation of a long, miserable wait. It was a Friday and so the Saudi Embassy was closed, but to make matters worse, it was also a religious holiday and nobody knew when it would reopen.

To add insult to injury, I managed to get food poisoning after visiting a French steak restaurant on my second night. It had been recommended as the best in town, which didn't say a lot to be fair, but that meant I spent the best part of a week holed up in the windowless bathroom of my cell, throwing my guts up. It was perhaps one of the worst experiences of my life; the agony of my stomach cramps was interrupted only by episodic projectile-vomiting all over the slimy bathroom walls.

Cockroaches crawled from nasty little holes behind the piping and I could hear a family of rats scuttling about in the wardrobe. The air conditioning was broken, and the TV didn't work. Even the fan kept me awake for five sleepless nights, because of its incessant creaking. It was too hot inside and too hot outside. The room smelt of diarrhoea and outside it smelt of shit too, from open sewers and broken drains. Even if I'd wanted to leave, I couldn't. I had a fever and I could barely move.

For days, I sweated and curled up in agony, the pain getting worse and worse. I lost all my energy and couldn't even raise a hand to swat away the flies anymore, so that they were soon crawling all over me. I thought that I might die there and then, an inglorious death in a miserable place far from home.

There was to be no celebrated spear through the face for me, only humiliation and an ignoble epitaph: *On the Horn, he died of filet mignon.*

16

The Secret Kingdom

They were a people of primary colours, or rather of black and white . . .
They were a dogmatic people, despising doubt . . . They knew only truth
and untruth, belief and unbelief without our hesitating retinue of finer
shades.

T.E. Lawrence

Just as I thought my awful nightmare might never end things seemed to take a turn for the better when I was told that my Saudi visa had finally been approved. By the time I arrived in the port of Jazan, I think I was delirious and couldn't quite believe I'd made it. I had first applied to get into Saudi Arabia six months before, going through the official channels. But there were no tourist visas to be had, so I'd had to apply for special dispensation from the Saudi Commission for Heritage and Tourism. I'd even written personal letters to Prince Salman bin Salman.

In my fevered, emaciated state, I'd given myself over to worry that my sneaking about in Yemen, and the subsequent implications that the Saudis knew I'd been there, meant there was no way I'd be allowed in. But after an honest conversation with the Saudi Embassy in London, it appears they suddenly changed their minds. I suspect it had something to do with the more outward-facing, progressive policies of the new Crown

Prince Mohammad bin Salman. He was due to visit Britain and had made advancements in recent months such as allowing women to drive, and had even proposed relaxing the rules on immigration and granting a limited number of tourist visas in due course anyway, so I guess he'd decided to let me in as the guinea pig.

I arrived in the Kingdom dazed and confused, but very much alive, and it was with a second wind that I faced the challenge ahead. And what a challenge it was. I'd only been given an eight-day visa to cover almost two thousand kilometres. Saudi Arabia presented the biggest country on my journey, and that meant averaging two hundred and eighty-five miles a day, through brutal heat and one of the most secretive police states in the world. I was expecting the worst.

I'd hardly been made to feel welcome by the constant toing and froing with the Saudi authorities over visas, and given its reputation as a place where human rights are abused in the most brutal ways, I can't say I was looking forward to the next week or so. Having seen first-hand the poverty and desperation in Yemen, caused by the Saudi bombing, as well as news reports of the stoning of women, hand-chopping and public beheadings, I arrived in Jazan feeling wary and cautious.

On top of that, I'd read so many conflicting accounts of Saudi Wahhabism and Salafist ideology being exported around the world, and seen its impact myself in places like Pakistan and Sudan, that I almost wanted to dislike the place. I'd been told the Saudis supported terrorism and were behind al-Qaeda and ISIS. The stereotype remained strong in my mind – wealthy sheikhs living extravagant lifestyles at the expense of a subdued, exploited and poorly educated majority; imams preaching hate and religious division; bearded thugs acting as hatchet men for the secret police; no art, no alcohol, no music and a country that kept its women under lock and key. It was my idea of hell.

I wandered through the port, past rows of dhows and fishing boats. At least I was back on the right continent, I thought to myself, in a bid to cheer myself up. I'd arranged to meet a local tour guide, Khaled, who would be with me through the country – that was the condition stipulated by the embassy on my visa. I'd been worried that I would have to be followed around by an armed escort, or a government agent, as I had in other police states, and so I was pleasantly surprised when a jolly man with little glasses and a friendly manner greeted me in the harbour car park.

'*Salaam alaikum*,' said Khaled, with a warm smile.

He looked more like a sheikh than a spy, in his long white dishdasha and red check shemagh. He was thickset and burly, but had a childlike smile that made his eyes shrink behind his tinted glasses. Only the black trainers poking out the bottom of his robes gave him away as a tour guide. He'd come from a very small pool of 'government approved' guides, of which he was apparently the best. But in spite of the smiles, I was sure he was under instructions to keep a close eye on me. In any case, I wanted a guide to show me around and it was going to be the best way to see as much of Saudi as possible in the time we had.

'Eight days,' he tutted as we got into his car. 'That's not enough.'

'I know,' I said. 'It's a long way.'

'A really long way. It's a shame as there's so much to see here, you could spend a whole week just in Jeddah, you won't believe.'

Quite frankly, I didn't believe. I'd fallen foul of traveller's fatigue at this point and merely wanted to get on with it and make it to the holy lands, where I knew I'd find the Middle East of my imagination. I knew little about Saudi Arabia, except what I'd read of T.E. Lawrence, and I'd be content if only I could fulfil a boyhood dream and see first-hand the Hejaz railway. That was my goal.

I knew that Mecca and Medina were both off-limits. There was to be no undercover, disguised sneakiness on this journey under the watchful eye of Khaled, no matter how jolly he seemed. It was his job to keep me out of trouble, and that meant sticking to the script. He was a tour guide after all, even though there were few international tourists, and he was used to carting Arabs around and showing them bits and pieces. But I was jaded and simply wanted to get moving, I'd had enough time stuck in one place recently.

Khaled revved the engine and off we went, leaving Jazan and the coast behind. 'We're going into the Asir Mountains,' he said. 'My homeland. Wait till you see it, it's beautiful.'

I looked out of the window. I saw only dusty streets and breeze-block compounds, stray dogs and cats lounging in doorways. It was much cleaner than Djibouti and Somalia, but there was something about the town that felt soulless and dismal. Perhaps it was because I saw virtually nobody on the streets. Shiny Land Cruisers with tinted windows sped along the highway, but nobody was out and about. It seemed like the Saudis did everything behind closed doors.

It wasn't long, though, until we left the suburbs behind and the road wound up into the rolling brown hills. To the south lay the Yemen border, only a few kilometres away. The tops of the mountains represented a no-man's-land, filled with landmines and barbed wire. It was the front line that had taken me so long to skirt around. But I was on the far side now. Oman, Salalah and Al Mahra seemed like an eternity ago. The last weeks had been

some of the most mentally difficult of all my time on expedition, and I was keen to put them behind me and move forward,
so I refrained from looking south. I was done with detours; the
only way ahead was north.

We drove for hours in the hills, passing village mosques and
high-walled farms. I saw a few village men leading camels down
a rocky wadi. They didn't look like the Saudis I'd imagined, not
at all like Khaled in his shining white robes and noble headscarf.
In fact, they looked almost identical to the Yemenis I'd met. The
sun was beginning to cast long shadows among the hills and it
was already time to be thinking about somewhere to sleep.

'Let's stay with a local family,' Khaled suggested. 'I know some
people in that place.' He pointed to a farm on top of a hill
overlooking the valley.

We arrived in time for dusk and were greeted by a group of
young men. They, too, resembled Yemenis. They all wore dark
sarongs and T-shirts with waistcoats, and khanjar curved daggers
in their belts. There was one small, but rather unique difference,
though. They all had colourful garlands of flowers in their long,
flowing black hair, and as a result looked like a troop of Morris
dancers.

'These are the Bin Amir tribe,' said Khaled. 'They're the same
as the Yemenis really. They are the descendants of the first Arabs;
these are the true indigenous Saudis.' I think he must have noted
my slight surprise.

'What's up . . . don't you wear flowers in your hair sometimes?'
He laughed.

I told him it was a rarity.

'We have many tribes here, and they're all different. The Bin
Amir think it is beautiful to wear flowers, both men and women.
They spend all day choosing the right flowers based on smell

and colour. They take it very seriously. Never mock a man with flowers in his hair, otherwise he'll cut your head off.'

I promised that it hadn't even crossed my mind.

The men invited us to join a feast. They had killed a goat and so we sat and joined them around the platter. I ate sparingly, not wanting a repeat of my Djibouti poisoning, and yet enough to be polite. I didn't want to get my head cut off.

The conversation went fairly quickly from the usual pleasantries of asking about each other's family and heaping platitudes on one another into enquiries about perceptions of Saudi Arabia abroad.

'What do the English think of us?' said Southi, a man of twenty-five.

I told him that few people knew much about his secretive home country and that our two nations were on decent enough terms, although we were a little confused as to why Saudi Arabia was attacking Yemen. I felt it was my duty to raise the issue, at least, given that I'd been there. I told him a little of what I'd seen just across the border.

'Yes, I do feel bad for the Yemeni people,' he said, with a look of genuine sympathy. 'They are very poor and long ago they were our Arab brothers, but now they are hiding the Iranian infidels and accepting their money. And Iranians are *kafir*.'

'What is kafir?' I asked him, surprised that he could show two such conflicting emotions in one breath.

'Kafir is non-believer. They're not Muslims, the Shi'as.' He went on, 'It's all part of Iran's plan to spread Shi'a ideas and now they are just across the border and they can easily attack us. Iran fired missiles from Yemen recently, they are using it to get closer and closer to us and they are trying to attack our capital. And our tribe, we are here right on the border, the first who will get hit by bullets.'

It was true that Iran-backed Houthi rebels in Yemen were firing rockets at Riyadh, but the Saudis were dropping bombs on the Yemenis. Shi'a Iran and Sunni Saudi were using Yemen as a battle ground for their proxy war and this young Saudi was another young Arab in the firing line.

Not for the first time on this trip, it occurred to me how complicated things were in this part of the world, and I thought it best to keep my mouth shut. Although I couldn't help wondering where Southi got his information from within the sealed walls of this police state.

The next morning we carried on north, passing through the village of Rojal, a remarkably well-kept example of Arabian mountain architecture. It wasn't quite as inspiring as the elusive Shibam or Sana'a in Yemen, but the tall, multi-storey adobe buildings with their red and green windows were impressive nonetheless. Despite the brand-new paved roads and the all-pervasive Toyotas everywhere, it was an example of the modern Arabia, new colliding with old at every turn. We stopped outside a little mosque for Khaled to pray and I found an old sheikh sitting on a veranda. He looked at least eighty years old. I sat down next to him and joined him in a glass of tea.

Unlike the youngsters of last night, he didn't seem in the least bit interested in me as a foreigner, or how Saudi Arabia was perceived by the world. He just wanted to show me his house. 'We built it in the 1950s,' he said. 'Back in those days everyone from the village would come and help. There was a real community in the tribe. In those days, there were no roads here in the mountains and everything was brought up by camel and donkey. People were much happier then. Now everyone is so busy and everyone wants to go to the towns.'

It seems that even in this oasis of traditional culture, there was still cause for complaint. Nothing, even here, was like it was in the good old days.

The road led back down towards the coast and that night we camped rough in the sand, but didn't get a wink of sleep because of the mosquitoes and the heat. It was too sweaty to cover up, and yet as soon as your skin was exposed, the little critters would be all over you. So the following morning, Khaled and I woke at four a.m. to try to get to Mecca before it was too hot. The plan was to cover five hundred kilometres today in order to allow a day of rest in Jeddah before embarking on the long road north into the Hejaz.

We arrived at the outskirts of Mecca at eight a.m. A sign directed all non-Muslims towards the ring road that circumvented the town. Only faithful followers of Islam were allowed to enter the holy site itself. Unlike in Burton's day, when a nifty disguise and a good grasp of Arabic would get you in, these days the pilgrims, whether on the *Hajj* or *Umrah*, needed all sorts of documentation to get through the security barriers – letters from your imam and mosque, pilgrim visas and accreditations from a tour company were all required to gain entrance.

'And in any case,' said Khaled, 'no Saudi would help an infidel to smuggle themselves in.'

'Why, what would happen?' I asked.

'Well, for a start it's illegal. You'd be arrested. Both of us would. But that's not what I'm talking about. As a Muslim it is *haram* – forbidden – to assist non-Muslims to go inside the holy city.'

Khaled smiled. 'Of course, if you'd like to convert and become a Muslim, then you would be welcome.'

We pulled up at the side of the motorway a few miles away from Mecca and Khaled told me to get out of the car. 'Look, there is the clock tower.' He pointed across the scrubland that morphed into the suburbs in a hazy blend. Beyond that, on the far side of the mountain, I could see the gigantic outline of the Abraj Al-Bait tower looming above the holy city. 'It's the biggest clock face in the world and I think the third tallest building,' said Khaled proudly. 'It's got hotels, shopping malls, penthouse suites, Pizza Hut and KFC.'

'There's a KFC in Mecca?' I said, a little surprised.

'There's three, I think. And seven McDonald's.' He shrugged. 'Just because we're Muslims doesn't mean we don't eat.'

'You know,' he carried on, 'people have been coming here for thousands of years. Even before the Prophet Muhammad was born, this place was holy. The Kaaba houses a piece of meteorite that the Bedouin used to come and want to see. Even the Jews and Christians used to come here to worship.'

'But not anymore,' I pointed out.

'No, of course not,' he said.

'Well, why not?' I asked. 'Why can't Christians come to see the meteorite anymore?'

'Because this is the holiest place in Islam,' he said, matter of factly. 'And as Muslims, we believe that non-believers will go to hell.'

I wanted to argue the point to see if he saw the irony in his line of argument.

'What makes Christians non-believers? They believe in something, it's just a different name for the same God,' I asked him.

He turned to me. 'There are certain things that you won't understand, because you're not a Muslim, Lev.'

I wasn't really sure how to respond to that. It was said without malice or pity, just as a fact.

'And what about in the days before Islam, before the seventh century when it was founded? Imagine if you'd been born then?'

'Well, Lev, I'd have been damned, without Islam to deliver me. We were a land of savages and barbarians before Allah came to Muhammad.'

I found it hard to relate to such dogmatic beliefs. But how could I? I'd grown up in a secular country, where religion is separate from the state, and with the freedom to believe in whatever I wanted. But here, the idea of Muslims – the people, the culture and the identity – and Islam, the ideology written in the pages of a religious book, were inextricably linked. In fact, as a theocracy they were one and the same: church and state, Muslim and Islam. There is no division between them. He could see that I was struggling with the gravity of his opinions and he gave me a kind smile.

'It's tricky, Lev, these are the rules in our country and that's just the way it goes.'

I couldn't help but think that perhaps his line of reasoning didn't account for some of the hypocrisy I'd encountered, particularly given the number of Saudis I'd seen in the Gulf who were quite happily getting drunk every weekend. But I was not here to stir up trouble, so I kept quiet.

As we drove around Mecca, however, it did occur to me how powerful this collective imagination could be. Every year, fifteen million of the 'devout' came here to share in a unity of belief, and to me it seemed a shame that it was only possible through the alienation of other faiths and a misplaced sense of superiority based on communal pride.

We arrived in Jeddah by late afternoon and were tired, so we checked into a hotel on the boulevard. An enormous Saudi flag fluttered from a gigantic mast. Jeddah had long been seen as the gateway to the holy mosques, and beyond that the Hejaz. These days it was fast becoming the new hub of the kingdom and had attracted people from all across the country to work on the up-and-coming building projects.

High-rise flats seemed to be in varying states of completion and the development was all-consuming. There were fast-food joints on every corner, sushi restaurants and hipster coffee bars. The walls of the hotels were covered in street art, and apart from the dress of the pedestrians, the promenade could quite easily look as if it belonged in Miami. It wasn't what I expected in Saudi Arabia at all.

Yes, most of the women were wearing black abayas, but certainly not all of them; in fact I saw several in colourful hijabs and even a few women in tight jeans, T-shirts and no headscarves at all. Most of the young men were wearing Western clothes and had a variety of fashionable haircuts. Street performers, beat boxers and musicians lined the walkways and defied the stereotype.

'Times are changing,' said Khaled. 'More than sixty per cent of the population are under thirty. Everyone is connected. We all use WhatsApp, Skype and Snapchat. I'm fifty-five and have Instagram. We've all got international friends. And the new Crown Prince is making sure that Saudi Arabia is keeping up. Personally, I've got my reservations about the youth of today, but that's probably because I'm an old man and don't understand, but times are changing and there's nothing we can do to resist it, so we may as well embrace it.'

The next day we set off to the north through the desert. The roadsides were picketed by troops of baboons, perched eagerly on the verge waiting for motorists to throw them the remains of their lunch. We travelled the four hundred kilometres to Medina in half a day, passing busloads of Pakistani pilgrims heading for the holy city, but again our road skirted around the city itself, which again was off-limits, and we were strictly directed by signs to keep out of the haram area. When we stopped at a service area to use the bathroom, I was approached by a Pakistani doctor, who told me he'd performed the pilgrimage twenty-four times. He asked very politely if I would like to be converted, right there in front of the toilets. I respectfully declined.

North of Medina, the landscape changed. It became more wild and rugged, and on both sides the highway was flanked by beautiful red mountains, which sparkled in the afternoon sun like distant flames. The desert was sprinkled with oases of date palms and twisted glades of acacia scrub. And on the left-hand side, I noticed a raised embankment that ran parallel to the road, disappearing into the distance ahead.

'That's the railway you're looking for,' said Khaled. 'It leads all the way to Damascus. Welcome to the Hejaz.'

17

Pillars of Wisdom: The Hejaz

Contentment is an inexhaustible treasure.
Saudi proverb

We arrived in Al-'Ula at dusk and spent the night in a small guesthouse, exhausted after so much driving. The next morning, though, I woke up early to explore and it was as if I'd woken up in paradise. Al-'Ula appeared to be a sleepy little oasis, lush and green. It was awash with colourful flowers that lined the roadside, and groves of palm trees and orange orchards in between the flaming red mountains that flanked the town.

It used to serve as a major stop-off point on the pilgrimage route from the north, during the days of the camel caravans, and well before that it was an ancient incense-trading centre that linked Arabian merchants with as far afield as Egypt and India. These days a new highway dissected the settlement in half. The 'new town' was host to a few shiny mosques and coffee shops and breeze-block apartments, but Khaled insisted there was more to see than that.

My trusty guide stopped the car in a dusty little side street and we got out to walk towards a large hill that dominated the horizon. Khaled led the way and I followed him up a carved stone staircase that seemed worn from the footsteps of centuries. At the top I discovered we were standing on the scorched remnants of an ancient fort.

'This used to be the centre of the pre-Islamic civilisation,' he said, as his white robes fluttered in the hot wind.

'Saudi Arabia is packed with history, dating back seven thousand years, and nobody even knows it, least of all the Arabs.'

From the ramparts, I looked out across the golden valley. It was as spectacular as anything I'd seen in Egypt or Jordan. For miles, date palm groves spread out like a vast, green blanket, backed up by sheer red cliffs and jagged, caramel mountains. And there, right below us, stretching out like a patchwork quilt of adobe, were hundreds of abandoned mud houses; an entire ghost city with not a human inhabitant in sight.

From the fortress walls, we descended into the maze. We entered a narrow passageway through an arch and it led us into another world. There were mounds of ancient bricks and masonry, mixed with old wooden beams, and shattered doorways leant against crumbling walls. It was a scene of apocalyptic archaeology.

'See that.' Khaled pointed to the keystone at the top of an arch. It was a huge wedge-shaped stone holding the doorway together.

'What is it?' I said, noticing that the stone was engraved with what appeared to be an inscription.

'It's Bronze Age, dating back two thousand, six hundred years,' he told me.

The eight hundred houses were centred around a large hill, dominated by a walled fortress that overlooked the valley.

'The last people left in 1983,' he said, kicking an old glass bottle aside. Old rags and clothes from then were strewn about the corridors and the rooms still had tin pots and pans on dusty shelves. It was as if the entire population had just got up and left one afternoon.

'In the eighties, Saudis started to realise that they didn't want to live in mud huts and tents anymore. The old Bedu ways became unfashionable and everyone wanted a house with an air-conditioning unit, a TV and a toilet. So, they all left and built a new town on the other side of the valley.'

Khaled smiled. 'You see, they have no concept of the past, especially anything that came before Islam. For a long time, Arabs have believed there is no beauty in dust and old houses. They are merely places to sleep and eat. Where you tourists see beauty and history, Saudis see rot and crumbling bricks. This place should be a UNESCO heritage site, and it's my job to make sure it is one day. I'm trying to tell my people we need to look after the old things and the old ways, so that we can preserve our heritage and legacy.'

He continued, 'Some people understand, but sadly not too many. They're too interested in getting the latest Toyota, or smart phone, but when they see the potential for tourism, maybe things will change. If there's money in it for them, then they'll save it, and *inshallah*, the new Crown Prince is changing things for the better and the tourists will come soon.'

We picked our way through the ruins back to the car and made our way out of the town and back to the desert, passing through a valley filled with vast sandstone stacks and natural arches that anywhere else in the world would be famous national monuments. There were huge black and yellow stones balanced on top of one another, and spines and pinnacles reaching into the azure sky. In the middle of the desert, there was one massive arch that stood out from all of them.

'That one is called Elephant Rock,' said Khaled, grinning with pride at the massive wonder.

We drove the car through the spectacular arcade. We must

have looked as tiny as a little ant in comparison to the mammoth cliffs dominating all around. We carried on, following desert trails to another valley, where cliffs towered above us on all sides. On a ledge, a hundred feet high, I noticed the cliff face was covered in ancient scribblings: pictures of antelope, dogs, horses and humans.

'These ancient petroglyphs are thousands of years old,' Khaled said. 'They were drawn by the first Arabs.'

It was an insight into a way of life that had lasted for millennia across the Arabian Peninsula; a life of hardship, of desert living and a daily battle for survival against the elements. The art showed sword fights and hunting; there were images of eagles and ostriches and sheep with vast curled horns; it was a culture at one with nature that seemed all but forgotten now.

One thing that hadn't changed, however, was the code of hospitality that had survived the ages intact.

We returned to the town to find a place to stay, and the next morning Khaled suggested that we attend Friday prayers at the mosque. Even though I'd been to plenty of mosques before, I was still pleasantly surprised to find that the imam had no problem letting a non-Muslim sit in and watch the proceedings. I'd got it into my head that because this was Saudi Arabia, it must be full of proselytising fanatics. I'd fallen for the generalisations and stereotypes that plague the media and our minds. I'd expected somehow to face withering looks and threats of forced conversion, but of course, none of this had happened.

The locals gathered outside the prayer hall to greet each other and shake hands, before removing their shoes and performing the ablutions. I entered with Khaled. He took his place on the mat and asked me to sit next to him, but I thought it better to stay at the back of the mosque with the teenagers, out of respect for those praying.

After the imam came in, the prayers began. He led with a sermon, which I gathered to be all about finding inner peace and respecting your neighbours. One of the kids explained the messages, while old men thumbed with their prayer beads. I found the prostrations mesmerising, and I couldn't help thinking that they must be quite healthy and good for one's joints. It wasn't too far removed from a form of yoga, and even the children and old men did the ceremony without fuss.

The service was refreshingly short. After half an hour, all the men were on their feet, shaking hands again, and then strolling back outside where a host of Land Cruisers sat in the car park, waiting to whisk them off for their Friday lunch.

'The imam has invited us to his house,' said Khaled. 'He wants us to eat with him.'

I eagerly accepted the offer, excited by the prospect of meeting the spiritual teacher, and finding out more about what it means to be a Muslim in the country that hosts the holiest sites in Islam.

His house was just around the corner on the main street. It was in a large compound surrounded by palm trees and high fences. The gates were open and we followed him through. He insisted on showing us around the communal rooms, as Khaled translated.

'The gates are always open to the community,' he said, with a warm smile. 'Anyone can come in and rest, at any time of day.'

The imam was a large man in his mid-fifties, who went by the name of Khalid Al-Muarei. He was wearing a brown cloak with golden trim, and a white cloth on his head. His moustache was shaved clean, leaving a long beard under his chin.

'Please, take a seat.' He motioned for me to sit on one of the cushions in the guest room. Rugs covered the walls and floors and we sat cross-legged, while a servant brought a platter of grilled goat and rice and bottles of Coca-Cola. A TV was blaring out music in the background.

'How do you like my country?' asked the imam.

I told him that I'd been welcomed with hospitality everywhere I'd been and was surprised at how liberal it appeared.

'We are very progressive. Don't believe all the things you hear on the news. We're not all terrorists, you know.'

It felt a bit impolite over lunch, but I thought I should ask some difficult questions, since I had the opportunity.

'What would you say to those people who accuse Saudi Arabia of funding terrorism?'

He shook his head and looked me in the eye.

'It is not true. That's it.'

'But this is where Osama bin Laden came from, isn't it? And there are a lot of people who believe that Daesh are being funded by Saudi Arabia. And what about Wahhabism?'

He smiled.

'I know you must ask these questions, so I will try to answer them, even though I am but a lowly cleric.' He took a swig on some Coke and stroked his beard before continuing.

'To begin with, Wahabbism is just a name. It means nothing. There are, of course, people who like to cause problems, but this is not limited to Saudi Arabia. Osama bin Laden was a terrorist with lots of money, who was only interested in power and fame. Terrorists come from all over, but they are not real Muslims. There are over a billion Muslims in the world and how many cause terror? Very few. In the Qu'ran it is said that whoever kills another human being, he will go to hell, especially if he kills fellow Muslims, and most people that terrorists kill are other

Muslims. Daesh are not real Muslims, they are crazy people. We do not support them. There are other powers in the world, you know, who do. I shall not say who they are.'

'Who?' I asked. I guessed he was referring to Western powers, as that was the great conspiracy theory that seemed so prevalent across the region.

'I think you already know,' he replied. 'But I will say this. The United States has much to gain by the chaos in the Middle East. If there is chaos, they have an excuse to try to control it and be here, taking the oil. But for us here in Saudi Arabia, the biggest terrorists are the Iranians. These people are the ones playing their games, so that we look bad.'

It was an all-too-familiar story that I'd heard all across the peninsula.

'But whatever the politics, remember this. Real Muslims, real Saudis, we just want peace and to worship Allah. That is all.'

With that he ate a grape and waved a hand to indicate that he'd had enough talking politics.

'Why don't you become a Muslim?' he said, with a casual shrug.

I liked the man, even though I knew we disagreed on plenty of things. I thought he was naïve to think that Wahabbism was only a name and that there was no implicit support of Islamism within the Saudi set-up. And yet he had a wry smile and a glint in his eye that betrayed a conviction in his beliefs without even a hint of arrogance. I thought I'd parley with him, if only to give him a different point of view.

'I like whisky,' I said to him.

He laughed out loud. 'That's a problem.'

'I also like art. Why can't Muslims draw pictures of living beings? It seems such a waste.' It was a question that had been nagging me for some time. I'd been dismayed to see ancient statues and pictures brutalised by fanatical Muslims from Egypt to Syria and Iraq over the last few years, and even recently I'd seen road signs of camels scrawled over – and I still hadn't figured out what was so offensive to the religion about an image of a face or a creature.

He pondered my question.

'Well, the Prophet Muhammad said that only God shall create images of living beings and it isn't for us humans to show pictures of people or animals, since we can never do the job as well as God.'

I pointed to the TV. 'Well, there's pictures of people coming out of that,' I said. 'And there's a photo of your face on your ID card. Surely that's the same?'

He screwed up his nose, before breaking into a smile.

'That's different. But I tell you what. If you become a Muslim, you can keep your art. I think Allah won't mind too much if you want to draw pictures.'

He patted me on the shoulder. 'But no whisky, okay?'

I told him I'd think about it, as we finished up our coffee. We shook hands and I thanked him for lunch before saying goodbye. I knew that I'd never find all the answers to my questions, and it was unfair to ask my host to speak for an entire religion and a whole country, but I'd come away feeling that he meant what he said. If his opinion was representative of most religious leaders in Saudi Arabia, and they were even half as pleasant as Khalid Al-'Muarei, then I was reassured that the mosques and madrassas weren't entirely to blame for espousing terror and fanaticism.

That afternoon, we left Al-'Ula to follow the road parallel to the old Hejaz railway. It was the moment I'd been waiting for and the most special personal experience of my time in Saudi

Arabia, if not the journey so far. When I'd watched the movie *Lawrence of Arabia* at the age of ten, I swore that one day I'd set foot on the tracks that earned him a place in British history as one of the greatest and most famous adventurers of all time.

I'd read *Seven Pillars of Wisdom* as a young army officer and took lessons from it during my deployment in Afghanistan a decade before. For all his controversy and faults, Lawrence was my hero. As we sped through the majestic red volcanic plains of the Hejaz, I mentioned as much to Khaled.

He grunted without looking at me.

'The man was a bastard. He was just a British spy who promised the Arabs gold, but it was all lies. Nothing good came of his mischief. Don't get me wrong, we hated the Turks and we wanted rid of the Ottoman Empire, but the Arabs, the Bedouin who he says he loved, they got nothing. We just swapped one foreign rule for another. No, I don't like Lawrence. Or your man Burton either. He sneaked into Mecca without permission. The only one I like is Thesiger. He lived with us Arabs and got to know us. He had no agenda other than wanting to learn about our ways, I think. Isn't that what travel should be all about?'

As the peaks grew higher in the distance, the dry river beds weaved between a fractured landscape made up of great boulders, jagged mounds and small groves of palm trees and lush acacia bushes, flowering with red and yellow blossom. We left the main road and followed a sandy track that led through a narrow valley.

As we came out onto a plain, I found the reward I'd been looking for. A sand-covered embankment ran in a straight line between the boulders, following the natural course of the wadi. It was, of course, the old railway line that we'd followed north, but here it was so indistinct that it was hard to tell what it was.

Khaled had never been here before and was reluctant to visit a place that for him symbolised a tainted past, but for me, I knew that I couldn't come this far and not see with my own eyes one of the original stations. This was Haddiyah.

The old Ottoman station, which appeared before us as an abandoned two-storey building, its grey bricks were now crumbling after a century of dereliction. There was no one else around and I climbed through a hole in the rusty wire fence to explore the scene of such monumental importance.

It was here that exactly a hundred and one years ago, Thomas Edward Lawrence, employed by the British army to raise a rebellion of the Arab tribes against Ottoman Turkish rule, had succeeded in blowing up a number of Turkish and German trains in the midst of the First World War. It was a guerrilla campaign that changed the course of history in the region and helped Britain and her allies to defeat Germany and the Central Powers – the Ottoman Empire, Austria-Hungary and Bulgaria.

Throughout my journey, I'd seen and felt the legacy of Britain's colonial rule. It was a subject that fascinated me as a student of history, and the reverberations are still very much apparent across the Arabian Peninsula, but I can't describe the sense of personal excitement and satisfaction at seeing for myself the place where Lawrence himself fought a battle. I followed the railway tracks, as Khaled watched on.

They were now mostly covered in sand, but all around lay the debris of battle. The cartridges and bullets had long since been swallowed up by the desert, but bits of twisted metal, ammunition tins and ration boxes littered the stony plain. Almost all the wooden sleepers of the railway line had disappeared, no doubt pilfered by nomadic Bedouin to use for firewood, but it was the fact that anything remained at all that astonished me.

Then I saw what I'd been looking for. A hundred metres away, at the base of a small hill, sat the twisted remains of a locomotive. At the front was the engine and behind it the metal frame of the carriages, complete with their wheels, doors, valves and pipes. The chassis was coloured a deep purple, its metal a uniform shade of sun-drenched rust. It rarely rains in the Hejaz, so it was in surprisingly good condition and the oxidisation was only surface level. The engine with its steam funnel was on its side; otherwise it was in impeccable shape and in no way looked more than a century old, but the date marking its construction was clear – 1911.

This was one of the several German-made trains that had been sold to the Turks to transport troops and weaponry to the front line against the British, and Lawrence had used dynamite to blow them up wherever he came across them. Only a few steps away was the hill where I presumed he and his men had lain in wait for the locomotive to steam around the bend. It would have to slow down to take the corner, making it the perfect ambush site. I walked to the top of the hill and crouched behind the largest boulder. I knew, somehow instinctively, that it was right here that Lawrence would have crouched just before he pushed down on the detonator box.

For the first time in a long time, I felt joyful to the point of awe. I'd finally fulfilled my dream, and equally importantly, I'd almost crossed Saudi Arabia. It was a watershed in my journey. I'd broken the back of the expedition and completed almost four thousand miles. As far as I could tell, the most difficult and dangerous parts of the trip were now behind me.

Ahead lay Jordan, a country I knew well – it was safe, and easily accessible, filled with friendly people and beautiful scenery – and beyond that was the Holy Land, and I was still on track to get there before Christmas. As I stood on the mound, in the footsteps of Lawrence, I congratulated myself on a job well done and looked forward to whatever the adventure might have in store next.

18

A Paradise of Sand

Who lives sees, but who travels, sees more.
Ibn Battutah

Over the course of the next few days, Khaled and I travelled
north, following the old railway until we reached the town of
Tabuk, and from there we headed to the border with Jordan,
where I said goodbye. Khaled, and the people he'd introduced
me to, had challenged all my preconceived ideas about Saudi
Arabia. He'd shown me a country struggling to come to terms
with modernity, but doing it nonetheless. I'd learned that it's not
an overnight process and there are still many dogmatic attitudes
that hindered progress, but amid the deserts and rocks, I'd also
found a country eager to embrace the benefits of technology,
communication and a more rational attitude.

I thanked Khaled for his insights. If nothing else, he'd
reminded me of the benefits of travelling with a good guide;
someone who knows the country and its customs well. I'd
realised how lonely it can be travelling without knowing the
language, and a decent travel companion can make all the
difference between a positive and negative travel experience, so
I was determined to find someone in Jordan who could help
me out, too. It was early December now and I had a couple of
weeks before Christmas to make it to Bethlehem. It was a

self-imposed deadline, but one that I couldn't miss. I'd invited my brother and parents and some good friends to meet me in the holy town, so I had a goal.

Khaled disappeared back to the south amid a dust cloud and I walked across the border into the Hashemite Kingdom towards Aqaba, following the same route Lawrence and his men had travelled in their bid to reach Damascus. For the next few hundred miles, I would be following one of the most ancient and important overland routes in the region, if not the world. It was a route steeped in history and legend, and I was eager to explore.

But first I needed a guide. Entering Jordan felt like a breath of fresh air. For the first time since Iraq, I saw women unveiled and without headscarves. Boys played football on the beach in shorts and old men sold ice cream and balloons under the palm trees. Children swam in the sea and teenagers did backflips into the water from a jetty. There was a festive atmosphere as families, both Muslim and Christian, sat around in the parks picnicking together. Music was pumping from radios and speakers all around.

I discovered it was the Prophet Muhammad's birthday and the whole country was on a national holiday. No wonder it felt like there was a party going on. The bay was filled with luxury yachts and the hotels sold beer. In fact, there was a street full of restaurants, bars and coffee shops, where young men with trendy beards and skinny jeans hung out smoking shisha. I sat down at a table in the Ali Baba restaurant and pondered where I might find a decent guide.

In the past I'd sourced my travel companions from all sorts of places; usually it was word of mouth, taking recommendations from friends working abroad: NGO workers, journalists and military types who knew the score. Sometimes I'd used official tourist guides, but more often than not they either had an agenda, or else they were a bit dull and only interested in the usual tourist sites, rather than showing me the underbelly of a country. Aqaba, and Jordan in general, was awash with tour agents given its heavy reliance on the tourism industry, so I was sure I'd find someone easily enough. That said, I wasn't prepared for what happened next.

As I waited for my coffee to arrive, I looked around the room. For the first time since the Gulf, I was in the company of other tourists. There were a few other Westerners in shorts and T-shirts enjoying a holiday. The local Jordanians were generally better dressed and were all busy laughing and chatting with their families. But in the corner, one man sat alone and stood out from the rest.

Wearing an off-white *jellabiya*, an oversize long-sleeved shirt, and a maroon headscarf that was wrapped around his forehead like a bandana rather than the usual Arab keffiyeh, he looked every inch like Captain Jack Sparrow. His hair was shoulder length, jet-black and curly, and he had a neatly trimmed moustache and goatee beard. His wrists were covered in bangles and he had tattoos on his forearms. But it was his eyes that drew me in. They were deep and mysterious and surrounded by thick kohl. Yes, he must be a pirate, I thought. What's more, he was happily getting stuck into a pint of beer. I knew, instantly, that he was my man. Without a second thought, I got up and walked over to him.

'Excuse me, do you speak English?' I said, hoping for the best.

The pirate looked me up and down, his face betraying no emotion whatsoever.

After a few seconds, he spoke. 'Why not?'

That was a relief, I thought.

'I don't suppose you would be interested in being my guide?'

He tilted his head, and took another slurp on his pint before responding.

'Why not?' he repeated.

Good start, I thought.

'Will you travel with me for two weeks, from here, all the way to the north of Jordan?'

He shrugged, finished his pint and stood up.

'Why not? Yalla.'

When you put yourself out there and pluck up the courage to talk to strangers and be open to new opportunities, the universe conspires to help you. I took my new mysterious guide's willingness to get up and join me as a sign. It was serendipity at its finest, and I felt like I was on a roll.

My new guide, it turned out, wasn't in fact a pirate; he was a Bedu by the name of Mishael Al-Faqeer. I agreed to meet him the following morning in the lobby of the guesthouse where I was staying. He turned up in the same clothes he'd been wearing the day before. The only addition was a tiny bag containing a spare pair of socks and a rolled-up, woollen brown cloak.

'Do you have a sleeping bag? Is that all the kit you have?' I asked. I thought that I travelled light, but he was taking it to the next level.

He chuckled. 'A sleeping bag? Bedu don't need sleeping bags. I grew up in a cave.'

With that we left the comfortable surroundings of Aqaba and trekked north-east into the sands of Wadi Rum.

Mishael was one of three million Bedouin living in Jordan. He'd grown up in the outskirts of Petra, brought up by his grandmother in a small cave hewn from the cliff face. Having left school at the age of ten, he was illiterate, but that hadn't stopped him seducing tourists with his natural charm and suave piratical looks – earning a living as a guide in the world-famous ruins nearby. I'd guessed him to be in his late thirties, but it turned out he was only twenty-five. Despite his youth, he'd been married for a couple of years already, to a Dutch girl who'd fallen in love with this enigma of the desert.

Mishael led the way in silence. He only spoke when I spoke to him. His English was acceptable, if not good, but he was simply a man of few words, content to take in the majesty of the scenery. I followed as we left the highway and made our way across the blood red plain towards a remote farm at the edge of the national park. This was the original Hajj route from the north. For hundreds of years, pilgrims and traders of the old silk and spice route had come this way by camel in both directions, and now I was to follow in their footsteps. Mishael led us down a trail towards the collection of shacks surrounded by a rickety wooden fence.

'It's my friend's house,' said Mishael. 'He will give us camels.'

We met Aude, another Bedouin, who agreed to come along as far as the northern edge of the Wadi Rum desert, which would take us five or so days to cross by foot.

It took him no time at all to assemble three camels, which were clearly used to load carrying and were as well-behaved as the ones we'd had in Dhofar. Aude was also in his mid-twenties and came with a serene aura. He couldn't speak a word of English, but had a calm, kind smile and I knew that I could trust both of them implicitly.

Mish and Aude walked, leading the camels by a long rein. Aude, despite being happily married with a baby, was clearly in love with his camels, and gave them a kiss and a hug at every opportunity. We trekked over a low ridge, leaving behind the last of the trees, and after two hours we found ourselves amid some of the most beautiful desert landscapes I'd ever seen.

Wadi Rum is one of the Middle East's most touristic destinations, bringing in more than a hundred thousand tourists a year, but the vast majority only have time to zip in and out on a jeep safari for a day or two, and stay in the main valley near to Wadi Rum village. Here in the south, we had the entire desert to ourselves. Vast escarpment rose on both sides, ancient sandstone tens of millions of years old, striking into the deep blue sky. It seemed to transform with the hours of the day and by mid-afternoon it had changed from golden yellow to deep scarlet. Above, buzzards soared high above the canyons seeking out their prey, but as I looked around there seemed to be no sign of life whatsoever.

'Let's make camp over there,' said Mishael, pointing at the base of a vast rock face. I was glad he'd suggested some shade. Even though by now it was late afternoon, it was still hot – not as hot as the Empty Quarter, but hot enough, and I was ready for a rest. We walked the quarter-mile to the bottom of the sandstone monolith and unpacked the camels.

'Follow me,' said Mishael, dumping his cloak in the sand and strolling back out into the hot sand.

'What are we looking for?' I asked.

'Firewood,' he said.

'But there are no trees.'

He just raised an eyebrow. 'We don't need trees.' At that he suddenly knelt down and motioned for me to do the same. I looked at the gravel and sand at my feet. Surely there was nothing but stones? Mishael brushed away the first layer of sand and began to dig with his bare hands. And then I remembered how Mahrouqi had discovered wood buried deep under the sand back in the Empty Quarter. It was a reminder that the old ways weren't completely forgotten. After a few seconds, Mish found what he was looking for. He unearthed a desiccated root, digging around the edges to make sure it didn't break off. What I thought was only a small twig, once excavated turned out to be a huge series of twisted branches almost a metre long.

'How did you know that was there?' I couldn't help but ask, still wondering at how he must have known.

Mishael shrugged. 'I'm Bedu, we just know.'

He sighed. 'The desert used to be filled with Bedu. Here, this valley was our home. When Lawrence was here, he found hundreds of families living only in tents. Nowadays everyone wants to live near the cities, even the Bedu nowadays have cars and houses. But me, I prefer a simple life. I would live out here forever, if only my wife would let me. I cannot write or read or drive, but I am happy here.'

With enough fuel to make a small campfire, we returned to the cliff base and made ourselves comfortable as Aude brewed up some sweet sage tea over the flames. He'd brought a chicken and he slow roasted that, too, along with some onions and rice. He even made his own bread from flour and water.

In the distance the sun set, casting long shadows from the rock stacks and causing the whole desert to turn blood red. The pillars appeared as melting candles rising from the wilderness; as if planted purely for the aesthetic pleasure of God himself. Soon a firmament of stars emerged from the depths of the heavens and for the first time in a very long time, I felt completely at peace. There was no phone signal, no internet, nothing to do. I'd long since read all my books and anyway, in this environment it somehow seemed inappropriate to want to transport my mind elsewhere.

Mishael and Aude began to sing old Bedu songs, and even the camels seemed to rest easy, chewing the cud and staring into the darkness. I listened and pondered the night sky, as a shooting star whooshed across the vast dome. The moon rose gradually, lighting up the alien panorama with such majesty that it was impossible not to feel instantly transported to another time; one in which material things meant nothing; where the only things that mattered were songs and love. In the flickering shadows of the fire, Mishael and Aude's dark faces seemed to dance in the half light, giving them an other-worldly appearance.

I felt as though this was what the real Arabia was all about – this was the real life of the Bedu nomads and therefore of mankind itself. This was the natural state of being for humans. With a belly full of food and a song in the air, what more can man ask for? There was no choice here but to simply exist in perfect harmony with one's surroundings. There was no struggle, except against one's self, and a belief in the benevolence of nature. Mishael had magicked fire from stones and thanked Allah for that ancient knowledge. For him and Aude this was perfection – not the shiny cities and desires of modernity – simply living, unburdened by the paradox of choice or worry about the future. And for me, for the first time on this journey, I realised it, too. I understood that I'd been so wrapped up with the purity of the journey and making sure that I was ticking all the boxes that I'd forgotten to exist and enjoy it.

For the next few days I forgot all about home; all about my own troubles; I forgot about the past and even about what lay ahead. I enjoyed the simplicity of desert life, living as a nomad. We'd walk all day, following indeterminate paths and ancient trails weaving through the enormous sand dunes. The terrain shifted and morphed from wide valleys to narrow gullies and great canyons. The landscape was at once Martian and alien, and yet to my inner nomad instantly familiar and hospitable. We'd eat when we were hungry, drink when we were thirsty and sleep when we were tired.

There was no need to set up tents – not that we even had any. We slept in caves or simply out in the open, like prehistoric hunter-gatherers. I would snuggle up inside my sleeping bag to keep off the night chill, but Aude and Mishael, used to the winter nights, just wrapped their cloaks around their ears and slept soundly till dawn. I knew when it was time to wake up, as the familiar smell of tobacco wafted through the air. Whereas Aude was a devout Muslim and prayed five times each day, Mishael began the morning with a ritual cigarette. I never saw him pray once.

The days passed with ease and on the fourth day, almost to my own sadness, we passed by Lawrence's spring, where my hero used to water his camels. Aude pointed to the waterfall, now all but dry and surrounded by local men selling handicrafts and carpets. It was filled with tourists and a signal that civilisation was nearby.

'Some of the very old people remember stories of Lawrence,' said Mishael. 'Are you from his tribe?' he asked.

I told him that I was. Speaking of my tribe, some English and American tourists took photographs of me, thinking I was a Bedu. Mishael nudged me and whispered with a wry smile.

'They think we're some sort of animal in the zoo. This is what it is like to be a tribal, but what to do?' He shrugged and smiled for the tourists. I smiled too and kept my mouth shut, not wanting to ruin their illusion.

An hour later, we reached the main road that led to Wadi Rum town, where we fed the camels and stopped for lunch in one of Aude's friends' houses. The next day we passed through a remote gorge filled with trees and exited the valley on its northern flank. When we reached the main road, Mishael and I said goodbye to Aude. He gave us a solemn nod, jumped on top of his favourite camel and raced off into the distance, assuring us that he could make the return journey in just two days.

The two of us flagged down a lift at the side of the road and jumped in the back of a passing pick-up truck, which was heading to Wadi Araba, over the mountains into a neighbouring valley. The driver, an old farmer named Karim, insisted we join him for lunch and tea at his home, a little shanty high among the jagged peaks. Jordanians are renowned even in the Arab world for their hospitality, especially the semi-nomadic Bedu, and Karim was no different. He fed us delicious *mansaf* – a sort of lamb biriyani – on a huge platter, with yoghurt and roasted nuts and raisins. After the meal, he gave us no choice but to accompany him into Wadi Musa, where he was off to place a bet on some illicit camel racing.

Later that evening we finally made it, exhausted but content, into Petra. Mishael was happy to be home and promised that after he'd said hello to his wife, he would show me around the archaeological sites.

There's a reason that Petra receives more than a thousand tourists a day. It's one of the wonders of the world and rightly acknowledged as a world heritage site. I thought back to the first time I'd visited Jordan in 2003, when the ticket office was little more than a roadside shack and backpackers used to be able to sneak in over the fence unnoticed. I'd camped in the ruins overnight then, but these days the whole place is surrounded by high security walls and the ticket booth resembles those at the entrance to vast football stadiums.

Hotels had sprung up all around the edges, along with bars, restaurants and souvenir shops. I was expecting the worst, and so made sure I woke up at four a.m. to beat the hordes. It was a worthwhile endeavour, as Mishael and I were the first inside and raced down the narrow sandstone gully to ensure we reached the famous Treasury monument first.

In a scene immortalised in *Indiana Jones and the Last Crusade*, a whip-cracking Harrison Ford rides horseback with Sean Connery to uncover the secret remains of an ancient kingdom. It was a piece of film that no doubt inspired many a young explorer to seek out hidden treasures, and I was as guilty as the rest. Mishael and I beamed with joy to see the wondrous building emerge from the carved cliff at dawn. Of course, inside, which is now off-limits, there is no hidden chamber containing the Holy Grail, or the ghosts of dead Crusaders – in fact it's merely a huge empty edifice, long since plundered of its treasures by its Bedu guardians, Mishael's distant ancestors.

'When I was a boy, we used to climb right to the top. We'd play in the graves and have competitions as to who could jump from the highest point,' he said. 'We'd go digging in the caves and see what we could find. Sometimes we'd find gold and silver coins, which we'd sell to the foreigners.'

'Do you think there is more hidden, or has it all been taken?' I asked.

Mishael shrugged. 'Every time it rains and the sand is washed away, we always find more treasure.'

We walked through the old Nabataean city with its intricately hewn tombs and monuments. We passed by the Roman city with its stone market street and temples. Beyond that we entered a narrow gully, where a staircase led us to the top of the mountain, from where the 'monastery' was hidden from view. Here, we had the place to ourselves. Many tourists were content with the view of the Treasury and didn't bother with the forty-five-minute trek up to the top, and so we spent the morning and afternoon simply admiring the view of the rock-tomb and the spectacular Valley of Moses, which stretched out beyond the mountains below.

Mishael regaled me with tales of his childhood, as other locals came and sat with us, offering tea and food. I thought back with nostalgia to the time that Alex and I had stood in exactly the same spot in 2003, at the tender age of twenty-one. Everything had now come full circle, and I'd fulfilled a promise that I'd made to Alex to return.

In the evening, Mishael invited me to eat mansaf in his brother's house and of course, I agreed. He led me down the mountain as the sun set somewhere beyond the Dead Sea, which remained tantalisingly out of view. In the darkness we descended to a hidden valley, somewhere outside the city limits, where a rocky outcrop was sheltered from the distant lights.

'Here is my family home,' said my guide. He pointed to a door at the entrance to a cave, where a candle flickered inside.

He shrugged and looked a little embarrassed. 'It's not finished yet.'

I told him that I felt enormously privileged that he should invite me at all.

Mishael's brother and his wife Ferozeh, who Mishael described as the 'Queen of the Bedu', were standing waiting for us. The cave itself was tiny; it was only one room filled with carpets that ensured it was warm year-round. A gas cooker was firing up a pot filled with boiled chicken, and a few vegetables were lined up, ready to be added to the pot. The walls were bare, apart from some tacky posters of imaginary landscapes and some family photographs. It was clear that these people were verging on poverty, and yet there was something about their way of life that was far richer than anything I'd seen before.

Ferozeh was the first to introduce herself and shake my hand. It was something I wasn't used to – a woman hadn't offered her hand to me in months – but Mishael insisted that the Bedu ladies in Jordan were the most liberal and emancipated of anywhere in the region.

'You're welcome to our little home,' said the lady in perfect English. 'This is my husband.' She waved at her man, who laughed.

'See, this is what happens when you come into a Bedu cave. The women are in charge!' He rolled his eyes.

'Oh, shut up,' she said in a joking manner. 'Otherwise you won't get any food.' She waved a ladle in his face with a wink and a smile.

Ferozeh spoke six languages fluently, including Chinese and Japanese. She'd never even been to school and had learned entirely off her own bat, so that she could talk with tourists and relieve them of a few dollars in exchange for handicrafts.

She looked me over and grinned. 'If we get some kohl on your eyes, you'd look like a Bedu, and then we'd welcome you into the family. It's a shame I'm already married, otherwise you could live here in my cave.' Her husband shrugged his shoulders and looked at me, rolling his eyes yet again. They clearly loved each other very much.

We sat down to eat and all night we laughed and joked, and

suddenly it occurred to me that even though I was with people from a culture so far removed from my own, I'd rarely felt so at home.

19

The Holy Land

He that gives should not remember, he that receives should never forget
The Talmud

For the next week, I travelled with Mishael over the central Jordanian highlands, usually just picking up lifts at the roadside and hitchhiking from town to town and village to village. We passed by the old Christian city of Madaba, with its Byzantine church and mosaics; we wandered around the ruins of the old Crusader castle at Shobak, and ate with shepherds in the Wadi Dana. We trekked past the tomb of Moses at Mount Nebo and looked down at the Dead Sea from the Mujib escarpment. The blue skies had now darkened with storm clouds and a distant thunder rumbled to the west. It was a timely reminder that winter was upon us, and the further north I travelled, the colder it had become.

We were in the second week of December now, and Christmas was almost here. The hills of the Holy Land shimmered in the distance on the far side of the lifeless lake. It was almost time to leave Arabia behind and enter the Levant. I was excited to be in a land of so much history; a place so vivid in my own imagination and one that I'd dreamt of returning to for such a long time.

I remembered my school nativity play again and my inauspicious introduction to the Middle East as the back end of a donkey, and allowed myself a little silent chuckle. I'd almost made it, I thought to myself.

'Yalla,' said Mishael. 'I want to see the Dead Sea.'

I'd promised him a night in a hotel. After camping out and staying in caves for so long, I wanted a shower, and down on the Dead Sea there was not much choice of accommodation apart from five-star hotels anyway, so I thought I'd treat him to a bit of luxury. Mishael hadn't stayed in any of his own country's resorts before, so for him it was an entertaining treat. He took great pleasure in wearing his Bedu dishdasha and headscarf and for once in his life feeling equal in wealth to the rich Arab holidaymakers.

'I feel like a sheikh,' he said to me over dinner, swilling some red wine with abandon, although he couldn't bring himself to ask the waiter for anything personally, and looked to me when he wanted to order more food and drink.

The highlight of Mishael's holiday, though, was donning a pair of board shorts and bathing in the Dead Sea like all the other tourists.

We made our way after that to the capital, Amman, where I spent a week or so making final preparations for the onward journey. There were still some logistical complications in store. I had no idea how I would get from Israel into Lebanon, since the border was closed, but I needed to ask around for local advice. The political situation had suddenly become more tricky, after President Donald Trump announced that he was going to move the US embassy in Israel from Tel Aviv to Jerusalem.

I watched news bulletins of protestors lining the streets in Gaza and the West Bank as riots erupted along the Palestinian borders. There was every chance of a renewed conflict. The situation in Syria was as bad as ever, and I'd heard some horror stories of kidnappings and murders in Lebanon, too. It made me realise that my journey was far from over, but I promised myself to push all that to the back of my mind, at least until I'd made it to Bethlehem and celebrated Christmas.

On 22 December I left Amman behind, saying goodbye to Mishael. We promised to remain friends, and despite his illiteracy, he added me on Facebook and we continued to communicate with the sole use of emojis. I travelled west through the green plantations along the River Jordan and the next day at dawn crossed the famous Allenby Bridge over the biblical river and into the ancient land of Palestine.

Just to set the record straight, before I continue, I'm calling it Palestine because that's what the vast majority of people who live in the West Bank call it. Technically, I was in the State of Palestine, or the Occupied Palestinian Territory as the International Court of Justice refers to it, and big red signs warned Israelis against entering. In fact, it was against the law for an Israeli to even enter the 'red zones'; if they did they could face death. The border was manned by Israeli Defence Force soldiers, however, and to all intents and purposes, and from an Israeli government standpoint, I was in Israel.

Despite the dire warnings that I'd be questioned for hours, and my passport would be ruined by the presence of an Israeli stamp, I was waved into the country by a very friendly and helpful Jewish soldier, who also happened to be a very beautiful girl in her mid-twenties, armed with an automatic weapon and some lethal lip gloss.

On the far side of customs, I was free to hitchhike down the road to Qasr al-Yahud, the baptismal site of Jesus. To navigate the complexities of this most controversial bit of land in the world, I knew I'd need to get the inside track from a local. I'd asked around when I was in Jordan and been recommended a guy named Saleh, and so I'd agreed to meet him at the place where Jesus was baptised by John the Baptist, 2,017 years ago.

The place was thronging with Christian pilgrims from all over the world: Americans, Russians, Filipinos, Nigerians and hordes of Chinese. They'd all come for one thing – to pay their devotions to the holy water of the River Jordan, now a mere trickle draining through a murky swamp. There were a handful of bored Israeli soldiers supervising the scene, but the pilgrims were busily dipping themselves in the fetid ponds and splashing the filthy water all over themselves, oblivious to their Jewish guards.

'I wouldn't be surprised if they caught bilharzia,' came a voice out of the crowd. I turned around to see a man about my own age, with a long beard and wearing thick glasses. He had an American accent and as I shook his hand, I noticed several fingers were missing.

'I'm Saleh,' he said. 'Don't get me wrong, though. I respect their devotion and their right to come here and pray. I believe that Jesus was here and that it was the place that John baptised him, I'm just genuinely concerned for all these poor people's health. They've come a long way, and I'd be very upset if they came to my country and caught some nasty disease from this foul river.'

He shrugged. 'Anyway, welcome to Palestine, you are my guest. I'd be delighted to show you around, but I'm guessing since it's Christmas Eve tomorrow, you want to get to Bethlehem?'

I told him that I did.

'And you like to walk?'

'Funnily enough, I do,' I said.

'Good, so do I. We'll walk to Bethlehem from Jericho,' he said. 'Yalla.'

We drove the thirty minutes to Jericho, and it was a reminder of the tiny distances involved in getting anywhere in the Holy Land. I'd been used to travelling hundreds of miles a day in Saudi Arabia and walking for eight hours a day in Jordan, but here everything was so close together, I thought it would be a shame not to walk between all the holy sites. It occurred to me to get a donkey to help carry my kit, but then I realised that might be a bit blasphemous. And anyway, my primary school nativity play had put me off them a long time ago. From a distance, I saw the ruins of Jericho and wanted desperately to see them.

'We'll come back and explore properly in a few days,' said Saleh. 'But if you want to get to Bethlehem by Christmas, then we should set off.'

I didn't want to rush and miss seeing more of the West Bank. There was a whole miniature nation to explore, places with such historical importance and current relevance, like Hebron, Nablus and of course, Jericho; yet at the same time I knew that I couldn't miss Christmas in the place that the world's biggest religion was born. We agreed to go and spend a few days in Bethlehem, and then come back to see more of Palestine, before heading to Jerusalem and beyond that into Israel itself, later on in the New Year.

So we went to a little supermarket on the outskirts of the town and stocked up on some provisions for the forty-kilometre walk. As we left the outskirts of Jericho, the suburbs soon gave way to low brown hills that were bare and windswept.

'This is the start of the Judean Desert,' said Saleh, wrapping his shemagh tightly around his neck to keep the chill away. 'It's where Jesus spent his forty days and forty nights in temptation.'

I looked around. There wasn't much temptation going on here these days, that's for sure. The undulating mounds seemed to roll on forever. The landscape was bleak and empty, something resembling an abandoned quarry, filled with scars and long-lost excavations, and yet . . . there was magic in the air. I could almost smell the roast turkey wafting over the mountains.

'The last bit is also the route that Mary and Joseph would have taken from Nazareth, so we're taking a well-trodden path,' said my guide.

Looking around, it certainly didn't feel that way. We'd crossed a main road earlier in the day, but other than a few dusty old military tracks, we walked along the stony footpaths that were now followed only by Bedu shepherds and the occasional pilgrim.

'Not many people come here on foot anymore,' said Saleh. 'The Christians come in big coaches from Jerusalem for a day trip with armed guards to see Bethlehem and some of the churches, but most people are too scared to take the trails and walk. It's a shame, because it's safe here . . . as long as you don't get involved in politics.'

'Let's leave that till after Christmas,' I suggested. Saleh smiled and nodded in agreement. And so we walked in a straight line across the desert, simply enjoying the silence and the gravel beneath our feet.

There's something revitalising about just walking. I'd realised it in Jordan, and I knew that there was only one way to enter Bethlehem and that was on foot. My mind was clear and full of excitement about reaching the Holy City. I'd invited my parents to come and visit for Christmas. My brother, Pete, was coming too, along with a few other friends. I'm not religious, but I still like to go to church at Christmas and spend it with my family and I knew it would be a dream come true for my mum and dad, and it would be good to socialise with people I'd sorely missed.

The plan was to celebrate Christmas in Bethlehem, and then travel together to Jerusalem and reach Tel Aviv a week later in time for New Year. After months on the roads, I was ready for a party and what better way to bring in 2018?

That night we reached a steep gorge inside Wadi Kidron, and on the far side I saw the silhouette of the monastery of Mar Saba, a fifth-century church that resembled a Tolkienesque fantasy fortress. It was made all the more enigmatic by the tolling of bells and distant chanting of monks. It was too late to cross the valley and reach the monastery that night, so instead I suggested sleeping in a cave overlooking the river that crashed through the mountains below.

'It used to be an old hermit's cave,' said Saleh, as we climbed through a hole in the rock. He seemed reluctant and insisted on putting up his tent inside the cave, even though it was covered from the elements.

'There's snakes and scorpions here,' he said. I told him that it was too cold for them at this time of year, but he was having none of it. I unfurled my roll mat and sleeping bag and laid down on the bare rock. We were sheltered well enough, but later that night after the fire died down, the temperature dropped to freezing and the wind bellowed across the valley. A solitary candle light glowed from a window in the monastery. Despite being far from home, I felt a smile creep across my face in the blackness of the night. I imagined the Holy Family two thousand years ago, also crossing the Judean Desert, heading towards what was then a small provincial town, sleeping in caves along the way.

Even now, little has changed. Perhaps Mary and Joseph slept here, or maybe the three kings as they travelled from the East. I gazed across the Kidron Valley and looked up into the night sky. The moon shone through a silver cloud and as I peered further, straining my eyes, the stars began to erupt, one by one. One in particular stood out, to the south-west, some interstellar luminary glowing brightly. I had no idea what it was called, but maybe, just maybe it was the star of Christmas.

We woke at dawn to a cold chill and the drizzle of light rain. Heavy clouds filled the sky and Saleh and I were in agreement that we shouldn't hang around.

'Let's cross the valley and get to Bethlehem,' he said. The footpath wended its way down the cliffside towards the great walls of the monastery, which now at six a.m. was deadly silent. I had for some reason expected the monks to be up and about doing their prayers, but the enormous wooden gates were firmly shut as we passed. I was hoping to drop in for a cup of tea, but nobody answered.

'It's a Sunday,' said Saleh. 'Even monks need a lie-in.'

So we carried on up the other side of the valley, following a trail that led to a dirt track, which in turn led to a paved road. From the top of the hill the first houses came into sight – they were the outskirts of Bethlehem. We'd made it.

As we got closer, the suburbs closed in and I noticed the spires of churches and the minarets of mosques vying for the skyline. There were domes, pylons and palm trees competing with a jumble of electricity lines and water towers. Most of the city was grey, plain and filled with concrete and breeze-block apartments, and yet here and there were flashes of colour: bright green painted walls, golden roofs and red terraces.

Probably the most vibrant of all, though, were the profusion of murals covering the walls of the town. It seemed that every square inch had been used to make political statements; of which the most well-known, of course, were the murals of Banksy – the infamous graffiti artist, who had a particular interest in promoting Palestine. The side of an industrial-looking warehouse was covered in one of his most thought-provoking pieces – a huge spray-painted figure of a masked protestor throwing a vase of flowers.

But I'd already decided to leave off the political stuff until I'd had a chance to see my parents, and anyway, it was Christmas Eve, and there were other things on my mind.

Saleh led me through the streets of the city, up steep hills into the very centre of town, where crowds were already beginning to gather. It was lunchtime now and as we headed to Manger Square, Saleh managed to push past the beefed-up security forces, flashing a press card to try to keep me out of trouble. After all, I had a big rucksack and a big beard, and that combination doesn't go down that well with Israeli soldiers.

I'd sent my parents a message to ask them to meet me in Manger Square, the spiritual heart of Bethlehem, where a huge Christmas tree took centre stage, right next to the Church of the Nativity. We fought through the massing crowds that were flanked with stalls and vendors selling Santa Claus hats and inflatable reindeer. It resembled a funfair more than a holy city. Everywhere there were flashing neon signs advertising Coca-Cola; baubles and bunting dangled from every street sign and the whole place had a kitsch, moneymaking feel.

It wasn't what I'd expected at all. Pickpockets and hawkers riddled the crowds and swarthy men with cropped beards whispered as we passed, offering drugs and money exchange.

On one level, it felt like the last days of Sodom and Gomorrah and yet, despite the awfulness of the in-your-face commercialism, once you looked beyond the blow-up snowmen and candy-floss machines towards the church itself, I was reminded why everyone was here.

I resigned myself to the theatrics and sat down with Saleh to enjoy a mulled wine.

'Hello, son.' I looked up. My mum, dad and brother Pete were standing in front of me, along with Dave, Simon, Tom, Ali, Janessa, Lian and my old walking partner, who'd come all the way from Mexico, Alberto. It was suddenly a right old reunion. I felt abashed that I might have brought my parents to a place that sat dearly in their Church of England parish imaginations and ruined the illusion. If I had, they showed no signs of showing it.

'Lovely to be here, son. How's your trip been?'

I hadn't seen my family in months, and suddenly here were all my mates, too. I was almost moved to tears by the fact that people had travelled halfway around the world so that we could spend it together.

'Great, thanks,' I said. Now wasn't the time to go into detail. If we wanted to find a space inside the church, we had to move quickly.

I dropped my bag at a nearby hotel and changed into some semi-fresh clothes, although I had only a pair of walking boots, and I felt rather scruffy entering one of the holiest religious sites in the world dressed as a rambler.

Saleh, who was nominally Muslim, said that he wouldn't be joining me in the Church of the Nativity, but we agreed to meet in a couple of days, whereupon we'd travel to Hebron and Jericho before crossing into Jerusalem, and he handed me over to a local Arab Christian named Fadi, who had secured my group access into the church itself – a process that takes months to organise.

'We've got the best spot in the house,' said the young man, who led us through the throngs and into the main entrance, which was a tiny wooden door that led into a stone porch, where security scanners blocked the way. We were unceremoniously patted down and searched by armed sentries. The queue filed around the block, but Fadi was well known to the guards and pushed us all right to the front. The Englishman in me reeled at such impolite behaviour, especially at Christmas, but Fadi insisted it was the only way to get inside on the busiest night of the year.

'Everyone is waiting for the Pope,' he said, referring to the Orthodox Pope Tawadros II of the Archdiocese of Jerusalem. All around, hundreds of devotees stood huddled together under the shining golden chandeliers. The church was split in two, with the Catholic part on one side and the Orthodox, Armenian section on the other. There was hardly room to move, but Fadi pulled us deeper and deeper into the crowds, until we reached a tiny doorway at the heart of the church, where some ancient steps led to a dark grotto.

'Follow me,' he whispered. Our group held each other's hands so that we didn't get lost in the hordes. 'Watch your head,' he warned us. I ducked as we passed through the passage and down the narrow corridor to a small cave. This was what we'd come for.

The cavity was tiny and packed with pilgrims, monks in robes and nuns. There seemed to be lots of youngsters – perhaps they were the only ones able to sustain the intense heat and humidity of the rarefied atmosphere. They were all chatting and singing and praying, not at all in unison. There was still an hour and a half to go till midnight when the mass would start, but Fadi told us to hold our ground, so we formed a solid circle right next to the stone where Jesus was supposed to have been born in a manger. I looked up at the blackened roof of the cave, and it was very much a cave, and not the wooden stable of the type you see on Christmas cards.

We waited and waited, watching as more and more people filed in and crushed themselves up against each other. It was hot and sweaty, but even my father, who isn't the most patient of people, seemed to be enjoying himself. And when the clock struck midnight and a procession of priests came in to light the candles and lead the hymns, a sense of electric harmony seemed to fill the room. My dad got down on one knee and restated his wedding vows to my mother. Everyone hugged each other and wished complete strangers a Merry Christmas. I knew for my parents it was a lifetime ambition fulfilled, and for me, too, this signified perhaps the biggest reward of my journey.

I was with family, friends and surrounded by happiness and love. I knew that this would be a moment I'd remember forever. Later, we spilled out into the perfect night and drank wine and shared stories into the early hours. The next day we all went out, joined by Fadi and his family, for Christmas lunch at a restaurant overlooking the shepherds' fields. There wasn't any turkey on the menu here, and we had to resort to rice and deep-fried chicken drumsticks, but none of that mattered. We laughed and joked and wore silly Santa hats and got very drunk on local wine.

For all the hardships I'd been through over the last months, everything was worth it – the risks, the hunger, the endless deserts and fear of kidnap. For a moment nothing else mattered, and even home didn't seem so far away now. I was almost on the final leg of my journey and it was easy to forget that I was in the middle of one of the most controversial and fought-over places on the planet. As we drank wine and laughed at Alberto's tales, dark political clouds were forming on the horizon.

Only a few days before, Donald Trump had announced that the US embassy was to be relocated from Tel Aviv to Jerusalem, effectively declaring Jerusalem as the official capital of Israel. The protests had already begun, and in the towns and villages of the West Bank and Gaza, thousands of Palestinians were preparing for a fight, and the Israelis were also readying themselves for war. There was talk of a new *intifada*, or Palestinian uprising, and in the corner of the restaurant the newsreels played out familiar scenes of violence and death. It was a harsh reminder that death and destruction were never far away in the Holy Land, and I knew that trouble lay in store.

20

The Road North

If one soldier knew what the other thinks, there would be no war.

Jewish proverb

I remembered back to the first time I visited the West Bank in 2003. It was during the second intifada, when Palestinians revolted against the state of Israel. The construction of the West Bank wall had started the year before and tensions had been high. But after the death of Yasser Arafat in 2004, the stage of the conflict moved predominantly to Gaza. Israel had begun to withdraw settlers and soldiers a year later, but retained control over the airspace and the coast. In retaliation, Gaza began firing rockets at Tel Aviv.

Meanwhile in the north of Israel, an incursion into Lebanon, in response to Hezbollah attacks, escalated into another war there. A couple of years later, Israel invaded Gaza again to prevent the rocket attacks from Hamas, but in 2014, Egypt brokered a ceasefire. Though relations were still strained, things had calmed down to some extent in recent years. There had even been direct peace talks and global attention on the idea of a two-state solution.

But things had taken a turn for the worse in the last few days. After Trump made his announcement about moving the US embassy, Palestinians across the country had taken to the streets and started marching. There were protests and riots and stone-throwing and the Israel Defence Forces retaliated by shooting several of the agitators, much to international condemnation.

I met up with Saleh and Fadi again on Boxing Day. I wanted to try to get a balanced viewpoint of the current situation, and Saleh seemed to have his head screwed on, despite his very obvious physical and emotional wounds, caused directly by his involvement in Palestinian affairs. Fadi was a Christian and I hoped he would give me a more objective viewpoint too.

'I was sixteen when it happened.' Saleh showed me his mangled hand. 'They left a bomb for us in a kids' playground. It was inside a tennis ball.'

'Who did?' I asked.

'The Israelis, of course. I guess it was the soldiers who'd made their own IED. People think us Palestinians are the terrorists, but they don't realise what we're up against here. The Israelis really hate us. They think the land is theirs, even though there are millions of us living here just wanting peace.'

'What happened?'

'I picked up the tennis ball and it exploded in my hand. They arrested me and blamed me for making it. I was put in jail for being a bomb-maker. They said I was a terrorist! I was just a sixteen-year-old kid.' He looked at the floor, wiping away a tear.

'Nobody will ever understand what it is like to live like this, behind walls, prisoners in our own country. We aren't terrorists, we're just people who want to be free. Of course, there are some trouble makers – there are everywhere – but I'm against extremists, whatever guise they come in. I suppose I'm a Muslim, but I'm not religious. I became disillusioned with Islam when Daesh started cutting people's heads off. They give Islam a bad name, but I think any extremists should be expelled wherever they go. I will fight anyone that comes to limit my freedoms, whatever religion they claim to be.'

He shook his head in visible anger. 'I heard that in England the Muslims don't celebrate Christmas. Well, let me tell them this. They aren't real Muslims. Jesus is a prophet in Islam and we should all celebrate his birth.' He gripped my hand and looked me in the eye. 'Merry Christmas,' he said sternly, 'and screw anyone that says anything different.'

Saleh smiled. I thought back to the poor Pakistani shopkeeper in Glasgow, who'd been murdered by a fellow 'Muslim' the previous year for offering Easter greetings to his Christian customers.

'But the Israelis are extremists, too,' Saleh carried on. 'I didn't say Jews. I don't mind Jews, but it's the Zionists who want to invade our lands and build walls and separate us, that are the real extremists. Look at that.' Saleh pointed at the infamous wall splitting the city in two. I looked up – the concrete monstrosity towered above the buildings and made it impossible to see what was on the other side. It was ten metres tall, covered in razor wire and CCTV cameras. 'There's even an automatic gun with a camera that can scan Palestinian faces and shoots them automatically.'

'What?' I asked in horror.

Fadi stepped in, shaking his head. 'It's a water cannon, it doesn't fire actual rounds. It's when protestors get too close to the wall.'

Saleh was on the verge of tears. 'Don't defend them, they're evil, the Israelis. They try and kill us, even you Christians, they don't care.'

Fadi shrugged. 'Who do you think built the wall?'

'What do you mean? The Israelis built it,' I said, confused.

'Who physically built the wall, I mean? You don't think the Jews lifted a finger, do you?'

I hadn't really thought of that.

'No, it was built by Palestinian Arab labourers, who wanted the cash. They didn't really think through the consequences. And the land that's been "invaded" by the Jews. Do you think they actually turned up with guns and kicked people off? No, of course not. They bought it from Palestinians, who sold it for hard cash.'

'Traitors!' shouted Saleh.

'Maybe,' said Fadi, 'but it's true. You need to look at both sides of the story.'

I gazed up at the wall. It was covered in anti-Israeli, anti-American and anti-British graffiti. There were huge caricatures of Donald Trump and Theresa May and other political figures, as well as more nuanced messages and slogans. The faces of Israeli soldiers could just be made out from behind the veiled screens of the watchtowers.

Whoever was complicit with the construction, I couldn't help thinking that walls solve nothing.

'Let me show you the real problems,' said Saleh. 'I'm going to take you to Hebron and the front line.'

Fadi shrugged. 'Go with him and see. Make up your own mind, just be careful. You don't need me there. We Christians are a small minority here, and we live between the Jews and Muslims. We barely get a say in matters, but when you're done, make sure you go to Jerusalem and see where all this started.'

I told him that I would. For the next couple of days, Saleh took me on a tour of the West Bank. We drove along empty highways that linked the notorious Jewish 'settlements', usually villages on defended hilltops resembling some sort of medieval fortress, with large walls, razor-wire fences and security cameras on every pole. All the houses looked alike – white stone-clad apartment blocks stacked on top of one another.

The Palestinian villages on the other hand were more roughshod and most didn't have access to water and needed to store their own in rooftop bowsers. The wall, now an omnipresent sight in the geography of the Holy Land, appeared in segments. Contrary to what most people think, it isn't a wall that simply encircles the West Bank itself; the wall is actually a series of walls, totalling some 440 miles long, often flanked by trenches and strips of no-man's-land – and most of it is inside the agreed jurisdiction of the West Bank.

Saleh pointed at the vast concrete partition. 'It's the Israeli attempt to separate our own communities. People can't even go and visit their family inside their own land, never mind over in what they call Israel. If I want to get to Tel Aviv to see my cousins, for instance, I need to get a special permit. And because of my record, I'll never be given it. When I was a boy, we used to sneak over there, through the valleys – but now, because of the wall, it's impossible. I'm a prisoner in my own home.'

We entered the outskirts of the city of Hebron, famous for being one of the most visibly divided cities anywhere in the world. After parking the car in the old town, we walked through the souk, past rows of Palestinian street vendors. They looked impoverished and miserable. On the far side of the old city walls, we came across an abandoned row of shops.

'It's been left to rot since the nineties, when all the locals were forced out. See the dividing lines. This is the Palestinian side, and over there is where the Zionists live.' Saleh pointed to the far side of the wall, to where modern villas lined the hillside. Some of them were only feet apart from their Palestinian neighbours' houses, right beneath the Israeli apartments, but the difference was stark. All the Palestinian windows seemed to be covered in metal bars. We walked down an alleyway, too, where the sky was part-obscured by a wire meshing covering the entire street.

'What's that for?' I asked naïvely.

Saleh shook his head. 'Look up there.' He pointed to a row of Israeli houses directly above the Palestinian shops.

'They throw rocks at us,' he said mournfully.

'Who do?' I asked him.

'The Jews. The settlers. And not just rocks either. Bottles of piss and all their litter – they throw it at us like we are animals, so we built this cage to stop the rocks. Everyone thinks that we are the rock throwers, but no, not here, it's those bastards up there.'

'Why?'

'Because they hate us. They think this land is theirs. They want to kill us all, they want us all to die. One of my friends has a nine-year-old girl. Last year some Jews threw broken bottles from up there. That window, out of their own house, and it hit her in the face. Now she has a scar forever. She almost died. Can you imagine? They do that to their own neighbours.'

I looked to a gate between the two communities. There was a section of IDF soldiers manning a checkpoint.

'And that goes to the Israeli side of Hebron?' I asked.

'Yes, but I'm not allowed to go there.'

'What about me? Can I?'

Saleh nodded, 'Yes, you're British, you can travel freely. See how unfair it is. There is no communication between the two communities at all. Go over and see for yourself, if you like, because I'm not allowed.'

Saleh waited for me while I walked up to the roadblock, and an Israeli soldier waved me through when I showed him my passport. I wanted to see for myself what an Israeli Jewish settlement looked like. I'd only heard one side of the story and knew that I should see what the settlers themselves had to say on the situation, if anyone would talk to me.

The streets seemed empty, apart from soldiers in their body armour and helmets, who stood in pairs on each street corner. I'd heard there were eight hundred or so settlers here, and twice as many soldiers to guard them. Whatever poverty the Palestinians lived in, I thought that the Jews who lived here must feel imprisoned, too. But it was, of course, of their own making. I wandered around for a bit, while the soldiers eyed me with suspicion. I tried to talk to one of them, but he was barely out of his teens, spoke no English and merely shook his head. He was only a kid, and probably as ignorant of the Palestinians as they were of the Jews. Just as I was about to give up and walk back across the border to find Saleh again, a car screeched to a halt, almost sending me flying.

An angry man wound down the window and started shouting at me in English. He had a strange accent, which seemed out of place, and at the time I couldn't put my finger on where it was from. There was a passenger sat next to him.

'Who are you? Stop harassing the soldiers. Are you a journalist? What are you doing here?'

'I'm just visiting. I want to meet a settler,' I told him.

'Why? You media bastards only show the Arab story, you never show what it's like for the Jews. We're surrounded here, those Arabs breed like rabbits and steal our land.'

I could place the accent now. It was South African.

'But since you're here, I'll tell you what it's like,' said Brandon, who was from Johannesburg.

His friend Danny was also an immigrant, but lived in Tel Aviv. Brandon got out of the car and stood with his hands on his hips. He looked like he'd punch me if I didn't listen to him.

'I am a Zionist. Do you know what that means? It means I want my own country. I came here because Hebron is a Jewish city and it always has been. We need to stand strong and look after one another – where else can we go? We've been thrown out of every country we've ever lived in, but not this one. This is our ancestral home. There was never anything called Palestine until the sixties. When the Jews came here in the forties, there were just a few shepherds here. There is no such thing as Palestine, do you hear me?'

I told him that I was listening.

'Good. People think there is a solution to this mess. A two-state solution! What a joke. Golda Meir said that when Palestinians lay down their arms, there will be peace. If Israel lays down her arms, there will be genocide. And she was right. We will never forgive the Palestinian leadership for what they made us do to them. I have nothing against Arabs. I don't want a wall. I want my children to go to school with Muslims. I have Arab friends, I employ dozens of them. I fought against apartheid in South Africa, and I will fight against it here, but two states is not the solution. We need to become one people, the Arabs are welcome in Israel, and the sooner that wall comes down the better. But THERE IS NO PALESTINE,' he shouted. 'Go tell that to your people.' And with that he got back in his car and sped off.

It was hard not to think that he had a point. Walls help no one; the problem here was a lack of communication and dialogue. There are no good guys and bad guys, only people.

After the horrors of Hebron, it was time to head back via the city of Jericho. I hadn't had any time to explore it properly before Christmas, as I was in a rush to get to Bethlehem, so I decided to return and see the biblical city. It was here where the famous walls were brought down by the prophet-soldier Joshua in about 1400 BC.

It's said that Jericho is the oldest city in the world. Mind you, I recalled that the inhabitants of Erbil said exactly the same, and having been to Eridu in Iraq too, I was reminded that wherever you go in Arabia, you're faced with mind-boggling antiquity and stiff competition among claimants. I hadn't even reached Damascus or Byblos yet, and if I saw both of them, then I would have been to all five contenders.

At any rate, it is said that the original Jericho dates back over ten thousand years – twice as old as the Pyramids of Egypt – and it is rightly considered to be one of the starting points of human civilisation. Who knows, perhaps it will be known to future generations as the place where civilisation ended, too. It certainly felt that way when I arrived.

I'd just finished walking around the ruined remains of the ancient walls, admiring the stacks of pottery and beautifully carved stone works, against the faint sound of the call to prayer as it drifted over the morning birdsong, when Saleh came running over.

'Lev, come quick. Follow me.'

'What's happening?'

'Just follow me and you'll see.'

I ran down the path and jumped in the back of Saleh's car and he sped off down a deserted road running to the west out of town. There seemed to be a crowd gathering underneath a highway checkpoint. I looked around and noticed that it was

LEVISON WOOD

only men and teenagers. The old men were sitting around outside the closed shops, watching as the youths massed.

Suddenly a car overtook ours and screeched to a halt underneath a large billboard. A kid, no older than fourteen, got out and opened the boot. It was full of old car tyres and he began unloading them. Other boys came over to help and before long a gang of them were rolling the tyres across the road to form a barrier, while others nearby were pulling down fence posts and dragging bits of barbed wire across the highway.

'Is this what I think it is?' I said.

Saleh smiled. 'There's gonna be a protest against Trump and the Americans and how they're supporting Israel. Let's stick around and see what happens.'

Saleh left the car parked at a safe distance behind, and led the way through the crowd right to the front. Some men in their twenties were busily donning masks and hoods. One of them poured a can of petrol over the tyres and set them alight, causing an immediate plume of thick black smoke to swirl into the air. Suddenly the atmosphere was changed from a peaceful Friday morning into one of ominous violence.

The young men began to chant. '*Allahu Akbar*,' they shouted and started forward, ahead of their defensive line, through the smoke and down the road, which was still filled with the debris of previous battles. A few hundred metres away, I saw their objective. At the side of the road, hidden by a fence, was a small Israeli bunker, and I noticed two soldiers in green uniforms standing alert with their rifles trained directly towards us. One of them was on his radio.

The mob ran forward, taunting the Israelis, but never getting too close. Out came the slingshots – home-made rope and leather concoctions that hadn't changed in their design, or lethality, since the time of David.

284

How times had changed, I thought to myself. Here were the Palestinians (the name itself is only another pronunciation of Philistine), descendants of Goliath, now forever reduced to taking the slingshot as their own mantle. And three hundred metres away were David's children, forming up behind armoured cars. I saw the little green figures, which from this distance looked like toy soldiers – except they were armed to the teeth with vehicle-mounted machine-guns, grenade launchers and tear-gas cannons. The roles were very much reversed. But this didn't stop the Palestinians trying their luck.

'They come out every Friday,' said Saleh, wrapping his red and white headscarf tightly around his face. 'It's so they can't identify me.'

One of the youngsters came over and gave me a scarf, too. 'Wear this,' he said, before running forward to pick up stones to throw.

'Wouldn't that make me a target?'

Saleh laughed. 'We're all targets here. They don't know who you are. They'll still shoot you.'

The mob edged forward and the boys began to lob their stones towards the soldiers. The Israelis held their line. They simply stood and waited.

The Palestinians seemed to be enjoying themselves. Some of the boys were laughing and joking and whooping with joy when a stone landed on target. Were it not for the impending threat of being shot by an Israeli sniper, it would have all been rather fun and festive, and that's certainly the impression I got from the youths.

'We love it,' one boy in a black mask said.

'Do you know why you are here? What have the Americans done?' I asked, wanting to see if they had a particular agenda.

He simply shrugged. 'I don't care. I'm just here to fight the Israelis,' he said, before winging off another rock. I wondered if for them it was a rite of passage, or even simply a habit, formed in solidarity with generations of Palestinians over the last seventy years.

After an hour, the riot grew more intense.

'It's not a riot,' implored Saleh.

'Well, these guys are throwing stones,' I told him, 'it's not just a protest is it? And let's be honest, they did start it.'

'Stones! That's all we have,' Saleh responded. 'Stones, not guns. Look over there at the Israelis. You'll see what they have soon.'

He had barely finished the sentence when the shooting began. I instinctively ducked and the mob all cowered. I heard something ping against a signpost nearby.

Thank God, I thought. It was only rubber bullets. More shots came, sending the Palestinians into disarray; they darted around, zigzagging to avoid the incoming rounds, but always they regrouped and pushed closer and closer to the Israelis, trying their best to keep up the rock throwing. Saleh bent down and picked up a bullet. It was indeed rubber, but Saleh took out a knife and spliced it in half.

'Look,' he said, thrusting the thing into my hand. 'It's metal inside.'

As I felt the weighty little object in the palm of my hand, I saw that there was a steel core.

'If this hits you in the face, it will kill you,' he said, with a fire in his eyes that I'd not noticed before. He was clearly keen to show the Israelis' indifference to the suffering of the Palestinians. 'When you go home, tell your people what you see.'

There was another bang, this time louder, and I noticed a trail of smoke hurtling towards us. There was a whoosh and a thud, the object missing my head by a couple of feet.

'What the fuck was that?'

'Tear gas, run!' shouted Saleh, amid the clamour.

Stupidly I ran straight through the thick white smoke, as one of the Palestinian boys kicked the round across the road, and someone else tried to cover it with a cardboard box.

Boom . . . there was another one. The Israelis were soon firing dozens of gas grenades directly at us. My eyes began to stream – the poison kicked into effect straight away. The sensation of burning was indescribable. I'd felt it before, in the army, when we had to experience pepper spray and CS gas first-hand, but I'd forgotten how awful it is.

'Come on,' said Saleh. 'We've had enough fun here, time to go.'

I couldn't help but agree.

As we went back to the car, with tears still streaming down our cheeks, I took a backward glance at the mob clashing. The Israelis had begun marching down the road, backed up by their Humvees and tanks, and the Palestinians were retreating to the burning tyres.

'It will go on all night, or until they all get bored, then it'll start all over again next Friday.'

It seemed bizarre to go from one extreme to the other, but that is the norm in Israel and the Palestinian territories. I said goodbye to Saleh back in Bethlehem, and walked alone over the hills and through the checkpoints into the suburbs of Jerusalem, which is only a few miles away. Soon, the barren limestone hills gave way to high-rise skyscrapers, apartment blocks and congested highways. Only the ancient city walls and the glistening dome of Al-Aqsa Mosque marked this out as an extraordinary city from a distance.

I'd made it to the holiest of the holies – the place where it all began. For the next week, I explored the beauty, intricacy and wonders of Jerusalem. I visited the place of the crucifixion, and the tomb of Jesus in the Church of the Holy Sepulchre. I was allowed inside Al-Aqsa Mosque and stood inside the Well of Souls. I touched the foundation stones in the Roman crypts and walked through the Damascus Gate. I felt the engravings of Maltese crosses – Crusader graffiti a thousand years old. I tiptoed along the haunted corridors of Yad Vashem, the World Holocaust Remembrance Centre, and laid a hand on the Western Wall.

Every inch of this city has a story to tell and I trod in the footsteps of time itself. The names of those warriors, demi-gods and saints, all of whom had prayed, fought and died here, came to mind in the very fabric of the stones I touched. Abraham, King David, Solomon, Alexander, Nero, Jesus, Muhammad, Richard the Lionheart, Einstein, Montgomery, Churchill: they'd all been here at some point, and it's impossible not to be overwhelmed by the scale of this town's importance throughout human history. With the company of friends and family, the expedition took on a more leisurely pace, and for a short while transformed into a real holiday.

We rented an Airbnb in Tel Aviv for a few days and lounged on the beach, partying until the early hours and generally having a good time. New Year's Eve passed in a suitably hedonistic fashion, and we all welcomed in 2018 with a thick head and new-found resolutions. I was happy to be surrounded by good friends and new memories. The glistening prospect of the Mediterranean Sea, in its winter golden hue, was glorious and reminded me that the end was in sight.

I said goodbye to my friends and family as the waves crashed on the sun-kissed beach. I hoped to see them in a few weeks, but I knew that the journey wasn't over yet. There were two hundred miles still to go to reach Byblos in Lebanon, and a whole host of challenges lay in my path. But I felt revitalised, reborn almost. It was a New Year that promised a new future and I was ready to take on whatever lay ahead.

And so off I went, walking along the promenade of the corniche, past the new city and the financial district, through the suburbs and up towards the old Roman ruins of Haifa and the Crusader fortress of Acre. It was a journey into the past, and yet also into the future.

I stared in wonder at the impregnable walls of the Akko castle, looking as grand and imposing as when the Knights Hospitaller had built it. Sometimes I'd walk and other times hitchhike, getting lifts with random strangers of all religions. I met Bahai students, who showed me their temple in Haifa, standing on top of a mountain like a little garden of paradise, with beautiful trees and manicured landscapes. I followed the coast and went inland over rolling hills and beautiful forests. Jews, Christians, Muslims, Druze and a host of all sorts of immigrants seemed to live in harmony, side by side. It was a world apart from the segregation of the West Bank.

With every step north, the landscape grew more and more familiar. Ahead lay the misty highlands surrounding the Sea of Galilee, where I stayed for a short while on a kibbutz as the guest of Jewish farmers. Here in Kadarim, the residents were mostly old hippies, remnants of a bygone age: the kibbutzim – Jews from around the world, who'd given up everything to live the Zionist dream. They worked in collective farms, giving up their salary for a community. Each day they worked together, growing crops or raising chickens, and each night they ate, danced and sang together.

Shani, a lifelong kibbutznik, and Mark, an east Londoner who'd moved here in 1992, welcomed me in with impeccable politeness. Despite being adamantly Zionist, they were both sympathetic to the Palestinian people and I couldn't have hoped for nicer hosts. Their life was tough, living in simple, small houses that reminded me of an army barracks, and eating in a communal kitchen. And yet they seemed content. They smoked weed and played the guitar and neither of them yearned for city life.

Shani drove me north to Metula, on the Lebanese border. The little town was nestled in these windswept highlands, which were now on the very front line against Israel's closest foes, Syria and Lebanon, and had been a closed frontier for decades. I knew there was little chance of crossing into either, but I wanted to get to the border to see with my own eyes what lay ahead.

The last few weeks had been enlightening, and in spite of the political complications, they had been enjoyable. But now I was about to enter no-man's-land and perhaps the most dangerous part of my journey so far.

21

Running the Gauntlet

When the sun shall be folded up; and when the stars shall fall; and when the mountains shall be made to pass away . . . and when the seas shall boil; and when the souls shall be joined again to their bodies . . . and when the books shall be laid open; and when the heavens shall be removed; and when hell shall burn fiercely; and when paradise shall be brought near: every soul shall know what it hath wrought.

Holy Qu'ran

The rain was getting heavier as we arrived in Metula, the northernmost town in Israel, which by now was shrouded in thick mist, so that I could barely see more than a hundred yards. Shani parked the car on the main street and suggested we stop for breakfast in a little café.

'I know a guy here who you should speak to,' she said, as we dashed through the pouring torrent, and jumped over the puddles that were filling the gutter overflow.

'It's always like this in January. I bet it reminds you of home,' she said, smiling, as a friendly restaurateur opened the door and welcomed us to sit by the fire.

Professor 'E' was already waiting for us, huddled in the corner of the bar. We hung our drenched coats by the fireplace and Shani greeted her old friend.

'*Shalom.*' He shook my hand with a vice-like grip. 'Sit down.'

I did as I was told. I was sodden, cold and feeling slightly downtrodden at the prospect of having to abandon the expedition without reaching Lebanon.

'The border is closed,' said the professor, a balding man with a scruffy moustache. He looked every inch the academic, but his eyes betrayed a knowing look and a life of intrigue.

'It's impossible to go to Lebanon from here. There are Druze families who have been torn apart for almost seventy years and haven't been able to see their relatives. We can only peer over the barbed wire into the no-man's-land.' He nodded out of the window, which was streaming with the heavy rain. On the other side of the road, beyond the wire fence, I could make out a blurry forest that disappeared in the fog.

'That's the enemy. On the far side of that wasteland is Hezbollah territory. You simply can't go there. There are minefields and unexploded bombs from half a century of war and they still fire rockets at us.'

I pulled out my phone and showed the professor a map.

'What about Syria? Is there a way to cross over the Golan Heights?'

He stared me in the eye and laughed.

'You're a bold young man.' He raised his eyebrows. 'You want to go to Syria?'

'Well, I want to go to Lebanon, but if I can't cross here, then the closest way is over the Golan Heights to Damascus.'

'You're right,' he said, 'but the Golan has been the front line since 1967 and is also closed.'

I told him I knew that, but I'd also heard rumours that some people had been able to cross in recent years, taking advantage of the chaos in Syria.

'Who told you that?' He suddenly looked serious.

I shrugged, pretending to know more than I did.

'Are you military?' he asked.

'I used to be,' I said. 'British Army. Parachute Regiment.' I knew that in some circumstances, a bit of a nod to my armed forces background could sometimes come in handy.

He leaned closer.

'Let me tell you something,' he whispered. 'ISIS are just across that border. If they catch you, they will kill you in the most awful way.'

I looked at the map. I'd often wondered how ISIS had managed to keep a stronghold buffered up against Israel for so long, when most of their enclaves had already been destroyed by Assad's army and the Russians. I could understand how they'd still held the land in the east, where they had free access to roam across the desert to Iraq, and could easily hide in the vast wastelands. But to be able to hold out here, while surrounded by Israel and the Iranian-backed Hezbollah militias that dominated southern Syria, simply didn't make sense. I told Professor E as much.

He glanced over his shoulder and then back at me.

'It's important you know this. And it's off the record by the way, but I'm not just a professor at the university. I also work for a certain government agency, if you know what I mean?'

'Mossad?' I asked.

'*Shhhh*,' Shani whispered. Clearly, she already knew.

'Yes. And the reason I'm telling you that is because I know what is happening over there. We are supporting them.'

'Them?' I asked.

'Daesh,' he whispered. 'We, the Israelis, are giving them medical support, vehicles, transport and anything else they need. If they get injured, we even bring them over to our hospitals and treat them.'

'Why?' I asked, shocked.

He smiled. 'Because we'd rather have those savages on our borders than Hezbollah or Assad's lot. They give us a convenient buffer, so that Iran can't get so close. You might think it's unsavoury, but it suits us, for now at least.'

I shook my head in disbelief. I thought all the rumours were conspiracy theories, but apparently not. I'd heard it straight from the horse's mouth. Of course, he could have been lying, but why would he?

'So, what you've heard about people crossing,' he continued, 'it's true. But trust me, they aren't the best fellow passengers.'

He chuckled and took a sip of his coffee.

'It's time to leave,' said Shani. 'There's only one option for you. You need to go back south to Jordan and cross that way. You might get across the border into Syria and from there go via Damascus into Lebanon. If you stick to the main roads and get yourself a Syrian government guide, then you stand a chance of making it, but I can't see any other option.'

Later that afternoon, Shani and I travelled to the east, following the border zones higher into the Golan Heights, where yellow signs indicated minefields and old tanks rusted at the side of the road – a symbol of decades of conflict. There were abandoned Syrian army bases, now overgrown with weeds, and trenches dug into the hillsides.

Despite the clouds and heavy rain, I could hear the dull thuds of mortars landing in the distance and the rattle of machine-gun fire; a reminder that up here, war was never far away. IDF soldiers patrolled the razor-wire entanglements, the only sign of humanity in the fog of war.

Peering from the relative safety of a concrete bunker, I saw movement beyond no-man's-land, through the grey mist a few hundred feet away. I couldn't tell who it was.

'It might be a local shepherd, or it might be an ISIS fighter,' whispered Shani. 'Who knows.'

I was suddenly filled with a feeling of panic. I knew that what lay beyond was an unknown entity. Syria had been chaos for years, and the prospect of running the gauntlet through the most dangerous country in the world was reckless, bordering on insanity. I knew it was madness, but I also knew that I'd come this far. I could literally smell the cedars of the Maronite highlands, and in the far distance make out the misty mountains of the anti-Lebanon range. I knew that, beyond their snow-capped peaks, lay my goal, Byblos – that most ancient of cities, and my final destination.

I'd survived the war in Iraq, the empty vastness of the Empty Quarter Desert, death threats in Yemen and the pirate-infested seas of the Gulf of Aden. I'd realised my dream of following in Lawrence's footsteps and celebrating Christmas in the Holy Land. There was one final hurdle, and I knew I couldn't give up now.

The highway to As-Suwayda was empty, shimmering in the haze of the late morning sun. No one was out on the roads and the only cars I could see were those burnt-out, black shells riddled with bullet holes, now abandoned in ditches at the side of the road. I wrapped the keffiyeh tightly around my face and walked north to the edge of the Syrian city. I felt as if I'd almost come full circle now. Al-Malikiyah, where I'd begun this journey, was only four hundred miles away to the north-east. And where I was right now, it looked to all intents and purposes exactly the same.

I was twenty-five miles inside Syria. Twenty-five miles from the safety of the Jordanian border, from where I'd come the day before. I'd taken the detour Shani had recommended, all the way back through Israel, over the River Jordan to Amman, and then struck north via the refugee camp at Zaatari, where I'd seen first-hand the victims of this seven-year conflict. Virtually all the children I'd met in the camp had no memory of their country other than war and extreme violence. For them, the only reality was the confines of this muddy campsite.

I'd met women whose children had been killed, men whose houses were burned down and children who'd lost their parents. It was tragedy in its worst form. And yet, in spite of it all, I'd discovered a surreal sense of hope among those refugees. Almost all the people I'd met wanted to go home, as soon as the war was over, and everyone I met begged and pleaded with me to go and visit their country. I'd had my doubts, of course, on whether it was the right thing to do; whether it was ethical to go to a war zone for the sake of writing a book about a journey.

But whatever doubts I had were banished by the words of those children who'd only ever *heard* of Damascus, Homs and Aleppo, and had never been to their own homes – and their smiles as they begged me to go and see their country for myself. So, armed with an official Syrian visa, I'd somehow been granted access to travel from the southern border all the way to Palmyra, Homs and Damascus.

I'd arranged to meet Nada, a Syrian woman, who'd agreed to escort me for my journey. I was surprised that the Syrian government – the Assad regime – had granted me a visa, let alone given me unrestricted access to visit as much of the government-controlled areas as I pleased. There was no military escort, no spy following me around and no bugged hotel rooms (as far as I was aware). I'd been told simply that I could report on whatever I wanted without caveat, because they were very confident that they were winning the war and had nothing to hide. Despite this astonishing freedom, I was probably still expecting something other than the diminutive lady in her late fifties who turned up to greet me.

Nada was wearing a hijab and smoking a cigarette when she arrived in a large 4x4 at the edge of town.

'You must be the English traveller?' she said, in very good English with an interesting accent.

'It's Finnish,' she said. 'I married a man from Finland and I spend half my time in Helsinki, but come back to Syria to work. I quite like the variety and frankly it's important to make sure people outside know what's really happening in my country.' She laughed.

I think I'd been half-expecting some exotic young girl, who would try to honey-trap me and enlist me as an Assad spy. Instead, I found myself with this eccentric woman, who I couldn't work out at all.

'Get in the car,' she said, with the air of a bossy school mistress. 'We have work to do!'

'Work?'

'Yes. You have work to do and so do I. I need to get us through Syria in one piece, and you need to go home alive, so you can tell everyone what you see here. That's your job.'

I guess she was right.

We drove through the suburbs of As-Suwayda, past the turn-off for Daraa. The town of Daraa was still in rebel hands, and parts of it were held by ISIS factions.

'Over there, the war is still raging,' said Nada. 'But it'll be over soon. The army has taken most of it back.'

In fact, in the last few weeks, Assad's Syrian Arab Army had regained control of more than half of the country, leaving only a few small enclaves of rebel militias, which were supported by NATO. I knew for a fact there were US and British Special Forces operating on the ground, not too far from where I was now, indirectly fighting against the very army that I was meant to be under the protection of. Nada was employed by a Syrian tour agency and had been vetted by the government to ensure her allegiance, but she wasn't some blind follower of Assad either. She was well aware of the regime's failings, and of their brutality at times. But she was very clear on who she preferred running the country.

'Given the choice, what is better?' she said. 'A leader who is harsh but can keep the country together, or a bunch of Islamist nut-job fuckers with big beards, who love cutting heads off?' I couldn't quite believe the language used by the little lady.

'Those bastards are stupid medieval assholes who are only interested in guns and power. They call themselves freedom fighters, rebels, ISIS or whatever. They're all the same. They're just immature pricks, who enjoy fighting. People think that ISIS are the worst, but there's al-Nusra, Jamaat al-Islam and the two thousand other groups of barbarians we have to worry about, too.'

The highway cut through the desert like a rusty knife, its edges scarred with rubble and debris. We drove past the village of Thalia, where the Druze inhabitants had formed a mobilisation squad to fight ISIS and al-Nusra, and old women had defended their homes with antique rifles and ancient shotguns. This was where the civil war had begun, and it was here that it was coming to an end. Quite what had changed, apart from the deaths of more than three hundred thousand people, I wasn't sure.

It took two hours to reach the south-eastern suburbs of Damascus, where the road split into roundabouts and flyovers. For the most part, it was empty. Nobody travelled south out of the city, and the shattered eastern suburbs around Ghouta and Douma were still in rebel hands.

'*Insurgent* hands. Or better still, *terrorist* hands,' Nada reprimanded me.'They are holed up like rats.They're imprisoning civilians as hostages, so that the government won't bomb them. They kill children and try and blame it on the government, and fake gas attacks so that the army looks bad. But wait and see, they'll be done for soon and we'll have our country back.'

I noticed how all the bridges were draped with Syrian flags and the walls were covered with posters of the president, sometimes alone, other times accompanied by grinning images of his allies, the Ayatollah Khomeini of Iran and, of course, President Putin. There were also the faded outlines of the ISIS emblem, now scrawled over and crossed out. Here, there was no doubt who was winning the war – and it wasn't the people we'd backed.

'You're a historian, aren't you?' Nada said, as we were waved through yet another checkpoint. The Syrian army had the roads fully under control, and every few hundred metres was a machine-gun post manned by a grizzly-looking fighter. Some were in regular uniforms wearing berets, and yet more were clearly militiamen in any combination of khaki and camouflage.

'I've studied a bit,' I told her.

'Well, I've done my research,' she said, 'and so have the government. They know you're a British officer, and they know everything else about you. Assad knows everything.' She winked conspiratorially. I couldn't tell if she was trying to scare me or wind me up.

'Let's go to Palmyra,' she said.

I was suddenly filled with both a sense of excitement and terror. Palmyra was two hundred and fifty kilometres away . . . in the wrong direction. It was almost halfway to Al-Malikiyah, where I'd begun four months earlier, and what's worse, it was almost right on the front line against ISIS.

'It's safe enough,' said Nada. I couldn't quite reconcile the blasé look of nonchalance of this little lady and the fact that she was suggesting we drive halfway across the Syrian desert to go and see the ruins of this once important town.

The explorer in me won over.

'Let's do it,' I said, and she smiled.

It took four hours to reach the oasis of Palmyra. It rose from the desert like a mirage. Overlooked by a flat-topped mountain topped by the crumbling citadel, the ruins of the ancient Semitic palaces lay spread across the plains. Roman arches and Greek temples littered the landscape in a glorious explosion of antiquity. I'd heard the worst, that Palmyra was no more, having been taken twice by ISIS. But as I got closer to the site, now more or less abandoned, I was relieved to see that much of it remained intact. Even the savagery of ISIS, it seems, couldn't defeat the architects of history.

'Fuck them,' said Nada. 'See, now we have it back.'

We passed a checkpoint into the archaeological site itself. I noticed the soldiers on guard; they were a mixture of Syrian soldiers, Afghan and Iranian mercenaries, and there, in the shade of a lean-to shelter, stood guard a handful of white men in Russian uniforms. The lads were all blond with piercing blue eyes. They wore light green camouflage smock jackets over blue and white T-shirts, almost the exact same uniform worn by their predecessors in Afghanistan thirty years before. Technically these were the enemy, but for today at least, they were my guardians. More importantly, they were the guardians of Palmyra, having recently liberated the town from ISIS rule.

'Let's get out and walk,' Nada said, as we parked the car under the shade of a date palm.

And so, under the watchful eye of the Russians, we strolled around the ruins.

For me it was a mixture of emotions. The damage was clear to see. Gone was the Triumphal Arch, and the gateway to the Citadel. The Temple of Baalshamin lay in sad wreckage, along with the Great Colonnade, although I was glad to see that many of the columns remained, and that the Baths of Diocletian and the Senate were for the most part undamaged.

I looked up in wonder at the infamous Roman Theatre, which once held gladiatorial contests, and in equally grim circumstances more recently, the executions of hundreds of men by Islamic State terrorists. The Temple of Baal was utterly demolished, blown up by these modern-day philistines, and now only the central gateway remained, and it was here, standing on top of the rubble, that I met Tarik Al-Assad.

'He's the son of the old head of antiquities at Palmyra Museum,' said Nada, introducing us. 'He has quite a story to tell.'

The man shook my hand. I guessed him to be about my age, with closely cropped hair. A sad look in his eyes betrayed an unknown tragedy.

'I work at the museum in Damascus,' he said, leading me through the piles of two-thousand-year-old masonry. 'And my father was in charge here. His name was Khaled, please don't forget it.'

Tarik stared at me with a long silence. I nodded.

'My father loved this place, he worked here for forty years. He was a historian and a hero, you know, it was because of him that Palmyra became a UNESCO world heritage site. When Daesh came here and took over, they arrested him, and me too. For weeks we had been taking the antiquities to a place in Damascus for safe keeping, because we knew that Daesh would steal them and sell them in Turkey. So when they came, my father told me to run and take my mother and brother away. So I escaped one night and hid from them.'

He paused. 'But my father refused to leave, even though he could have. He said that his place was here in Palmyra, even if it meant he had to die. Daesh were stupid and thought there was gold hidden in the ruins and they beat my father and asked him where he had hidden it. When he told them that there was no gold, they started blowing things up. Then when they realised it was just old stones, they asked him where the antiquities were. He refused to tell them anything.'

Tarik stuttered his words and I noticed a tear running down his cheek.

'One day, on the eighteenth of August 2015, they took him to the crossroads by the mosque, just over there.' He pointed beyond the gate to the shattered remnants of the modern town, where a bullet-strewn minaret jutted miserably into a grey sky.

'They forced him to kneel down on the pavement and ...'

Tarik looked at the floor and wiped his eyes, before looking directly into mine.

'They cut his head off with a sword.' He winced and gazed off into the distance and fell into silence. Nada was looking intently at me, as she stood in the background. 'He was eighty-three years old.'

Suddenly Tarik pulled out his phone from his pocket and opened up his file of photographs. He forced the phone into my hand. 'Look at that.'

I peered at the screen with disbelief. The image was of a body, hanging upside down from a traffic light, with a decapitated head on the floor in a pool of blood underneath on the pavement. The bloated and battered head still wore a pair of broken spectacles.

'It's my father,' said Tarik, with a forced smile. 'I still have his glasses.'

Shocked, I didn't know what to say, and Tarik, the man whose father had been murdered for no crime other than defending his country's heritage, put his hand on my shoulder as if to comfort me.

'Just remember his name, that's all I ask. Khaled Al-Assad.'

The clouds darkened and it was time to leave.

22

The Final Battle

In peace, sons bury their fathers. In war, fathers bury their sons.
Herodotus

A Russian soldier stopped us at the checkpoint west of Palmyra, next to the ancient Druze castle of Tadmur.

'*Dobry den*,' he grunted in Russian. Good afternoon.

He asked for our papers and Nada flashed our regime press cards. He eyed my passport as I looked at him. I tried to decipher the badges on his uniform, to figure out which unit he was in. I knew from my intelligence sources that the two main groups of Russians in the region were mercenaries from a mysterious private army called 'Wagner group', as well as Chechen militiamen drawn from the elite ranks of the Spetznatz. The Russians had been supporting Assad with air strikes on rebel units, and in recent months had deployed Special Forces troops and private fighters on the ground to act as advisors and military police.

I looked at the soldier. He couldn't have been a day over twenty-one and I suddenly felt very sorry for him. He couldn't have grown a beard, even if he'd wanted to, and looked hot and uncomfortable in his uniform and body armour, surrounded by a ragtag bunch of Syrian commandos. A couple of miles down the road, we stopped at a petrol station to refuel our car and I went to get a cup of tea from the shop.

As I was waiting to be served, a shiny white coach pulled up outside and dozens of armed men piled out. Like the Russians, most of them seemed to be in their late teens and early twenties, but these men were definitely Arabs, and most of them wore long beards and some had long curly hair tied up with black bandanas.

I froze and for a second I thought that ISIS might have turned up. I shuffled into the corner to try to make myself less conspicuous. Luckily, I had a decent beard and blended in pretty well as a Syrian, but still I admit that for a moment I feared that I'd finally pushed my luck too far.

'*Salaam, kaif halak*,' said a young man, 'how are you?', swinging an AK-47 over his shoulder. He wore olive-green webbing around his chest and grenades dangled from his pockets.

'Wa alaikum as-salaam,' I replied.

'*Min ayi balad ant?*'

I only had a very basic understanding of Arabic, but I knew he was asking where I was from. There was no point in lying.

'England,' I said, fearing the worst.

The lad broke into a grin. 'Welcome!' he said in English. I love England.'

Phew, I thought to myself. 'Where are you from?' I asked him back.

He stared at me with an earnest look and held my gaze for a few seconds before replying.

'ISIS,' he said solemnly.

My heart skipped a beat and I was silent. He then started

laughing uncontrollably.

'Just kidding, I'm from Lebanon.' He said, enjoying the fact I almost shat myself. 'We're Hezbollah.'

'Oh, nice to meet you,' I said with a gulp.

'We're off to the front. Should be fun.'

'Yes, I'm sure,' I said. 'How long for?'

'This deployment is only a few weeks. I've just finished school, so it's like my gap year.'

He smiled and patted his machine-gun, before handing me a Coca-Cola.

'Here, it's on me. Add me on Facebook, I'm coming to England soon. I've just finished my application form for Leeds University.'

With that a burly sergeant came in and shouted for the troops to get back on the bus and they all shuffled out, finishing their cigarettes and waving goodbye.

It occurred to me just how complicated this war was. Here we had Russians supporting pro-Assad militias, a stone's throw away from the rebel Free Syrian Army, supported by Turkey, the US and the UK. Fighting them, to the east were the Jaish al-Fatah and Tahrir al-Sham, factions of al-Qaeda, directly funded – *allegedly* – by Saudi Arabia and Qatar, both of whom, of course, are funded and supported by Turkey, the US and the UK.

Iran, a firm ally of Assad, was sending in Afghan Hazara tribesmen to fight alongside Hezbollah from Lebanon, in order to defeat the al-Nusra Front – an organisation sponsored by Qatar, which is, believe it or not, a firm ally of Iran, and bizarrely, a mediator for the Taliban in Afghanistan, who really do not like the Hazara.

The Kurds, to the north, were still being bombed and invaded by Turkey and yet were themselves being helped by the US and the UK to fight against al-Nusra and of course, ISIS, who, if Professor E was to be believed, were being directly assisted by Israel.

What a bloody mess.

We drove west towards Homs and reached the city by nightfall. It was almost dark when we found ourselves in a small hotel next to a fried chicken restaurant, on the main avenue that led to the old town.

'We'll stay here for the night and we'll meet Hayat,' Nada told me.

Hayat was a government official, who worked for the Ministry of Information. She had offered to show me the devastation of the city, which had seen some of the heaviest fighting in all Syria after being under siege for three years.

After a troubled sleep, punctuated by sporadic gunfire in the distance, we woke early and drove down towards the district of Warik, where we met Hayat, a middle-aged woman wearing thick makeup and a black leather jacket. Her eyebrows were painted on and she greeted me with a forced smile, stained with a lifetime of cigarette smoke.

We walked together for some time along a road that was flanked by now derelict gardens and allotments, overgrown with weeds. For some reason it reminded me of home: Stoke-on-Trent, when I was a boy in the eighties. I remembered going for walks with my grandfather in Hanley Park and, remarkably, the view was almost identical.

Hayat told me about the war, about how the 'terrorists' had taken control of Homs in 2011 and dug in for three years, before it was finally 'liberated by the government'. I wondered how her version of the story would differ from that of one of the thousands of Sunni residents who tried to rise up against Assad's brutality.

'I want to show you the truth,' she said, as we rounded a corner. I stood still in horror as the panorama before me assaulted my vision. Two ragged children were frolicking in a playground, holding each other's hands as they slid down a dirty orange slide. The roundabout creaked as it spun. Behind the park was a scene of the kind of devastation I hadn't seen since Mosul. The entire neighbourhood had been demolished; rubble was piled up fifty feet high and not a single building had remained unscarred.

Whole apartment frontages were ripped apart by shells and bombs, leaving a naked skeleton of grey, forlorn destruction. The streets of the old city were filled with bullet cases, burnt-out cars and twisted relics of former peace; dishwashers, sofas and chairs were strewn across the road. In some waste ground, a Ferris wheel stood as a grisly monument to what seemed like time before the apocalypse. We wandered through the dereliction. It was a scene all too familiar.

This was the Syria of the news reports, it was the Middle East we'd all become accustomed to, but even such indoctrination could never prepare my own brain for the incomprehensible scenes of such savagery and violence. This was Dresden and Hiroshima after the bombs had fallen. This was real life Armageddon. Death and annihilation was everywhere; school textbooks littered the rooms, alongside filthy teddy bears, ripped Qu'rans, shattered pots and soiled nappies. Shoes and torn clothes were mixed with masonry and broken plaster, like some gruesome modern art installation.

The walls that were still erect were all sprayed with rocket holes and the graffitied slogans of the various fighting groups that had battled among the ruins over the years. Hayat began to sob as she gently picked up a family photograph album from the floor of a house. She dusted it off and opened it up, her tears dripping into the mummified pages.

'Dead. All of them,' she cried. 'Thousands of people dead, and for what?'

She shook her head and placed the book down next to a children's toy – a fluffy smiling heart.

It seemed the old city was empty, utterly abandoned, but no. The little children we'd seen in the playground ran past us and scuttled up the shell of a staircase into the rubble and up some stairs.

'People are starting to return, but look at what they must live among,' said Nada, placing a hand on Hayat's shoulder.

I turned around, hearing the squeaking noise of a bicycle wheel. It was an old man, with a vacant look in his eyes, pushing an ancient bike with a makeshift basket filled with empty bottles and metal tools. He nodded with sadness.

'Where are you going?' asked Hayat.

'Home' was his simple reply. I followed him along the street as he picked his way through mountains of warped debris.

The word echoed through my mind, as I watched the poor man enter the charred hole that had been his porch. He shone a torch into the murky shadows of what was once a room, and was now just a void. 'We have no water. Please tell your people to send us water,' he whimpered.

'Yalla,' muttered Hayat. 'Leave him to his misery. There's nothing we can do here.'

She tugged on my arm and I walked away, feebly pressing forty dollars into his hand, as the only gesture I could think of.

We left the tragedy of the old city in the half light of the afternoon, as the sun disappeared below the jagged remnants of the shattered mosque. Hayat insisted that we stay with her in her apartment. Nada agreed that it was the safest place, and so we followed her in our car to a part of the city that seemed to have avoided at least some of the fighting. The building was grey and reminded me of the kind of London council flats that were built in the 1960s. The elevator didn't work, so we trudged up the stairs to where Hayat let us in.

Her flat was small and grungy. Fluorescent strip lighting and exposed bulbs dangled from the ceilings, giving the place a harsh, industrial feel. I noticed that in one corner was a shrine: a display cabinet with an ornate gilded Qu'ran and prayer beads, and some framed verses of the hadiths. In the other corner of the room was another display cabinet, similar to the first, and yet this one was filled with Christian figurines. There was a crucifix leaning against the wall, and a little porcelain statue of the Virgin Mary. I had no idea if Hayat was Muslim or Christian, and I supposed it didn't really matter. I was a guest in her house and she was glad to have us.

She fumbled about in a pantry and came back with two beers and a bottle of arak. Nada didn't drink, but Hayat poured me a double and we toasted peace in Syria. I saw that on the walls of the living room was a third shrine, a photograph of a young man in uniform. I'd seen these kinds of pictures before – they often adorned the roadsides in Middle Eastern war zones – shrines to the martyrs of the war.

'Who is he?' I asked.

'My son, Mohamed.' Hayat smiled, wiping away another tear. 'He was killed three years ago in Daraa by Nusra. He was twenty-one.'

The tales of horror were endless, it seemed. Hayat told me how he'd volunteered to fight for the Syrian army after the opposition took the south.

'He wanted to fight for his country and not see it overrun with terrorists,' she said. 'He joined with his friends and they were all in the same unit, and then one day, in August 2014, he found himself surrounded by the enemy in a house. He did what any good boy would do, and called me on his mobile. He tried to reassure me that everything would be okay, but I knew by his voice that it would be the last time I ever heard from him. He said goodbye. I heard a bang. Then the line went dead.'

We sat in silence. I was welling up with emotion myself at the sight of this poor woman who'd lost her son, regardless of which side she was on. I asked if she would ever forgive them.

'Forgive them?' She shook her head and fell silent. A minute passed, and I thought perhaps I should never have asked. I felt rather self-conscious as she mulled over my dumb question.

'They're probably dead anyway,' she eventually responded. 'They were young boys, too, I'm sure. All dead. I must forgive them, I must forgive all those who push for war, and I must forgive myself. Hatred gets us nowhere. I must forgive, because otherwise all of this was for nothing. All we want for now is peace. I have to forgive for the sake of Syria.'

That night I was given the only spare bed in the house. It was that of Mohamed, Hayat's son, a twenty-one-year-old soldier. I didn't really know what to feel about sleeping in his bed, surrounded by his belongings. On the bedside table and a desk were spread out his meagre effects: army dog tags, childhood photos, a military belt and his beret, some toys, and medals for sporting achievements and, leaning up against the wall, his rifle, a polished AK-47, still loaded with a full magazine of 7.62 rounds.

Despite being on the front line in Syria, sleeping in a dead man's bed, surrounded by those who were technically the enemy,

I felt a surge of empathy and understanding such as I'd never experienced before. I knew that I'd never take anything personally again. If that woman could forgive the people who killed her son, then I could certainly let go of whatever insignificant niggles were bothering me. I'd seen and experienced it all and knew that life would never be the same again.

When I got home, I'd make sure never to take anything for granted. I'd tell those around me how much they meant to me, I'd forgive those who'd hurt me and I'd never lose my temper again. I realised there and then that nothing else matters but kindness, compassion, forgiveness and love. I slept soundly that night as machine-guns and rockets drilled the horizon, and I dreamt of home. I felt myself holding my grandad's hand as I walked through the green and brown allotments of Hanley Park in Stoke-on-Trent, beneath a grey sky.

23

Land of Milk and Honey

Behold, I will liken you to a cedar in Lebanon, with fair branches and forest shade.

Ezekiel 31:3, *The Holy Bible*

Legend has it that the Prophet Muhammad looked down on Damascus from Jebel Qassioun, the mountain to the north-west of the city, and refused to descend, saying that man could only enter the gates of Paradise once.

Perhaps because of the desperation I'd seen for much of my journey through Syria, I felt wholly unprepared for what I was about to encounter. I arrived at the gates of Damascus expecting the worst. Nada drove me through the now familiar chicane of military checkpoints and police barriers that blockaded every entry point into the capital city.

'Take off your seatbelt,' she told me, as we approached the armed sentries.

'Why?' I asked, confused. She raised an eyebrow, as if to tell me not to ask stupid questions.

'Because they'll think you're a terrorist, of course. Only terrorists wear seatbelts.' She tutted.

'Of course,' I said, slightly bewildered.

High-rise buildings and concrete apartment blocks flanked the main thoroughfare through the sprawling suburbs, yet these,

313

unlike in Homs and Palmyra, were unscathed and bustling with life. The streets were busy, and traffic jams slowed us down as we moved closer to the fabled walls.

'We'll have to walk from here,' said Nada, parking the vehicle in a car park just outside the vast stone blockades. Here, like everywhere else, Assad's face loomed down from billboards and posters and the Syrian flag fluttered from every lamppost. Soldiers lurked at every corner, looking alert and menacing. It wasn't surprising – the war raged on in the Damascene suburb of East Gouta, and we'd heard that last night the rebels fired mortars into the city from only two miles away, killing five civilians. There were rumours of more chemical weapons being used, and nobody seemed to know who the culprit was. It was just part of daily life here. But Nada assured me that inside the walls, things were different.

We entered the old city via the Al-Hamidiya Souq, and immediately found ourselves thrown into the chaos of the market. Hawkers and vendors sold dates and fruit piled three feet high. Men in red waistcoats and Fez hats poured coffee from silver pots, and the whole street smelled of the aroma of frankincense, spices and perfumes, which gave the atmosphere a heady excitement. As I walked through the covered bazaar, its black roof pockmarked with bullet holes from distant conflicts, rays of light shone through and the roof seemed to sparkle like a firmament of stars.

I think I'd finally found the Arabia I was looking for and it was here, in the most unlikely of places. At the end of the market stalls, enormous columns flanked the gateway – relics of Roman civilisation – and these, in turn, opened up to reveal a cobbled square and the vast citadel, dominating the wooden balconies and warren of alleyways that snaked through this most ancient of cities. The great Umayyad Mosque glistened like a jewel in the centre of the jumble, where sparkling marble courtyards glimmered in the afternoon sun above the tomb of John the Baptist. Golden rays slanted through the warren of passages and the whole scene reminded me of some medieval theatre.

Among the labyrinthine streets were hidden gems: secret hammams, smoky coffee shops and smiths' forges selling silver, bronze swords and antique Damascene steel. There were still tourist shops open, all of them lined with twinkling fairy lights. They sold the usual array of Bedu carpets, old coins and postcards from a bygone era. The shopkeepers sat outside on little plastic stools, smoking shisha pipes, still waiting after seven years for the tourists to come back.

'One day they will return,' said Nada. 'They never miss a day, these shopkeepers. They live in hope that the war will end, and each morning at seven o'clock the shutters go up and they light a bowl of frankincense to ward away evil spirits. They never sell anything, but at least they have hope, and that, these days, is in short supply.'

'Come, let me show you something,' she said, leading me down a stone staircase, around the manicured gardens of the fortress and into a busy alleyway. The sun was about to set and a flicker of green lights seemed to erupt around the city. They were the lights of the mosques and within the minute the call to prayer sounded over the minarets.

As we weaved through the crowds of locals, I took stock of the sheer liberality of the place. School girls in knee-length skirts were out in little groups taking selfies on their smart phones; some of them approached me and began to flirt outrageously. I couldn't quite believe it, but Nada just laughed. 'People here have always been liberal. Look around, I'm pretty much the only woman wearing a hijab. Nobody minds here, Assad has kept this place secular and he's the only one protecting the minorities: Christians, Yazidis and Druze. Imagine if the Islamists had taken over, you wouldn't see any of this.'

She pointed to a man in a snazzy waistcoat and tight trousers, strutting along the pavement. He was incredibly camp and I assumed gay. She was right, there's no way he'd be allowed to dress like that under any of the other groups vying for power. Nestled between mosques and churches were a plethora of wine bars, fancy restaurants, pubs and nightclubs, preparing for the evening's festivities. There were no tourists and hadn't been for years; these hipster hangouts were very much for the locals – Christians and Muslims alike.

Regardless of what the pious might like to think, in my experience at least, alcohol is drunk widely and more often than I'd expected, openly throughout the Middle East. But here in Damascus, where life came and went easily, the youngsters took their nightlife seriously. Dance music throbbed from hidden cellars and young men and women sat in street cafés smoking shisha pipes, without a care in the world, it seemed – even as the sound of mortars thudded in the distance just a few miles away.

'What did you expect?' said Nada. 'We can't let a war get in the way of our lives. People need normality. They need to carry on. People still go to work, do their chores, fall in love, get married and have children. They party, they go out, they're allowed to have fun. Come, see that there.' She pointed to a coffee shop in the street, where locals had begun to sit down. 'Let's get a seat before it gets too busy.'

And so we sat down at a table in the corner of the room. It was straight out of a scene from the *Arabian Nights*; the walls were filled with swords and treasure and the wooden beams revealed a history dating back hundreds of years.

'It's the oldest café in Damascus, it's called Al-Nawfara, which means fountain, because this used to be an old bath house,' said Nada.

Old men smoked shisha in their dishdashas, sitting next to off-duty soldiers, and there were families, too. All sorts of people had come to sip *qahwa* – Arabic coffee – or sweet mint tea. But the real reason they flocked here wasn't for the beverages, it was for the entertainment.

'He's here,' whispered Nada, with an air of reverence. Through the door walked an old man with a wise face, dressed in a long, brown cloak hemmed with gold. On his head he wore a tassled red Fez and he carried a long silver sword in his right hand.

'Who's that?' I asked, in astonishment at the sight of this Ottoman apparition.

'His name is Ahmad Tayab, the *Hakawati* of Damascus. He's a storyteller.'

The old man, whose graceful entry was greeted with whoops and cheers by the audience, sat down on a raised throne at the back of the room. He adjusted his robes and made himself comfortable, causing the crowd to fall silent with a mere cough. He had the air of a warrior king, like Odysseus returned from his ordeals – about to recite glorious poetry. And that is exactly what he did.

Ahmad Tayab opened a large old book that was rested on his lap and he began to read, quietly at first; but then with growing alacrity and volume, he regaled the crowd. Nada translated for me, but I cursed myself for my lack of Arabic. If ever I wanted to know this elusive tongue, it was here and now, listening to the tales of the *Hakawati* in Damascus.

'It's a story from the *Arabian Nights*,' she said in a hushed voice, glowing with pride. 'It's called the tale of the ruined man.' She winked at me. 'I think you'll like it.'

Nada waited for the storyteller to finish his sentence before each interpretation.

'There was once a man from Baghdad. He was very wealthy, but prone to bad luck and for whatever reason he lost all his money and became so poor that he was forced to work in back-breaking hard labour. He became sad and fed up with his life, until one day he fell asleep and had a dream. In the dream a voice came to him and it told him to go on a journey to Cairo.'

Nada raised her eyebrows. 'Cairo, in Egypt.'

I nodded and begged her to continue.

'Well,' the story continued, 'the adventure would be long and dangerous and fraught with many perils, but at the end of it he would find his fortune and live happily ever after. "Go and seek it," the voice had said to him.'

I felt myself drifting into the story, as Nada spoke gently in English, recounting the undulating verse of Ahmad Tayab, the storyteller. With each sentence he raised his sword and slapped it down, giving a dramatic whoosh, and the crowd erupted with joy and laughter.

'So, the poor man,' Nada continued, 'he listened to the voice in his dream and went on an adventure to seek his fortune. It took him a long time to reach Egypt, but when he did finally make it to Cairo he was so tired he fell asleep in a mosque on the outskirts of town. As fate would have it, that night some thieves entered the mosque and used it as a base from which to break into the house next door with the intention of robbing it.'

The sword whooshed through the air again, amid chants of *Ali Baba, Ali Baba!* Nada grinned.

'The neighbours heard the robbers and awoke, scaring them off. The constabulary were called and the guards searched high and low, but could not find the thieves. They did, however, find the man from Baghdad sleeping in the mosque. Of course, they arrested him and beat him to within an inch of his life, until the sheriff arrived to question him.

'"Where are you from, you thief?" the sheriff asked the man.

'"Baghdad," he said solemnly.

'"And what brought you to Cairo?" asked the sheriff.

'"I saw in a dream one who said to me, "Thy fortune is at Cairo; go thither to it." But when I came, the fortune that he promised me proved to be the beating I had of thee," said the man from Baghdad.

'The sheriff laughed out loud, and said, "Oh ye of little wit, three times have I too seen in a dream one who told me of a house in Baghdad." The sheriff went on to describe the house and that in the garden there was a fountain, under which was buried a great deal of treasure.

'"In my dream, the voice told me to go thither and take it," he said, shaking his head. "And yet I didn't go, for fear of making such a foolish journey. But thou of little wit has journeyed from place to place, on the faith of a dream, which was but an illusion of sleep."

'Then the sheriff gave the man from Baghdad some money to help him get home to his native land and freed him at once. The man from Baghdad went home, and on the way, he pondered the dream of the sheriff. When he returned to his own city, he followed the sheriff's directions to the letter and found that they led him to his own home. Of course, he went into his house and into the garden to his fountain, where he dug and dug and found a great deal of buried treasure.'

Nada turned to me and smiled, 'And thus Allah gave him an abundant fortune.'

She finished the translation just as Ahmad Tayab, the storyteller of Damascus, slammed the book closed and raised his sword triumphantly.

Even here in the midst of a war, the power of tradition and storytelling had triumphed against all odds. Life goes on, I thought to myself. And the tale had reminded me that mine must, too, and it was time to go home.

Nada took to me to the Lebanese border, where we said goodbye at the side of the main road. In a way, I was sad to be leaving Syria behind. In spite of all the tragedy, I'd come away with a deep sense of hope. I was under no illusion that there would not be many more months of conflict in store for that poor country, and that inevitably it would end as it started, with Assad still at the helm. But the human spirit seemed to live on in a way that I could never have imagined.

I hitched a lift from Chtaura at the southern end of the Bekaa Valley towards the town of Baalbek. I felt a weight drop from my shoulders, as I looked around to see vineyards and beautiful valleys. To the west was the faint outline of the Lebanon Mountains, my final obstacle to cross before reaching the shores of the Mediterranean. I felt as if I'd left the Middle East and re-entered Europe. Despite the ominous presence of Hezbollah flags fluttering from telegraph poles, it had an entirely different feel to where I'd come from. Green fields replaced sandy deserts, and tall oak and pine trees replaced the ubiquitous palm.

The minibus I rode in dropped me off at the turning to Baalbek, and I decided to walk into the outskirts of town. This was the heartland of Hezbollah, and I'd had mixed reports about how I might be treated. Of course, the official line was stay well away, and I'd read all the horror stories of kidnappings, murder and terror attacks. But the team back home had been looking into the reality of the threats and we'd all come to the conclusion that it should be safe enough to transit the Bekaa Valley, and in any case, it was the best route to Byblos.

As it happened, I was pleasantly surprised by the welcome I received. As I was walking down the road, I came by a row of grocery shops, where a local man invited me in for a tea. When I explained that I was hitchhiking to Baalbek and had just come from Syria, he made a phone call, and after five minutes one of his relatives turned up in a BMW car. He was a young lad who spoke good English.

'My name is Hadi,' said the twenty-five-year-old. 'I will take care of you here.'

'Thanks,' I said, getting in the car. We drove through the village to his house, a two-storey villa on the edge of the plain. It had good views to the east towards the Syrian border, as well as across the valley to the mountains. From here, beyond the lush vineyards, I could see the snow-capped peaks glistening in the afternoon sun.

'*Marhaba*,' he said, with a kind smile, welcoming me into his parents' house.

'My parents live in the city, but we have this as a second home for when family and honoured guests want to stay.' It was plain and it seemed unfinished from the outside, as if they were waiting for something.

'The war over there slowed things down,' Hadi said, 'so we didn't want to spend all of our money on the house till Daesh was defeated. You know, they came within a mile of here.' He pointed out the window to the waste ground outside.

As I sat down, some more boys entered.

'These are my brothers, Hussain and Alushi.'

The elder one was perhaps in his early thirties and wore a leather jacket; the younger one seemed very shy and gave a respectful nod in my direction. Hadi shouted something in Arabic and the youngster disappeared off to bring tea and a platter of fruit.

'He's only sixteen,' said my newfound friend, 'but he's very good at things.'

'What things?' I asked.

'Anything. He's a genius,' said Hadi, with a smile. 'Play the piano,' he said to the boy.

Alushi nodded and sat down at a grand piano that was in the corner of the room. He began to play. Suddenly Beethoven's Piano Concerto No. 5 filled the room, played with such exquisite delicacy and grace that it was impossible to imagine that it emanated from the fingers of a sixteen-year-old. It was as if the entire Middle East's problems melted away all at once. I sat in dumbstruck awe, as the lad seamlessly transitioned into Vivaldi's Four Seasons and the notes danced off the bare walls and out across the fields.

'What would you like me to play?' he asked, expressionless.

I thought for a second. Why not my old Regimental march?

'Wagner. "Ride of the Valkyries", do you know it?' The boy shook his head.

I hummed the tune for him and in less than thirty seconds he was playing it almost perfectly, much to the delight of his older brothers.

'He's like this with everything. Sports, Alushi is the best gymnast in Lebanon, and can run faster than anyone. Maths, he's a freak and can do all the numbers. If only we had some money and we could send him abroad, he'd win a Nobel prize.'

With that, Hadi poured us some tea. I asked him more about the threat of ISIS.

'You must have been terrified, if they were that close.'

'Of course,' he said, 'but we protected ourselves. You know, we have Hezbollah.'

I knew that this was Hezbollah territory, and that it was a designated terrorist group, sponsored by Iran and used in Syria to support Assad, but I wasn't fully aware of how they operated inside the country alongside the legitimate government. Lebanon is a pretty progressive country, with an elected democratic republic, and the constitution insists on a fair representation of the ethnic and religious factions.

It's also the most ethnically diverse population in the whole Middle East, and in an effort to keep everyone happy, the president is always a Maronite Christian, the speaker of the parliament must be a Shi'a and the prime minister a Sunni Muslim.

From what I understood, despite ongoing tensions with Israel to the south, Syria to the east and some sabre-rattling from Saudi Arabia, Lebanon was relatively stable. The Lebanese Armed Forces were a strong power, with backing from the US and Britain, and even some of my old military colleagues were in the country training their border force. And yet, alongside all that was a paramilitary Islamist anomaly: Hezbollah. What on earth were they all about?

'They're just Shi'a volunteers,' said Hadi, with a nonchalant wave, 'like youth workers.' He shrugged. 'Everyone here is Hezbollah. My brother is in the organisation.'

I quickly looked across the room to Hussain, who smiled and raised an eyebrow.

'Oh,' I mumbled.

'Don't worry. We're not terrorists. That's what everyone thinks in the West, isn't it? We're just protecting the country's interests. It was Hezbollah that defeated Daesh on the borders, not the army, although we often work with them. We're generally on the same side.'

Hussain came and sat next to me, with a cup of tea in one hand and a closed fist in the other.

'Here,' he said. 'I have a gift for you.' He dropped something into my palm and I looked down.

It was a bronze coin. At first, I thought it might be an antique, but no, it was strangely new, with swirling Arabic writing, and yet I didn't recognise which country it came from.

Hussain grinned. 'It's an Islamic State coin. I got it from Syria. You can keep it.'

I thanked him.

'We're normal guys, we volunteer to defend the Shi'a faith against the aggressors, and you know who they are, don't you.'

I knew what he was going to say. 'Israel and Saudi Arabia.'

'Exactly,' he said. 'But it's nasty politics. The Israelis invaded us and so we must fight them. The Saudis want to destroy us, too, but we won't let them. We will fight to the last man if we need to. But we always remember that it's just a game. You know, some people like to party, right?'

'Sure.'

'Some people like to play the piano, like Alushi here.'

'Sure.'

'You. You like to travel, climb mountains and to walk.'

'I guess so.'

'Many people like to make money.' He chuckled. 'I'm one of those.'

'And here, in the Middle East, some people like to play games with other people's lives. It's not nice, but that's the way it is. And so, what can we do? We must play the game better than other people, otherwise we will be destroyed. And it's as simple as that. At the end of the day, there are no good guys or bad guys, people are just people.'

That evening, Hadi drove me to Baalbek and we walked around the old town to see the ancient Roman ruins. What appeared before me were arguably the best-preserved Roman temples in the world outside Italy. A vast structure, almost intact, had what are thought to be the largest known ancient blocks of stone in the world, carved intricately to architectural perfection, which have survived two thousand years and countless wars. As we ambled through the columns, I chuckled to myself at how appropriate it was that the great temple was dedicated to Bacchus, the Roman name for Dionysus: god of ritual madness, religious ecstasy and wine, all rolled into one.

Outside, street vendors sold Hezbollah T-shirts, baseball caps and keyrings, and the last rays of sun shone through the ancient arches, giving the place a warm glow. To the west, the snowy peaks shimmered in clouds of bronze. We returned to sleep at Hadi's house that night, where he agreed to escort me over the mountains to the Maronite highlands tomorrow, for the final leg of my journey.

24

Where It All Began

Trust in dreams, for in them is hidden the gate to eternity.
Kahlil Gibran

'I can get us a lift to Aainata,' said Hadi the next morning at dawn, waking me up with freshly brewed coffee. 'My friend Ali has a car and he can be here in thirty minutes, so yalla, get up.'

I rubbed my eyes and stuffed my belongings into my rucksack. I'd looked at the map last night. Aainata was at the base of the Lebanon Mountains, the dividing line between the Bekaa Valley, which was settled by the Shi'a Muslims, and the Maronite Christian highlands. Nobody seemed to know if the road was open or not, as there were rumours that there was still some snow on the high passes, and if the road was closed, I was unsure that we'd be able to walk it, since I had no cold-weather gear.

'Let's give it a go,' said Hadi, full of enthusiasm. 'I've never been there before, so it'll be an adventure.'

'You've never been there before?' I asked, surprised, since it was only twenty miles distant and forty minutes away by car.

Ali arrived in a brand-new Land Cruiser, which must have been worth a fortune. He was wearing a leather jacket, with a pistol tucked into his jeans. It turned out Ali was a Hezbollah intelligence officer, and in spite of his deadly appearance, he was full of beans and very charming.

'I think you are very crazy for going over the mountains,' he told us, with genuine concern. 'Look,' he said, pointing to the looming peaks. 'Much snow.'

'We'll be fine,' I said, bolstered with confidence that the end was near. Ali the spy just shrugged and drove on in silence to the village of Aainata on the slopes of the valley. The village was nothing but a collection of small farms, and a paved road that zigzagged up the hill.

'I'll see how far I can get you. The next town is Bsharre, but that is over thirty kilometres away.'

Thirty kilometres is a long walk on the flat, never mind over a snow-covered high pass. I looked up. It was a bright, warm sunny morning, but I knew that if the clouds came in, it would be a rather different story. Still, I'd committed now. Hadi was keen as mustard to go for a winter walk and Ali had to go to work – back to spying for Hezbollah.

Soon enough the paved road disintegrated into a rough dirt track, with endless switchbacks, and we began to gain height and ascend above the trees. With each turn, the view back down across the Bekaa Valley became more and more wondrous, as the green plains stretched for as far as the eye could see.

'I'm really sorry,' said Ali, as the vehicle came to a halt. 'I can't go any further.' We pulled over in a lay-by and I looked ahead. We had almost reached the snowline and a thin layer had covered the track ahead. 'The wheels will slip and it's too dangerous.'

'That's okay,' I said. 'You've brought us a few kilometres closer than I'd expected.' He'd shaved off seven clicks from the journey, so I was more hopeful.

'I'm excited,' said Hadi, grinning ear to ear. In truth, so was I. Despite the fact that I was wearing suede desert boots and jeans, and my only jacket was a waxed cotton Belstaff number,

I was determined to get up and over the hill and see what lay beyond.

We both waved goodbye to Ali the spy, who wished us luck, and with that we plodded off up the hill. The trail was easy to follow at first; we simply walked along the embankment where the concrete balustrades poked out above the snow. We hopped from one to the next in a bid to keep our feet dry. Hadi was enjoying himself at first, but as the morning wore on, it became apparent that he was not used to walking very far, so we had to slow down.

After the first twelve kilometres, we'd almost reached the high pass itself, but the snow was getting deeper and deeper, and we couldn't keep dry any longer. With a deep sigh, we trudged through the knee-deep powder, getting wetter and wetter with each minute that passed.

The bright skies gave way to a mist that drifted from the far side of the mountain and soon we were engulfed in a thick fog, which made it impossible to see more than ten feet beyond. As we gained height, the clouds lowered and so did the temperature. By noon, it was below freezing and we were both drenched through, shivering with every step. I looked at Hadi. He seemed to have lost his sense of humour and become introverted, walking in silence. We had better get over this hill soon, I thought to myself, otherwise there will be trouble.

Up and up we went, deeper into the fog, until it was a complete white-out. I was cold, wet and worried. Arabia wasn't supposed to be like this, I thought. We kept going, though, and there were times when I had to pull Hadi physically up the hill through waist-deep snowdrifts. There was no going back; we had reached the threshold, and point of no return. I knew we were closer to Bsharre than Aainata and so we had to continue. Just a couple more miles and we'd reach the highest point.

So we carried on. I was buoyed by the thought of a warm fire and a hearty meal. Bsharre was high up on the plateau, but I'd heard there were a couple of lodges and a restaurant. My mind began to wander. First, I found myself transported back to my childhood, sledging in the snow that Christmas in 1987 with my father, I remembered those formative visions of a biblical east, imagined through six-year-old eyes through the lens of a school nativity. I thought back to my first forays in the Middle East as a student, then as a soldier. I found myself dreaming of the past, away from the snow and into some desert oasis. As I struggled to force my legs through the freezing slush, I thought back over the previous months, of the joys and hardships and friendships forged out of a very messy region. I'd travelled through thirteen countries, all very different in many ways, yet the omnipresent desert had remained all the while.

Sometimes it was close, the sand beneath my toes as it was in the Empty Quarter, and in Sir Bani Yas and the trenches of Iraq; other times it was far, like a tantalising genie on the horizon, or a watchful goddess in the form of a distant dune against a glistening gulf; but it was always there, from Syria to Yemen, Somalia to Jordan and the Holy Land. And yet here I was, high on a distant mountain covered in snow, dreaming of another place and another time. I wondered if Odysseus had felt this way on his return to Ithaca, faced with his final hurdle.

My thoughts drifted to my own home, back to my family, friends and life in London. I thought of what was to come, and of the future – the welcome-home parties and joyful reunions, the good food and good wine. I thought about what Dave and Simon and I could do to celebrate the end of the journey, and I thought about the pledge I'd made to myself after this one – no more big expeditions. Enough was enough. I had been promising myself a more settled life for the last three years now, and finally there was light at the end of the tunnel. Arabia had been my nemesis, and yet, against all odds I had somehow survived, well, at least until now.

'Snap out of it!' I said to myself, out loud. 'Live in the moment.' How many times did I need to be reminded of the fact that the only reality is the here and now.

I pulled myself together. I knew that I had to get myself and Hadi back to reality, whatever that might be. Our survival depended on it, and it's funny when you realise that, how quickly you stop daydreaming. These jagged mountains, I knew, were the gateway to home.

After another half an hour, utterly exhausted, we reached the summit of the pass. Somewhere in the whiteness was Mount Lebanon itself, throne of the gods and revered in antiquity, and yet there was nothing to suggest a peak, because the visibility was so low. Suddenly the ground flattened out for a while, and then, following only the arrow pointer on my Google Maps, we began to descend. Winds swirled and gnashed at our faces. Only our frosty shemaghs kept our noses from dropping off. Hadi plodded on in silence, and I used every ounce of my strength to push him onward and encourage him to stick with it.

Then, as quickly as it had come, the fog simply disappeared. I looked down, and a gap in the clouds revealed where we were. A few miles beneath us, I saw the rejoicing colour green: wide, lush valleys and great cedar forests spread out below us, and there in the middle was a small village. I could see chalets and a church and smoke billowing out from a farmer's shed. Hadi smiled. I couldn't tell if he was delirious or not.

'Are we in heaven?' he asked.

'I think we just might be,' I said. 'Come on, yalla.' I patted him on the shoulder and we bounced down the mountain, slipping and sliding down a near vertical slope to the edge of the village.

Two hours later and we'd made it. We were soaked through with sweat and snow and there wasn't an inch of either of us that was dry. We had to jump over a few barbed-wire fences and wade across some freezing cold streams to get to the farmer's fields, which were all still covered in snow, but at least we were alive. Following the smell of wood smoke, I dragged Hadi into the nearest lodge. It was a small hotel for locals, who used the village as a base to go skiing. It was empty inside, but a barman invited us to sit by the fire and strip off our wet clothes. I tried to revive Hadi with some water and a Coke, but within minutes he had sprawled out on a sofa with a smile and fallen fast asleep, his socks still dangling above the fireplace.

As Hadi snoozed, I felt myself relax into the comfort of the chair and think about some of the contradictions and complexities I'd encountered on my journey. I had come to Arabia in search of some answers to my questions. I'd wanted to try to define a region, but had found it undefinable. I was still no closer to discovering what made an Arab an Arab. I didn't feel like I had so much as scraped beneath the surface of Islam, nor could I congratulate myself on coming away with any real grasp of why war, division and violence seemed to be such a prevalent part of human nature in this part of the world.

My only conclusions were personal. I had come to realise that while stereotypes served their purpose for an outsider looking in, they were useless once you'd faced them head on. It's in human nature to build walls and fuel hostility. Tribalism creates divisions, which in turn brings unity to the few. But for society to flourish and develop, walls must come down, and only through open-mindedness, courage and education can ignorance and fear be defeated. There was a long way to go here in Arabia, and my romantic notions of innocence had all but been destroyed.

There was no purity here in that sense. And yet, I'd come away with hope. I'd made new friends and thought of the incredible sense of hospitality that I'd received along the way. I thought of my guides: the ambitious Omer, the traumatised Amar and the egotistical Mahrouqi. I thought of the brave Abshir and the noble Hadi in Dhofar. I thought of Khaled and his determination to show me the human side of Saudi Arabia, of the freedom-loving and humble Mishael, of the emotional Saleh and the friendly Fadi, and in Israel of thoughtful Shani and in Syria, the gallant Nada. These were the people I would think of when I remembered this journey.

The next morning, I arranged for Hadi to take a taxi back to Baalbek. He'd had enough adventure for one trip, and he was quite sure he'd been to heaven in any case, so there was no point travelling further. He would take the long way round, all the way via the coast and Beirut. It would take a couple of days for him to get home, but he didn't seem to mind. I determined to carry on my journey in the same vein as I'd started, so after waving goodbye, I walked out of the hotel and through one of the only remaining cedar forests in Lebanon, called the Cedars of God. And for good reason – they dated back to the very start of civilisation. These trees dated back millennia and legend has it that the oldest among them was three thousand years old.

These were the very trees the Phoenicians used to build their merchant ships; the same trees the ancient Egyptians used in mummifying their emperors. The trees are referred to by the Assyrians, Babylonians and Persians. The Romans venerated them and King Solomon used the wood to build the Israelites their temple in Jerusalem. Even Queen Victoria, horrified at their destruction, built a wall to protect them.

These living monuments to history loomed large above me as I trudged through the snow, their magical branches arcing under the weight of fresh icicles. Robins and ravens danced above the bows and the tracks of a fox led to a secret lair. It was all quite enchanted, and I wondered if perhaps this might be the real garden of Eden, and the biblical scholars had got their geography wrong by a few hundred miles after all.

I walked down through the Qadisha Valley. The snow had melted now, giving way to a verdant paradise filled with deep gorges, plentiful lakes and sublime waterfalls. These were the Maronite highlands and I'd crossed back into Christendom. Vineyards filled the lush slopes and at each village I saw little churches, and there hidden away in the valley, I stumbled upon the monastery of St Anthony. By coincidence, it happened to be the saint's day and it was filled with Lebanese Christian pilgrims, who came to worship the hermit.

It was there, outside the church door, that I encountered a man in a rough brown monk's habit, who was lighting a candle at the shrine. Walid greeted me warmly and I assumed he must live in the monastery. I assumed an air of reverence in the face of the holy man.

'How long have you been a monk here for?' I asked.

He burst out laughing.

'I'm no monk,' he said. 'I'm just visiting, I'm a taxi driver.' He chuckled again. 'I'm just wearing these robes as a penance to get forgiveness. I must wear them for seventy days in total. I've only got a week left, thank God.'

'Oh,' I said, slightly surprised. 'May I ask what you did to receive such a punishment?'

Walid raised an eyebrow. It was only then that I noticed scars on his face and tattoos on his knuckles.

'I shot a guy. He was annoying me.'

I kept my mouth shut after that. Never ask a question you don't want an answer to, I thought, as we strolled through the magical gardens towards a cave in the side of the hill.

'Where are you going?' Walid asked. I explained my journey in brief, and that I was almost at its end.

'My God!' he exclaimed.

Pilgrims were queuing to get inside the cave, but Walid quickly shoved them out of the way and pulled me by the arm into the dark cavern.

'May I pray for you?' he said solemnly, with a glint of insanity in his eyes.

'Sure,' I said, not wanting to run the risk of annoying him.

Inside the cave, the only light was from hundreds of candles flickering on an altar, causing shadows to dance around the walls. At the back of the cave were chains dangling from pins, hammered into the rock face.

'What are they?' I asked.

'That's where we used to chain up mad people,' said Walid. 'It cured them of their sickness after a few days.'

I gulped.

Walid opened his arms and muttered at an icon of St Anthony, which was next to a crucifix on the altar. I stood still, pondering my adventures with a little smile. I was nearly there, and yet, at every turn, there was the chance for adventure, if only you looked for it. People are people, wherever you are, and I'd come out of this journey, not only alive, but surprisingly hopeful, determined to seek the best in myself and others.

After he'd finished, Walid made the sign of the cross on his chest, turned to me and smiled.

'I asked God to keep you safe for the rest of your journey, you crazy bastard.'

He suddenly put a hand to his mouth. 'Oh shit, I just swore. Now I have to wear this for an extra day.'

I laughed, but he was deadly serious and shook his head in disappointment.

'Can I take you to where you need to go? Maybe God will see that as an act of kindness and forgive me.'

Well, in my hitchhiking mantra, I always say the best experiences are born of serendipity, and everyone deserves a second chance; so I agreed, and who was I to stand in the way of Walid getting out of his habit? The mad monk-taxi driver led me out of the grounds of the monastery to a car park, where a battered old taxi lay covered in bird shit and rust.

'Yalla,' he said, with a smile.

'Yalla,' I replied.

We drove down through the valley, past ancient villages and beautiful towns that reminded me of the Alps. We passed by Hadath al Jabbah, Harissa and the waterfalls of Balou Balaa. I could almost smell the Mediterranean now. Long pampas grass swayed in the late afternoon wind as we reached a viewpoint near to Aannaya on 17 January 2018.

As we rounded the bend of the hills, the clouds were glowing red, casting an auburn glow across the valleys below, and there I could see my goal. Glinting under a dying sun was the golden Mediterranean and at its shores, I could see the coast. A little town spread out along the distant cliffs. It was Byblos, the place where it all began.

'Welcome to the land of God,' said Walid, beaming with pride.

Walid dropped me off at a small hotel in the village by the main road, where I spent my final night. The next morning, eager to get to the coast, I woke up early, only to discover that the view was obscured by mist and drizzle.

Sod's law, I thought. But I wasn't about to wait. After a meagre breakfast of boiled egg and instant coffee, I hauled my rucksack on for the last time and walked. I walked and walked, through muddy lanes and across farmers' fields, through orange and lemon orchards, through the mist and through drizzle. There was just twelve kilometres left to push and I wasn't about to let crappy weather dampen my spirits.

I realised something on that little walk down the mountain. I felt a certain sadness that I was nearing the end. I'd chosen Byblos as an arbitrary finish – the destination didn't matter as much as the journey itself. It was that I should be celebrating, not lamenting a grey day and a bit of rain. I'd learned a lot of things on this journey, but perhaps no lesson more valuable than no matter how bad the situation may seem, only you – inside yourself – have the ability to let it get you down.

In every difficulty is an opportunity, and a challenge one must face. One can either accept defeat and move on, or one can keep striving to be the master of one's own fate. I decided that this was my journey, nobody else's, and I'd made the rules all along. I chose to be happy with the situation, embrace the obstacles and try to learn from them.

Byblos came into view again in the form of low-rise industrial buildings, concrete factories and gated villas. This was the oldest city in the world; the place that monotheistic religion began – where the Canaanites decreed that there was one God – and the Israelites agreed with them, and yet called theirs something different.

This was the centre of Phoenician society, which resulted in Europe becoming the centre of the world. It was the launchpad of civilisation itself, and the first signpost I saw directed visitors to McDonald's.

But I didn't care. What was purity in any case, other than a sense of wellbeing that the present is all that matters. There is no need to worry about the past, because it's gone, and the future hasn't happened yet. If I'd learned anything at all, it is to enjoy the moment and be thankful for whatever you have, right here, right now.

Alhamdulillah, as the Muslims say. All praise be to God (or whatever entity or spirit, or philosophy you choose to engage with).

With a spring in my step I bounded through the suburbs, sensing my way to the sea. Soon the modern drabness gave way to the more reverent stones of the old city, and just as I arrived at the ancient walls, as if by magic, the grey clouds broke and a ray of sunshine pierced the sky like a bronze sword. I slowed down my pace. Enjoy the moment, I reminded myself, there's no rush.

The magenta flowers of the bougainvillea seemed to suddenly feel closer and appeared more vibrant; the stones smoother and the aroma of frankincense, wafting from doorways, all the more fragrant. Everything seemed colourful and energetic and full of hope.

I picked my way through the alleyways and cobbled streets, past the old Crusader fort, the Roman theatre and the necropolis. Tall cypress trees hemmed in the Temple of the Obelisks and the Bronze-Age ramparts, and long-forgotten graves jutted from primeval mounds. Alexander stood here once, and this was the place that Lawrence studied Arabic. Burton and Thesiger, too, came here for their holidays, but even that didn't matter to me now.

I ambled through the leafy lanes, simply enjoying the warmth of the noontime sun, now bursting with passion through the silver clouds. I rounded a final corner and the medieval harbour opened up in front of me. It was filled with little wooden fishing boats and a kind of light reserved for only the most magical of days. I sloshed my way over the flooded corniche to a stone breakwater that jutted out from the quay into the stormy sea.

To the left, the beach spread out along a palm-fringed shoreline all to the way to Beirut, which appeared as a hazy apparition in the far distance. To the right, cafés and boutique hotels lined the cliffs, reminding me that this wasn't an illusion. This really was the Mediterranean, and my journey was at an end. I'd reached the gateway to Europe. I dumped my bag on a stone and briefly contemplated doing what I'd done so many times before, and ending my journey by jumping head first into the sea. But looking down at the jagged rocks and the crashing waves of a cold winter ocean, I thought better of it.

Back in England, life went on as before. I returned to find a green and pleasant land, where water was free and there are no deserts to cross. Arabia returned to its familiar sanctuary, a faraway land that occasionally explodes on our television screens. It dissipated with time, melting back into the recesses of my mind and memory. I carried on, though, with a renewed feeling that we should perhaps care a little more about those faraway places.

And I knew, deep down in my heart, that if I closed my eyes and stayed quiet, then maybe I could just about recall the feeling of the sand beneath my feet; the muezzin singing his chant above the domes of Jerusalem; and the laughter of the Bedouin in the caves of Petra.

Acknowledgements

I was once given some invaluable advice: 'To achieve great things, you must surround yourself with great people.' No expedition, of course, is a one-man show. I think it is clear to the reader that such a long journey anywhere, let alone one through such a contested region, must require the help and assistance of a great team, and as a result the acknowledgements for this book require more than any other I've undertaken.

There are many people that I must thank for their advice, help and assistance before during and after the expedition. This journey really began way back in 2003, when the late Alex Coutselos and I set off to backpack home from Cairo. Alex is sorely missed, and his legacy lives on in so many ways.

The planning for such a mammoth task took months of bureaucracy, emails and logistical wrangling, and all of this was down to the tenacity and sheer guts of two people: Dave Luke and Simon Buxton. They were both instrumental in the making of this journey, which would not have been possible without them. I'm only sorry that there wasn't enough space in this book to recount all our adventures together. In addition, I must thank Neil Bonner for his filming and directorship; Tom Cross, who joined for the second half; and Charlotte Tottenham for her invaluable assistance throughout.

I would like to humbly thank HRH the Prince of Wales for

his sage advice before embarking. The start of my expedition was made smooth with the help of my old friend, Omer 'Chomani' Hussein, as well as Dr Nawzad Kameran Al-Salihi, Sheikh Karwan Barzani, Jim Fidell, Saad Wadi Khamis and the Kurdistan Regional Government. I owe my security and access in Iraq to Amar. In the Iraqi marshes, I was well looked after by Jassim Al-Asadi, Azzam Alwash, Razzaq Jabbar Sabbon (Abu Haider) and Salwa Um Haider. In Bahrain, I was warmly welcomed by Jesus Florido-Banqueri and all the team of the Bahrain Tourism board. In the UAE, Charlie Taylor at Jumeirah and my friends, Griff Freedman and Katherine Kearsey, gave me some much-needed R&R.

I received extensive Omani expertise from Major General Richard Stanford MBE, Nabs El Busaidy, Mark Evans, Charlie Dalziel, Major Dom Dias and Major Nick Le Crerar, and 'Mahrouqi' Ahmed Haroub Hamed guided me safely through the Empty Quarter desert. Hadi Al Hikmani and his skilled troop of Jebeli guides – Ali Said Al Hikmani, Salim Suhail Al Hikmani, Saïd Suhail Al Hikmani and Saïd Salim Al Hikmani – kept us safe in the mountains of Dhofar. I was accompanied by Matthew Fisher, Michael Greep, Emmanuel Ansah, Nutan Rai, Stephen Turner and Harry Card, courtesy of the Endeavour Fund, and these brave warriors made the steep escarpments of the Dhofar peninsula even more of a joy.

In Yemen, I am indebted to my fixer, whom I have called 'Abshir' for security reasons, to Sultan Abdallah bin Essa bin Ali Al Afrar, Colonel 'H', and the invaluable advice of a man whom I will simply call John.

Through the HALO trust team, I was introduced to Hersi Abdirizak, who was a great help in Somaliland. My access to Saudi Arabia was arranged with the help of HRH Sultan bin

Salman, as well as the very helpful Richard Wildash, Jim Tanner, Richard Cowley and Jamana al Rashid. It was my knowledgeable guide, Khaled Al Took, who truly brought the sands of the kingdom to life.

I am indebted to HRH King Abdullah II of Jordan and his chief of staff, Jafar Hassan, for their hospitality and assistance, and George David and Ahmad Ashour at the Royal Film Commission of Jordan. Also, to Mustafa Khalifeh, Qais Tweissi, Salem Sabah Al Zalabia, Aude Eid Salem and above all, to Mishael al Faqueer for being my guide through his beautiful lands.

In the West Bank, I was looked after by Salah Abu Laban and Fadi AbouAkleh, and in Israel by Shani Amihay Boneh. In Syria, I was enormously grateful for the wisdom and insight of my guide, Nada Kettunen. In Lebanon, Hadi Obeid and the staff of the British Embassy in Lebanon were all a great help.

I am grateful too for the support of all those companies and organisations who helped out: Sicuro, Global Rescue, Horus, Rotana Hotels, Jumeirah Group, the Bahrain Tourist Board, Nomad Travel, Leica, Belstaff, IWC, Oliver Sweeney and Sky Vision.

Across the Arabian Peninsula, I was helped by a number of generous individuals and organisations from the charity sector, including Camilla Kinchin from UNICEF and the staff at Zaatari Camp; Richard Scott at the HALO Trust; Chris Forbes at Save the Children; Ole Solvang at the Norwegian Refugee Council; Matt Timblin, Belkis Wille at Human Rights Watch; and David Wiseman of the Endeavour Fund.

And in no particular order, to all of the following for their words of wisdom, floor space, companionship on the trail, or just a cup of tea: Nigel Winser and Shane Winser at the Royal Geographical Society, Ben Wright, Charles Dalziel, Patrick

Mark, Steve Tidmarsh, Tracey Saunders, Josh Baker, Nadia Hardman, Lottie Gimlette, Paddy Nicholl, Sam Browne, Rich Bowyer, Ruthie, Ronnie, Dahlia and Dana Markus, Imran Zawwar, Doc McKerr, Ben Ross, Isobel Abdulhoel, Oz Katerji, Colonel Sharon Gat, Noam Shalev, Julia Civettuolo Haddad, Tom Bodkin, Mary Martin, Luca Alfatti, Chris Wright, Doug Muirhead, Toby Woodbridge, Jude Carnegie, Ceci Alonzo, Claire Arrowsmith, Tes Mendoza and Elin Kongevold.

It was reassuring to know that I was in the safe hands of Mike Kennedy, Elinor Buxton and Sean Nelson, who kept tabs from afar.

Thanks to all of those who came to visit and boost morale over Christmas and New Year – my wonderful parents and my brother Pete, and my friends, Ash Bhardwaj, Andrea Thompson, Lian Michelson, Ali Naushahi, Janessa Wells, Michael Walford-Williams, Harry Pilcher; and to Alberto Caceres, who also joined for parts of the expedition.

As ever, I owe the book to my fabulous agent, Jo Cantello, and Rupert Lancaster at my publisher, Hodder & Stoughton, as well as all of the team involved, especially Kerry Hood, Cameron Myers and Barry Johnston.

I'd like to thank Jenny Walker for giving me a critic's eye from a local perspective, Neil Gower for the fabulous maps, and Ella Jackson, to whom I must give special thanks for the beautiful cover and wonderful times throughout the writing of this book.

Finally, my gratitude to the people of Syria, Iraq, Kuwait, Bahrain, the UAE, Oman, Yemen, Somalia, Somaliland, Djibouti, Saudi Arabia, Jordan, Palestine, Israel and Lebanon for their generosity and kindness.

Picture Acknowledgements

© Juliya Ka / Shutterstock: 4, bottom.

© Simon Buxton: 4, top left. 9, bottom. 14, middle. 15, bottom. 16, bottom.

© Trinity Mirror / Mirrorpix / Alamy Stock Photo: 1, top left.

© Umar Shariff / Shutterstock.com: 5, top.

All other images © Levison Wood

Index

Please note that the article Al- at the start of names is ignored in alphabetic sorting (e.g., Al-Qaeda is under Q)